Birthing God's Mighty Warriors

By Rachel Scott

PRESS

The Vision

I must begin this book by sharing with you a vision that the Lord has given me about a special generation who will walk the earth before the Lord returns.

I believe that some of these people may already be walking the earth, but many more must be saved, and some have not even been born yet! "Let this be written for a future generation that a people *not yet born* may praise the Lord" (Psalm 102:18). A large group in this generation will be children and young people whom God brings to earth in these final generations *for such a time as this* (Esther 4:14). The following is my vision of what this generation will be about.

There is a generation coming who will walk with God as intimately as Enoch walked with Him (Genesis 5:24). They will be so *completely in love with the Lord* that they will follow Him wherever He leads them and be consumed with His purposes. They will not be afraid to be martyred and will be a living testimony in all the earth. "They will not love their lives so much that they shrink back from death" (Revelation 12:11).

Their love for the Lord will cause great revivals to sweep the earth, bringing untold millions into the kingdom of God to join the ranks of worshippers awaiting the sudden return of their bridegroom Savior Jesus Christ. This will be a spiritual generation that will consist of people of all ages, yet within this generation there will be children unlike any that the world has ever known. It is for the hope of these children that this book has been written. There is an anointed generation of children that ***must come*** to the earth to prepare the way of the Lord.

> *"From the lips of children and infants you have ordained praise*
> *because of your enemies to silence the foe and the avenger"*
> *(Psalm 8:2).*

The Bible says that a little child will lead them (Isaiah 11:6). Jesus said that we cannot enter the kingdom of God unless we come as a child (Matthew 18:3) and that the kingdom of God belongs to the children (Matthew 19:14).

Children play a significant role in allowing the hearts of men to see a *unified generation of* people ready to meet the Lord, because children possess a unique innocence and a tenderness that allows the Holy Spirit to have His way with them.

Many of the anticipated children will be the Godly offspring of mothers and fathers who revere the name of Jesus and who also have a strong desire to follow Him. Some will be born to unsaved parents, yet God's grace will be upon them and they will find the Lord and will also lead their families to Him. Their salvation will come as the result of the prayers prayed by previous generations of believers who faithfully prayed for the unsaved in their country and in foreign lands. At this time in history, God will ripen those prayers and allow these children to be born—children destined to know Him!

In families where God has been the Lord for several generations, specific spiritual gifts will be released upon the next generation to continue to be passed down from generation to generation. "His children will be mighty in the land; the generation of the upright will be blessed" (Psalm 112:2). These Godly parents will nurture, raise and train up these children. "Fathers will tell their children about your faithfulness" (Isaiah 38:19). These young children will be "like arrows in the hands of a warrior" (Psalm 127:4)

Many parents today who walk with God are already seeing that their children have spiritual awareness and gifts that resemble those of adults. The Body of Christ as a group is seeing an increase of this blessing every day, and it will continue to increase in preparation for the seasons to come. (Haggai 2:9)

As these special warriors are being created in God's secret place (the womb), they will be *with God* and will be ready to serve Him from birth (Luke 1:15). Like John the Baptist, they will be born knowing their destiny before them. "From birth I have relied on you; you brought me forth from my mother's womb. I will ever praise you (Psalm 71:6).

Many of these children will possess characteristics that will remind us of righteous men of old. They will have the faith of Abraham, the humility of Moses, the conquering spirit of Joshua, the servant's heart of Ruth, the worshipper's heart of David, the prophetic eye of Jeremiah and Isaiah; they will dwell in the miraculous like Elijah, possess the boldness of Paul, and have the knowledge of Esther that they have come into the Kingdom "for such a time as this" (Esther 4:14).

They will be lights in the darkness no matter where they go and will not possess the *fears* of previous generations because they will be rooted and grounded in the Lord. This will cause the Lord's hand to be upon them (Luke 1:66) as they march in unison and respond to the voice of the Holy Spirit. Their lives will not be about *themselves* or *fulfilling their own desires* because they will be consumed with the things of the Lord.

On the other hand the enemy is preparing his army for battle. Believers don't need to *fear* the other side, but we do need to be aware that they exist. I believe that there are children being born right now who already desire to promote the enemy's agenda. Some are chosen in the womb through satanic rituals or other forms of evil. The only hope these children have is to find Christ, but until they do, they will be increasingly susceptible to the deeds and plans of the enemy.

As the world sinks deeper into the darkness that will eventually lead it to embrace the Anti-Christ, both sides will continue to prepare their armies. No matter when this time comes in history, the bottom line is that there will be a generation of people who will be alive on earth awaiting their Bridegroom Jesus to come for them. This generation of believers will be God's army, fighting the lies of the enemy and being *over-comers* until that time comes (Rev 2:7, 11, 17, 26; 3:5, 12, 21).

Many believe that we are presently living in the last generations before Christ returns. The children that we are birthing right now are the beginnings of this end-time army of worshippers who will prepare the way of the Lord.

> *"See, I will send my messenger, who will prepare the way before*
> *me. Then suddenly the Lord you are seeking will come.."*
> *(Malachi 3:1).*

But before any of this can come to pass, these anointed children *must be born*! They each need parents who will be open to what God wants to do within their own families and be visionaries of God's great purposes. In order for these children to be part of God's end-time army, they must first be *conceived* and be allowed to be brought to earth.

This is not to be taken lightly! The enemy has tried hard to convince God's people that children are a *personal choice* and a *hardship*. He has successfully fooled the Body of Christ into *greatly limiting their offspring;* he is trying to limit God's army from being born. The enemy would like never to see these generations conceived or born, for they are the final generations prophesied who will be awaiting God's triumphant climax of history.

Mom and Dad, it is time to overcome the enemy's lie and grasp hold of the task at hand. As parents we have been given the privilege that *no other generation has ever been given before:* To BIRTH the END-TIME ARMY of the LIVING GOD!

MOM and DAD, it's time to be . . . Birthing
God's Mighty Warriors!!

Thankyou

I wish to thank the many people who made this book project possible. First my husband Christopher for having the angelic dream that started this whole journey. I want to thank him for all of his love, support and Godly insight. I wish to thank my son Shawn, *my computer whiz kid*, who rescued me more than once from my computer inadequacies. Ashley, Heather and Courtney who allowed me time on the computer while they kept house and took care of Judah, Destiny and Haven who were all born during this process. I want to thank my dear friend Soula who spent hours helping me correct my manuscript and also encouraged me, uplifted me and pushed me to *"get this book out!"* I wish to thank Mary Jo for being the best proofreader. I wish to thank Debbie for the prayerful support and all of the other girlfriends who read various parts of my manuscript and encouraged me to *stay the course*. To all I am truly grateful. Thankyou! Last but certainly not least I wish to thank the Lord for giving me wisdom to understand His message of hope and for allowing me to take part in preparing the way of the Lord. To Him I am forever grateful.

Dedication

This book is dedicated to a new generation who desires to
discover God's best for their marriage.
To those who seek to love the Lord with a love that says,
"I am willing to do whatever it takes to follow all of Your ways,
no matter what it might cost me."
This is for those who desire to pay the price for holiness,
even if those around them think that they are foolish
or simply do not understand.
This is for those who realize that what God is doing on the earth in
this hour is not about them, but about the name of the Lord being
glorified. These are those who are not afraid to be completely
surrendered to following the Lord wherever He may lead them....
A blessing for the Righteous:

Blessed are all who fear the Lord, who walk in His ways
You will eat the fruit of your labor,
Blessings and prosperity will be yours
Your wife will be a fruitful vine within your house
Your sons will be olive shoots around your table
Thus is the man blessed who fears the Lord
May the Lord bless you from Zion all of the days of your life
May you see the prosperity of God's people and may you
live to see your grandchildren.
(Psalm 128)

Table Of Contents

Preface

I feel the message of this book is the voice of one calling in the desert, sounding an alarm to God's people, calling today's generations to come back to Him.

God is saying to you:

"Prepare the way for the Lord, make straight paths for Him." (Mark 1:3)

"See I will send you the prophet Elijah before that great and terrible day of the Lord comes. He will turn the hearts of the Fathers back to the children and the hearts of the children to their Fathers or else I will come and strike the land with a curse" (Malachi 4:5,6).

The enemy has the ability to blind both believers and nonbelievers so that they miss the light of the gospel of Christ (2 Corinthians 4:4). In this book I want to expose an area where God's wonderful people have been blindsided by the enemy. They have been making choices that are bringing their lives various forms of *death* and they don't even realize the source of their pain.

Our sins in the area of family planning have caused our land to be struck with a curse because we have not received all of the children that God had planned for our lives. We are reaping the sorrows of our sins.

God wants to reveal to us our areas of sin so that the curse can be removed and the hearts of the Fathers can turn back to the hearts of the children so together they can, "Prepare the way of the Lord."

God has plans to forgive us (2 Chronicles 7:14), prosper us, bring us hope and a future (Jeremiah 29:11) and He doesn't want us to miss His blessings anymore. God is sending us a clear call that it is *time to wake up!*

> *"Wake up, O sleeper! Rise from the dead*
> *and Christ will shine on you" (Ephesians 5:4).*

This book is the beginning of an adventure. It will begin a life-long quest to follow the Lord in a new way. I will take the *age old theme* of birthing children and shed some new light in the hope that you will discover some Biblical truths that God's people need to remember once again.

I am convinced that this is a message that is *burning in the heart of God for His people.* We are in the greatest time period *ever* to be birthing children and you may not realize that God might want you to consider having another child. Even if you have all of the children that you think that you want, or if you have not decided if you want more or if you have not even began to start your family yet, I believe that the Lord wants to give you a new understanding of what it means to be given a child. Children play an important role in God's plan for the future and in your vision of understanding God's purposes for your own life.

It is time for God's people to consider His way because our own way has brought us disaster, *death* and destruction. We are suffering from cancer, divorce, loss of marital intimacy, great spiritual loss, sorrow and rejection. We are wounded. We need to make choices with our family planning that line up with God's plan so that our present lives and future generations can walk in God's full and abundant blessing.

Few people realize how much is at stake at this time! Many people buy into society's beliefs about family planning because they are misinformed. I feel it is my responsibility to alert you to the fact that the enemy has a plan to *destroy your seed* and *rob you of your scriptural inheritance*! I also want to share with you how much the medical advances of the last seventy years in the field of family planning may not have offered the best choices for God's people. Many of God's people may be making decisions that go against God's moral code simply because the medical community has made certain advances available. These advances have no scriptural basis and are not for the people who love the Lord!

Now more than ever we need to be clear about what God is saying about children so that we do not become confused about the ideas adopted by those in our society who do not bow the knee to Jesus Christ our Lord and Savior (Romans 14:11). We know that Satan is a liar! (John 8:44). It's time to expose his lies so that the light of the gospel can transform our old mindsets and turn us toward the plans and purposes of the Lord.

When the Lord gave me this understanding about the importance of being open to birthing His children, it really was not something that I was searching for. I had read the book of Revelations several times and knew that this would be a volatile time on earth, but I never stopped to think that I could personally have a part to play in birthing children who might be on earth during the time that leads up to the return of the Lord. I had not grasped the idea that I, my children, my grand children or my great grand children might be a part of that privilege. They might be the very people alive to take part in some of the events of this final book of Revelations! This alone is deep. Try and grasp this. We are the *chosen generations* and the envied groups that are alive on planet earth at this critical time.

As this message is revealed to your heart my biggest prayer is that you will try to *be open* to what God may want to say to you. I believe that the Lord desires to challenge you and to birth a new vision in you to serve Him. Please allow yourself to hear a new message and consider God's way.

This is a message of hope for all generations to read, to think about and to absorb so that our future generations may be blessed. I am saddened that many in my generation (thirty-five years and older) may have already missed a large part of God's blessing because so many have chosen to follow the family planning ideas of society. My prayer is that this group will return to God (Zechariah 1:3,4) and listen, repent, become healed if needed and possibly bear more children if the Lord so desires. My prayer is for those in the next generations to learn from our mistakes so that they do not fall into the devil's trap. If the next generation will listen, I believe that God will caution them to *avoid* the physical, emotional and spiritual judgments that birth control use and sterilization can bring. In the area of family planning there is a wonderful plan that God has for this generation to discover. If they will do things God's way it will bring *life* to their bodies, *life* to their emotions, *life* to their marriages and *great wealth* to their spiritual lives.

My prayer for each and every person who reads this book is that they will allow the Lord to open their hearts and minds so that they can discover His plan and experience the wonder of Birthing God's Mighty Warriors.

Introduction

I have always been the type of person who asked theological questions that no one could answer. This happened often in my Sunday School classes and during the six years that I attended Christian school. I would raise my hand and ask a very valid and thoughtful question, but the teacher either could not answer my question or, sometimes it seemed did not want to answer my question. Teachers often challenged me to go find the answer myself and report back. This usually sent me on a journey to find the answers in Scripture.

About eight years ago I found myself once again asking questions for which no one seemed to have an answer. This time the subject was *family planning* and whether believers should consider sterilization. I was asking this because my husband was considering a vasectomy, and I was not in complete agreement. We sought counsel from Godly people, but once again I asked questions that no one could answer, and once again God graciously led me on a personal journey to search out His Scriptural truths. During this process I also found medical data to support my Scriptural conclusions. As I searched God's Word, what I found truly amazed me. I found *God's beautiful plan for marriage,* which is something that no one had ever told me about during the forty-two years that I have faithfully attended church.

My research has drawn me to the conclusion that many of God's dear people have no idea what God has to say about *family planning in marriage.* This should be of great concern because we are at a pivotal time in the history of the world. My curiosity compelled me to ask questions that maybe God's people also need to be asking themselves, because God does have answers.[1]

My most compelling conclusion was that most people do not realize how much God would like to have a say in what they choose to do with their families and how much He desires to bless them with children!

Before I begin, though, I would like to share my own journey of how God led me to desire to research this subject in the first place. My story will help you understand my own situation and how God graciously showed me His greater vision.

My husband and I both grew up in Christian homes and both have attended church every Sunday since we were born. We were high school sweethearts after we met twenty-seven years ago at the church youth group. He says that it was love at first sight, and I agree. We have been married for twenty-three years now, and we have an amazing marriage based on Scripture and mutual agreements. We both received Christ as our Savior when we were very young, and we both grew up knowing and loving the Lord. His grace has kept us faithfully serving Him for more than thirty-nine years.

We presently have seven children and are expecting our eighth. We desire for the Lord to bless us with even more children if He chooses. Every time that we have another child, my husband says, "I think we are done," but then God surprises us with another blessing. We believe that staying open to His call in this area of our lives is what He desires of us; however, we have not always been open to this possibility. In fact, we used to feel the exact opposite.

When we first got married, twenty-three years ago in 1980, we were both in agreement that *we did not want a large family.* I was from a family of three children and my husband was from a family of five children, and yet we felt that two children would be enough for us. We felt that a large family would be expensive and would require a lot of work, and we wanted the *freedom* to do other things with our lives instead of being burdened with raising a large family. Also, *we could not see the purpose of having a lot of children.* Even though we had both been brought up in Bible-believing homes and churches, neither of us had ever heard a sermon on the subject of family planning and were ignorant about God's truths concerning families. *We formed our beliefs and attitudes from movies, TV, society, comments in our Sunday School classes, and the other couples that we met through our church or in our neighborhood.*

At every church that we have ever attended, we knew couples who had been sterilized. Several years ago, we began to notice increasing numbers of couples in our age group (35 year and older) who were sharing their *sterilization* stories with us. The husband or wife would make a comment about how the husband was feeling because he had just been "fixed." They would laugh and joke about him not being "quite up to snuff," or the husband would share how the wife had just gotten her tubes tied after the delivery of their last baby and how *happy* he was that he would not have to *worry* about any more children coming.

Every time I heard one of these couples tell their stories, something inside me would cringe. I knew these people loved the Lord, but something was not right about the idea of sterilization. My heart was aching for them, but I really did not know why, nor could I understand why I cared. After all, it really was not any of my business. This nagging feeling always occurred whenever the subject was discussed. I just knew that something was not quite right and that the spirit of God was trying to tell me something.

When I was growing up in the sixties and seventies, it was becoming increasingly popular for women to be on *the pill* and to have their tubes tied. I remember that my mother was against both of these options. She was a preacher's daughter, and her parents never used birth control. Even though my mother used birth control herself, she thought that *the pill* was evil. She believed that it was causing the breakdown of the family because it made having an affair easier, and most important she felt that it was bad for a woman's health. Many of her friends were suffering complications as the result of being on *the pill* and my mom cautioned me that using unnatural and artificial hormones affect a person's long-term health. When I was getting married she persuaded me not to go on *the pill*, but my OB/GYN prescribed it anyway. Being eighteen and in college, I especially did not want to get pregnant. So in the beginning of our marriage, I reluctantly went on it. Thankfully it made me ill, and I was stopped taking it several months later.

I remember also how my mother was very opposed to a woman getting her tubes tied. She thought that this too was wrong and went against God's plan. She would always tell me not to ever have my tubes tied because, "You never know if you might want to have more children someday and it is unscriptural for a person to make assumptions about their future."

My mother often tried to talk her friends out of their decisions to have their tubes tied, but most of the time their minds were made up and her suggestions fell on deaf ears. Every one of these women have now admitted to her that they regretted their decisions and were struggling to live with the consequences of their choices. Seeing these older woman suffer caused me to develop my own opinion on this subject, even though I had not really thought it out. My opinion was not a Scriptural opinion but a rational idea based on my mother's wisdom and these other women's mistakes. I knew that I would never want to have my tubes tied, but my husband felt differently about male sterilization.

He had been raised in a churchgoing family with five children, and they did not have the luxuries that many families enjoy today. This *lack* caused him to desire to have a small family so that he could give them all the things that he had never enjoyed. After we had our son in 1983 (when I was 21 years old and he was 24 years old), he was content to have no more children. But after a few years, I began yearning for a daughter to make our family more complete. Since we had already discussed having two children, after some time I was able to convince him that I would be unfulfilled if we did not at least try to have a little girl.

When our son was four years old, my husband finally agreed to another baby. God faithfully blessed us with a daughter in 1988. We both felt that our family was now complete. Since we were both under thirty, neither one of us wanted to be sterilized yet, but in our minds, we were finished having children and had completed our family.

Both my husband and I always feared pregnancy, so we were extremely careful to use a contraceptive every time that we made love. We were *never* careless and were very confident that *we were in control* of our situation. Then three years later, I thought I had a flu virus and I found out that I was pregnant. We were in shock! *Both of us were upset,* particularly my husband. Neither one of us wanted more children and felt that God had let us down. As the pregnancy progressed, we began to get used to the idea of having another child, and by the time our third child was born, the Lord had turned our hearts around so much that we realized how much we really wanted another baby. We also realized that God must know a really good reason why we needed another child because we couldn't figure it out ourselves.

My husband loved our new daughter from the moment he saw her, but he continued to be upset about our family and their growing needs. He was running his own business, and our finances were very unpredictable. When we were experiencing our leaner months, he especially feared raising children that he could not afford. He did not want to see his children miss the same things that he had missed. The reality that this could happen upset him greatly. God did watch over us faithfully, and somehow after our third child's birth in 1991, we were able to manage.

The pressure increased greatly when three years later we experienced another birth control failure and I became pregnant again. We were both shocked and upset again, but this time it really upset my husband. He could not understand why God was bringing added responsibility and why his children might not be able to have all of the things that he had envisioned for them. During this pregnancy he began to talk about getting a vasectomy. He wanted an end to the possibility of any more children because he was afraid of the expenses. It was not that he did not love our children; in fact, he was and is a very caring and loving father. It was the financial responsibility of supporting them and their future lives that concerned him so much.

During this pregnancy, the more that he talked about getting a vasectomy the more upset I became. I did not believe in sterilization and somehow I knew that it was not the right thing to do. He wanted to get a vasectomy, but I could not agree. I was pregnant and emotional and was not sure if I wanted this child to be my last one.

Every time that we talked about it he became very upset with me. Deep down I just knew that God was doing something with us. During this pregnancy our finances hit a big slump even though my husband worked harder than ever. As he felt the unbearable financial pressures closing in on him, he felt that he had to take the situation into his own hands. The city that we lived in also did not help the situation very much because there were huge billboards posted on all the main highways advertising a no-scalpel vasectomy clinic with quick results. He called the vasectomy clinic to price the surgery.

As soon as I gave birth, he was anxiously waiting for my agreement, but I just could not find any peace about it. Since we could not agree, and we did not have any Scripture to guide us, we decided to seek counsel from our pastor. Our pastor told my husband that this kind of decision must be one of agreement between a husband and a wife and that he should not get a vasectomy unless I was in agreement with him. Since I could not agree, we were at a stalemate waiting for one of us to change our mind. This was when God supernaturally stepped in.

One night, when our new daughter was several months old, my husband had a dream. In the dream, an angel of the Lord appeared before him holding a flaming sword and the angel said, ***"Do not abort the plan of the Lord*!"** Christopher immediately woke up. He was freaked out, to say the least. He woke me up and told me that God had said that he could not have a vasectomy. I said something to the effect of, "Wow! This is big! Do you know what this means? Something great is about to happen or someone great is supposed to be coming through our family lineage for God to send an angel just to tell you not to have a vasectomy. This is wild and wonderful!"

He decided not to have the vasectomy, but even after the angel dream he was still very concerned about how we were going to afford four children and maybe even more some day. Because God is so faithful in His love for us, the Holy Spirit began to open both of our eyes to the truths in God's Word concerning children. Our finances were already in a lean period during this pregnancy, even though my husband worked so very hard. After the fourth baby was born the finances still did not improve much. But God was faithful and merciful to us. I believe that the Lord was working on my husband's heart and mine. After that dream, Christopher would say that he would not mind raising a larger family if we at least had the money to do it. He began to be *more open* to God and began to believe that He has a plan for families that we knew little about. He switched careers and the Lord began to bless him in his new job. The more open he became, the more the Lord blessed him. By this time, I had begun to research Scripture for answers to what God was trying to tell us. I wanted to find out what God said about children. As the Lord revealed his Scriptural truths to me and I began to share them with Christopher, our agreement led God to show us His hand at work over our family in a way that we had never imagined before.

After the angel dream, we still continued to use birth control. God had to reveal His plan to us in Scripture and He had to grow our faith so that when four years later when we found ourselves expecting our fifth child, Christopher and I were in complete agreement. Christopher was no longer upset at the thought of another child; in fact, he was very excited. This was a true testimony of how God had used His truth from Scripture and our circumstances to change his heart and mine. During this pregnancy he liked telling people that his wife was pregnant with his fifth child, just to see their reaction. It did not even bother him when the rudest remarks were made by believers who gave him a negative response. He no longer cared what they thought. Somehow we both knew that this child was going to be a very special blessing for us.

As the delivery date drew near, we were having trouble choosing a name for our fifth child, mostly because every one of our children wanted to have a part in picking the name. It seemed that everyone had an opinion. We both kept praying for peace about what to name this special child. We had several names picked out for a boy and several for a girl, but they did not seem to fit for one reason or another. The importance of naming our children is another very powerful truth that the Lord had revealed to us, so naming this baby was very significant.

On the way to the hospital we both suddenly agreed that if it was a boy, his name would be *Judah*, which means "Praise." Since we are a family that loves to worship and sing together, we felt that adding another praiser to our crew would be quite a blessing. Judah came into our life on Mother's Day morning 1999, with all of the children present and several other special girlfriends. The name Judah/Praise immediately fit our bubbly baby boy.

When I got home from the hospital, I looked up the story of Rachel and Leah in Genesis and was amazed to read the Scriptural account of these two women and their competition to bear children for Jacob. When Leah had Judah she said, "This time I will praise the Lord!" With tears in my eyes I realized why we had named our baby Judah. With this fifth child, this time we had really praised the Lord! God had changed both of our hearts and had begun to grow our faith to trust Him more. Because of what God had revealed to us in Scripture, we now knew the value of a child and highly valued our ability to receive God's gift of life.

After Judah was born, the Lord began to really convict our hearts about trying to *control* our family planning. The Lord placed a deep desire in both of us to give this area of our lives completely over to Him. This was a new reality for us. We had never trusted the Lord with our family plan before. This was really a big deal for us. *We were not sure we could trust the Lord with something as great as the size of our family.* We are very fertile people, so trusting God with this could mean many, many more children. But the more we prayed about it and read the Word, the more the Lord began to convince us to at least *be open* to allowing Him to choose the size of our family.

It was spoken over our family that the birth of our fifth child would be a time of great breakthroughs. As soon as Judah was born, the Lord financially prospered our family. We learned the secret to financial wealth when it comes to the argument of not having enough money for children. God *never* brings the increase until *after* the child is born. God's Word says, "The children of the righteous will not have to beg for bread" (Psalm 37:25). He will provide for His children once they are born.

Within a year and a half of Judah's birth, the Lord opened my womb again and surprised us with another child. We had never had children this close together before! If we had the choice, we would have waited at least two to three more years. But God chose otherwise and now that our sixth child, a daughter, is three years old, it has worked out fine. This child was born in 2001 and came as the result of trusting the Lord with our family planning. As a result of this decision, my husband's salary doubled. As before, we did not have a name picked out for her until we drove out of the hospital parking lot, when suddenly the name ***Destiny*** came to me. I knew that the Lord was speaking. We had received a valuable treasure in learning to trust God in this area. This trust has placed the *destiny* of our family in the Lord's hands instead of our own.

Then in 2002, He blessed us again with a little daughter that we named ***Haven.*** Our home and family have become *our haven* of rest, happiness, laughter, and joy. I often wonder what I would be doing if the Lord had not blessed me with this many children. If it had been left up to me, I would have only had the first two. I plead ignorance! I had *no idea* what God could do with my life. But I often think that if that had happened, today I would only have my first two: a twenty–one-year-old son and a sixteen-year-old daughter. If I had no more children I would probably be working a full-time job in broadcasting or I might have pursued law school or psychology. I am not the type who could just sit at home all of the time; because of my personality, I have a need to be busier. Maybe I would have owned my own business or gone back to earn a few more college degrees. My husband says maybe we would have taken a few more vacations. Maybe my sixteen-year-old would have gotten her dream sports car when she turned sixteen, instead of the cute little Nissan that we got her.

Would I have been less busy if I had fewer children? Probably not. In fact I might have even been busier had I chosen another kind of life. Would I have had more money? Maybe. If I were working full-time, I am sure our combined income would be more than it is now. It is safe to assume that if I did not have the rest of my children, I might have a few more dollars to spend. But then again, I still might not be better off! It is just as easy to spend money when you are raising two children as it is when you are raising seven children! There are always expenses, and more money to spend just means more toys to buy.

I would not trade what I have today for all the wealth that I could accumulate in a million lifetimes! God has blessed us with many material possessions and the children to enjoy them with as well. I *love* what God has given me! I thank the Lord every day for giving me children as my blessings. I am forty-two, pregnant with my eighth child, and the mother of a twenty-one–year-old and six others, three of whom are little ones. It is fabulous! I am trying to love and cherish every moment of it. He has given me the *motherly wisdom* and *foresight* to realize how quickly time is slipping through my fingers.

This decision to trust God was not an easy one, but we know that it was the right one for us. It requires our faith to be renewed daily. It requires us to trust Him with all that we have including our future and we are comfortable knowing that He holds our future in His hand. My husband and I do not know how many more *mighty warriors* the Lord will allow to come through our loins, but we are open and will welcome each and every one. There is an excitement as we anticipate who God may bring us next. This makes us eager and grateful to be able to receive from Him again.

As you read the pages of this book. I pray that the Lord will help you see that *family planning* is something that our loving *Heavenly Father* cares greatly about. I believe that God will speak something special to each person. These are exciting times to be living in as we participate with the Lord to bring the people here who He desires to send. These individuals will participate in the final generations as members of His spiritual army. What an exciting and awesome privilege!

CHAPTER 1

Mary, Can I Borrow Your Womb?

*The womb, which houses the unborn baby, is a special
place of mystery where God perfects His creation.
Every woman has the opportunity to allow God to use her womb.
There are many blessings, some obvious and some hidden,
for the woman who walks this road with God—the woman
who is willing to be God's handmaiden.*

When I gave birth to my seventh child, a precious baby girl, God allowed that *beautiful little life* to come into my hands and again I was overwhelmed with *His love* for me. Once again He was giving me the privilege of birthing another *mighty warrior* and allowing me the opportunity to train up this child into righteousness. It thrills me to be able to participate in this wonderful process called *motherhood*.

Each time that I give birth it seems like God is giving me a deeper understanding of the awesome role that He has reserved exclusively for women. As women give of ourselves to God, we help fulfill His desire to bring the generations of mankind to earth. Through the miracle of birth, He allows us to experience the *power of God* as new life passes through our bodies and comes to this planet!

A WOMAN'S CALLING IS CONNECTED TO HER WOMB

In the Garden of Eden, the thing that made Eve different from Adam apart from the obvious differences in her physical anatomy, was the fact that she possessed an added bonus. Eve was a man creature with a womb, a *womb-man*! Her body had the ability to house, nurture, and feed another human being. This particular gift had not been given to Adam! This one thing separates the females from the males and makes the role of the female particularly *special* because this is something that only the woman's body is capable of doing.

Since Eve possessed a womb before Adam and Eve sinned, God was already planning to use her body to be the house of new life. The womb was the special place where He would work His creation. God would unite the microscopic egg and sperm so that it could grow into a beautiful new person (Isaiah 64:8). As God forms new life in the womb (Psalm 100:3), He gives the woman the added pleasure of meeting this new human being *before* anyone else can, because God's creation happens inside of her body. This pleasurable bonding time is God's way of saying "thank you" to her for allowing Him to use her body. Isn't this amazing?

Being able to grow new life is a very special event for a woman, and yet it is not always something that a woman wants to experience. Some women are afraid and unwilling to surrender themselves. As a woman I can sympathize with their position. Pregnancy can be very hard physically, and caring for young children is a sacrifice. In fact, raising children involves a lifetime of sacrifices! When we do participate in this process of motherhood, I believe that God honors our choices and sends supernatural grace to those who ask for His help (2 Corinthians 9:8). But still, even with God's help, some women believe the whole ordeal just seems overwhelming.

Does God understand a woman's struggles with this? I believe that He does. The Bible reveals the beautiful love of the Father's heart for women and their willingness to take part in thie process of birth through the example of the encounter between the angel Gabriel and the Virgin Mary. The Lord cared about the thoughts and feelings of Mary so much that He sent an angel to announce His plans to her and to get a *response* from this very special woman.

In order to grasp the depth of this visitation from God, it is necessary to separate ourselves from the viewpoints of our Western culture and try to understand this event in the cultural period in which it occurred. In Biblical times, it was the custom for men to treat women with very little respect. Women were often viewed as having menial value and many times were treated as sub-humans. Most women were denied their basic rights and could easily be bought or sold if their husband or master wished to do so.

God did not see Mary this way. The beauty of God is revealed in how He honored her womanhood. He cared about Mary and valued her as a person and as a woman. His desire was for Mary to be happy. He did not want to impose *His will* on a young maiden who may not have wanted the responsibility of caring for a child who would be the Savior of the World. God knew that this was going to be a big job, and He cared enough about her to send an angel to announce His plans and to see if she would be willing to surrender her life for the purposes of God.

In the gospel of Luke (1:28-38) we can read the account of the angel Gabriel's visit to the Virgin Mary. God sent Gabriel down from Heaven to tell Mary that she was highly favored of the Lord and that God was with her. He also said that soon she would be *with child* and that this child would be special, for he would be the Savior of all mankind. What we need to understand in this passage is that God did not send Gabriel to tell Mary that she *must* birth Jesus. Gabriel came to announce God's plan and to see *if Mary was willing* to submit to God's will.

After giving Mary the details of how this would come about, the angel waited for Mary's reply. . . .

Mary had a choice to make.

Through the angel God was asking, "*Mary, can I borrow your womb? Mary, can I use you?*"

God was seeking her willingness to birth Jesus, her agreement with His plan.

What Mary needed to decide was if she wanted to have a child and sacrifice her life for this purpose.

She could have told Gabriel a contemporary answer, "Tell God, 'No, thank You.' I have other more important things to do with my life right now. Joseph and I want to spend time with each other before we have children, and there are some things that we need to buy first, and I need to focus on my career and find my place in this world. Raising a child will take a lot of work, and I don't want to waste my time doing that right now. But tell God, 'Thanks for thinking of me.'"

Of course we know that she did not say anything like this, but that her response was an overwhelming *"Yes! Do unto me according to what you have spoken. I am God's servant and He can use me (my womb to house and nurture the Savior of the world). I am a willing participant!"*

Mary made a wise choice. Her first love was towards God, and this made her open to His plans and purposes over her own wishes and desires. Her willingness to cooperate created a place for her in God that allowed her to be blessed above all women (Luke 1:42). She said, "From now on all the nations of the earth will call me blessed" (Luke 1:48).

Our wonderfully loving God valued the wishes of Mary enough to give her a choice. God knew Mary's heart and knew that she would say *"Yes,"* but I believe that if Mary had said *"No,"* then God would not have used her. God's way is never to *force servanthood* on anyone but to find people who are willing to be open to his plan (Psalm 2:11, Isaiah 56:6, Revelation 7:15, 22:3).

God did not want to force Mary to be the mother of Jesus, and He is not looking to force any woman to be a mother. I believe that the Lord knows the stress that pregnancy and birth can bring. I also believe that He knows the fears that many women have concerning the whole mothering process. God knows that it is not easy to birth children and raise them. It is a role that any person could easily discount as being too much trouble, especially in our society which does not value sacrifices that look as if they are insignificant.

People want to believe that their time on earth has value. Many people see motherhood as a small contribution because it appears to be something that any woman can do. This attitude has contributed to the downfall of society. We place *little value* upon families and the future, and we act like the role of mothering is so easy that any woman should be able to have a family and be able to juggle a career as well. This is why many women do not want to say that they are *only mothers,* yet this role is something that *God views as precious* and a wonderful way to contribute to His plan.

*The Lord is looking for people who will be
willing and open to His plan.*

He is looking for *Godly women who will be willing to lay down their lives for the sake of the call*—women who will look past what they think their own personal plans and dreams *should be* and see that *motherhood* is their highest calling. He is looking for those handmaidens who will say to Him, "Do unto *me* according to your word. I am a willing servant"—women who will see their wombs as holy unto the Lord, who will lay their lives upon the altar just like Mary did, and who will say,

"Lord, I lay my life down so that Your mighty warriors can come to earth. I will allow You to keep my womb and my heart open so that Your plans will come forth on the earth. Use ME, Lord!!"

THE WOMB IS A PLACE OF HOLY SIGNIFICANCE TO GOD

How many women ever stop and focus on the fact that they have a *womb?* To most women it is something that women *have,* but is rarely talked about. Even though it is part of their physical makeup, women usually do not sit around discussing their wombs unless they are telling a female medical horror story. Wombs are not bragged about or compared from one woman to the next like other female body parts. In our society *wombs* have not gained the focus of our attention.

Most Godly women do not realize that the Bible actually talks about *this amazing organ* and places a real value upon it (Judges 13:5, Psalm 139:13, Isaiah 49:1, Jeremiah 1:5, Luke 1:15). God gave the womb to women for a very important reason, and the Bible tells us some wonderful things about our wombs. One of the clearest truths is that Jesus came to earth through his mother's womb. This is an interesting observation. Why did Jesus, the Savior of the World have to come to earth this way?

God could have brought Jesus here through many other means other than a simple woman's womb.

For example:

One day Jesus could have just appeared on earth as a grown man teaching in the temple, or . . .

He could have made a grand entrance by flying in on the clouds, or . . .

The angel Gabriel could have visited Mary and handed her a baby.

God did not have to choose the womb of an ordinary, yet very accepting, young woman. He must have been trying to communicate something to mankind about *the importance of birth.*

I believe that *the womb* must hold *a large degree of spiritual significance* or else Jesus would not have needed to experience *being in His mother's womb* before He came to earth. He must have *needed to experience the womb* in order to relate to mankind in some way. Since the King of Kings and Lord of Lords voluntarily submitted to come to earth through the womb, God was communicating to us that the *preparation process* that takes place in the womb is something special that *all* must experience. No person after Eve ever came here without first being conceived, grown in the womb, which is God's special hiding place, and then experiencing the transition from the womb to the world. If Jesus submitted to this, then there *must be something to gain* from the entire conception to birth experience—*something that even God wanted to put Himself through.*

The Bible speaks about the womb in several places. Scripture describes how *God spoke* and the world came into existence (Genesis 1:3). It also tells us how He took dirt and formed man and woman in His image (Genesis 1:26).

After creation was completed, then God rested (Genesis 2:2). From that point on, God did not create another human being in the same way, but He chose to use another passageway to bring mankind to earth. *That passageway was through the door of our mother's womb.*

Every person after Adam and Eve had to have a mother and a father (with the exception of Jesus) to conceive him. Then each person *including Jesus* had to grow inside of his mother's womb and participate in the experience of his own birth.

God has never chosen any other way in the history of mankind to allow humans to come to earth except through the human womb! Think about this: he has clearly made *the womb the only doorway.*

THE WOMB IS THE ONLY DOORWAY TO EARTH

This is significant! Enoch and Elijah were allowed to *leave* earth without the doorway of death but *no one comes* to earth without the womb.

Nicodemus had understanding of this doorway when he questioned Jesus about being born again in John 3:4: "Surely (a man) cannot enter a second time into His mother's womb to be born!"

Since Scripture so clearly establishes that the womb is the only doorway to earth then *God must be the doorkeeper of that door*, for no one comes to earth unless God allows them to come!

As the doorkeeper, God has to find an available womb to open in order to bring each human being to earth. He even chose to do this to bring Jesus (God in the flesh) to earth.

The fact that God Himself submitted to this process tells us that participation in birth is a *holy event* and that *it must be <u>very</u> important!*

Just as Scripture establishes that the *womb is a doorway*, it also describes it in another significant way. In Psalm 139, King David describes the womb as being an *experience with God,* a special time of preparation: "He who made you and formed you in the womb"

(Isaiah 44:2). This preparation was something that Jesus (God in the flesh) felt was a necessary part of the human experience. In the womb, He experienced a process of preparation just like every other human being.

> You created my inmost being and knit me together in my mother's womb. I praise you because I am fearfully and wonderfully made. Your works are wonderful; I know that very well. My frame was not hidden from you when I was made in the secret place; when I was woven together in the depths of the earth your eyes saw my unformed body (Psalm 139:13-16).

David calls the womb the *secret place,* a place where God creates a new person in secret. It is a place where man is not supposed to put his eyes to invade or disturb God's Holy work. It is a quiet place where the unformed child is in the presence of God, as his soul and spirit are being created by Him.

David also calls it *a place hidden in the depths of the earth*, as if it is a spiritual pocket deep inside the earth where man cannot go, but not too far from God's eyes. David's description established the womb as a *secret place of creation and holiness for God and child.*

THE WOMB MAY ALSO BE A PLACE OF HOLY PREPARATION

"In His hand is the life of every creature and the breath of all mankind" (Job 12:10).

Since David so beautifully shows us that it is a place where the presence of God is evident, maybe the Lord *talks* to the baby being formed; maybe the *baby experiences God* before birth. The Bible does not really describe the details of *our womb experience,* but David leads us to believe that something *very special* and significant to God does happen deep inside of a woman's body.

This is where God prepared Jesus.

The Bible also speaks about the womb as being *a place where people are chosen.* Just as Jesus was already chosen before conception, the Bible tells of other people who were chosen and set apart for service to God while still in the womb.

Samson was chosen in the womb to be a Nazirite and set apart for God *(Judges 13:5).*

Isaiah was chosen in the womb to be a prophet (Isaiah 49:1).

Jeremiah was called by God from the womb to be a prophet (Jeremiah 1:5).

John the Baptist was filled with the Holy Spirit from the womb (Luke 1:15).

The Apostle Paul was chosen in the womb to preach to the Gentiles (Galatians 1:15).

The Nation of Israel was made and formed in *God's spiritual womb* to be set apart as a nation unto Himself (Isaiah 44:2,24, 49:1,5).

Therefore, if someone can be chosen and set apart for sevice unto God while still in the womb, somehow the womb must be a place to ready the person for their unique calling.

The Bible also speaks of the *womb as being an origination point for God's creation,* from which the sea bursts forth (Job 38:8), where ice and frost are born (Job 38:29), and where the dawn originates (Psalm 110:3). This womb of creation is hidden from man, as Job stated in Job 42:3: "things too wonderful for man to know."

Does God have a womb? Scripture does say that God has loins (Ezekiel 1:27), but it does not tell us that He has a womb. It only shows us that *God borrows wombs from women so that He can bring forth His creation. In reality a woman's womb is really God's womb! WOW!*

Could God have created a womb for Himself? Of course; He is God. He could have whatever He wants, but He has not chosen to have a womb. Instead He has chosen to *borrow the womb* from the woman and make her role a vital part of His plan. He planned this from the beginning, because Eve had a womb before she sinned. By making women's wombs significant, the Lord seems to be communicating a special message to women. He desires to validate our womanhood through opening our eyes to see that our womb is valuable to Him for He accomplishes his purposes through us! Our womb is a special place of new beginnings and *should never* be taken for granted.

Most women do not realize what an awesome privilege it is to have a womb; it is something that no man has and no man can ever have! Men have no idea what is going on inside the heart of a woman as a new life is being created inside of her physical body. Every little kick and movement is a reminder of her thoughts, plans, and dreams for a child that is not yet born. This is a privilege that God chose to give exclusively to women. Men will never experience the same anticipation that a woman feels as she looks forward to the first time that she will hold her precious little baby in her arms and comfort its little cries and cancel all of its fears. Many women express that the days during which their bodies are creating new life are some of the most cherished days of their entire lives. This precious experience was created by God for women only.

I believe that God chose to create women this way so that both husbands and wives would have a valuable and unique role to play in creating new life. The male contributes the seed, and the woman contributes the egg, yet she makes the baby. They both share in the process, but the woman gets to actually experience the creation happening inside her body. The fruit of the womb is a new creation that is equally the husband's and equally the wife's, and this new child literally fulfills the Bible verse that says, "The two shall become one flesh" (Genesis 2:24). This is an awesome miracle!

Women of God, I want you to see that this is not something to be taken lightly!

God considers our wombs to be *holy,* yet in today's society we are seeing far too many women not wanting to take part in this *holy act* of motherhood. Many reason out whether they want to be *with child* or not. They want to plan this event around their career or personal plans. Many women feel that they have far too much to offer to be wasting their prime years *mothering a bunch of kids.* They believe that they have other *more important things* to do with their lives. Sadly, they do not realize that in God's eyes, nothing is as valuable as birthing God's eternal creations and raising them to serve Him. Everything else can potentially fade away. This is why being a *mommy* is so vitally important—it builds the future.

This was why Paul counseled young women to get married, have children, and manage their homes (1 Timothy 5:14), and also why he encouraged women to love their husbands and children and older women to train the younger women to be happy mothers of children (Titus 2:4). Many women in our society have not been taught the long-term value of motherhood. The attitude that women should find "better" things to be doing is not limited to the unchurched community. Even among God's people, there are women who do not understand the deep role of motherhood because it has not been taught to them. Many women who are seeking to be Godly in other areas of their lives have not been shown the powerful significance of their role as mothers. This is why giving God Lordship over something like their ability to control the number of children that they will have seems so unusual. After birthing what they feel is the number of children that "feels" correct to them, they then "move on" to other options instead of maintaining a lifetime availability to birth additional children if God so desires.

They have believed the awful LIE of the enemy!

I say this because if God has shown a woman that He has great plans for her life, then *all* of those plans will come true when she is also open to fulfilling her role of motherhood. When a woman allows *her body to be used of God* and submits to her role of birthing God's mighty warriors, she is taking part in the greatest contribution of her lifetime. God sees her heart's other desires.

Submitting to His Lordship in this area takes a lot of faith—the kind of faith that will move mountains (Matthew 17:20). In the eyes of God, children *are never* something that would prevent people from fulfilling their dreams! *To God, birthing and training Godly children is the fulfillment of a woman's greatest dream* (Proverbs 31:26) Building a family is a role that lasts far past this lifetime *(Psalm 127:3)*. Oh, to be used of God! This is why Rebekah's brothers blessed her and told her: "Our sister, may you increase to thousands upon thousands, may your offspring possess the gates of the enemies" (Genesis 24:60).

There is too much pressure for women in today's churches to find *other roles* apart from motherhood, and this is why so many women among God's people are *unhappy* and *confused* about what they should be doing with their lives. They are searching for their purpose because they do not understand what their most significant role is. Thank goodness that the great women of the Bible like Eve, Sarah, Rebekah, Jochebed, Hannah, Elizabeth, Mary, and Eunice saw that motherhood was their most valuable contribution!

We all need to realize that ever since time began, God has been using women and our wombs to bring life to this planet. We are highly called of God to take part in this process. The Lord values us and wants to celebrate our womanhood with us by *blessing us* with children.

This great blessing was not something that God only meant for the women of the Bible. *This is a message for today's Christian mom*, who goes to the mall, serves in the PTA, and enjoys crafts. This is God's calling to the woman who could easily spend her life pursuing other interests and personal fulfillments. Today God is asking *you* to consider serving Him by allowing Him to fill your womb with the children that He has *specially planned* for your womb to carry. This is something beautiful that needs to be embraced.

Women of God, there is *power* being released here, and it starts inside of our wombs. The calling of motherhood is the highest one for women, yet most women have never realized how *powerful* this motherhood calling is.

WE ARE BRINGING LIFE TO THIS PLANET!

Each time that a woman gives birth to a child, *she loans herself, her womb, and her body to God* so that He can send His special creation to earth.

Women are the *stars on the stage of life.* Women get to present God's newest gift to the world—a gift that can only come through a womb on loan to God!

Are you a handmaiden of the Lord who is willing to lay down your life so that your womb can be open and available for the Lord?

Do not be afraid. . . .

I know that for many of you, your heart is agreeing with this message, but you are scared. This is understandable fear. Most women do not want to be pregnant non-stop, and the enemy will tell you that this is what will happen if you submit to the Lord in this area. The enemy is so afraid that you might heed this message of the Lord that he will try to use fears to make you think that:

> You will not have a life outside of diapers and bottles.
> You will not have any money.
> Your health will go to pot.
> You are crazy to obey God.

This is what the Lord says to you:

> Do not fear for I am with you.
> Do not be dismayed for I am your God.
> I will strengthen you and help you.
> I will rescue you with my righteous right hand (Isaiah 41:10).

The Lord knows your fears and the lies that the enemy tells you. He also knows the plan that He has to bless you with when you give this area of your life over to Him. Jesus Christ is calling you as the lover of your soul to submit *your will* to Him, to trust Him with your physical body and your life. *Because you love Him, don't you want to obey Him and be open to the possibilities of what He might do through your willing submission?*

> *"For I know the plans I have for you" says the Lord, "*
> *Plans to prosper you and not to harm you, plans to*
> *give you a hope and a future" (Jeremiah 29:11).*

Put aside the lies of the enemy and say, *"Yes, I will trust You!"* to the Lord Jesus.

PRAYER for the Wife:

Oh, Lord, thank You that You made me special by giving me a womb. I thank You that it is a place of holiness to You. I want my womb to be available so that You can accomplish Your plans and purposes through me. Help me to see past my own plans and dreams to realize that my highest calling is motherhood. I will gladly receive Your creation into my physical body. I am Your humble and willing handmaiden. Please see my heart, my physical capabilities, my finances, and my willingness to participate with You. Help me, Lord, to lay down my life on the altar as I give all of my fears to You. Lord, I place my hope and my trust in You. I love You, Lord. Amen.

PRAYER for the Husband:

Lord, I thank You that my wife has a womb and that it is a place of special beginnings. Lord, please help me to be sensitive to her needs and understand that her willingness to participate with You is a sacrifice for her. Help me to honor her role as a wife and a mother and always to remember that without her participation the children that You are blessing me with could not come to earth. Thank You, Lord, for this blessing. Amen.

CHAPTER 2

The First Real Commandment

"Be Fruitful and Multiply"

"God blessed them and said, "Be fruitful and increase in number,
fill the earth and subdue it. Rule over the fish of the sea,
the birds of the air and over every living creature
that moves on the ground" (Genesis 1:28).

Anyone who has raised small children knows that parents spend a great deal of discipline time helping their children get acquainted with learning the proper way to behave in the world. Parents will constantly be either praising their children's good behavior or guiding them to behave more appropriately. When parents are helping their children make better choices, parents will say "No!" or "Don't touch that, because it can hurt you!" or "Don't do that, it isn't nice!" They are cautioning their little ones to stay away from trouble.

One of our greatest desires as parents is that our children will listen to us, because we believe that we know what is best for them. By helping them learn the rules of this world, we are pointing them in the proper direction so that they can grow up to be successful and productive members of society. We also hope that our constant care will promote trust and loyalty in them so that as they grow, our wisdom and advice can help them avoid the pitfalls of life.

I believe that our Heavenly Daddy, the Almighty Father God, believes the same thing about us. He created us to be His children, and He knows what is best for us. He gave us His Word, and He put information in the Bible that would help us make proper choices for our lives as we walk down the road of life. In the same way that we want our children to desire to listen to us, I believe that God desires that we listen to His wisdom and obey His guidelines for life. If He asks us to do something, then we need to listen! If He tells us in His Word that a particular thing is bad for us, then He wants us to listen and avoid that thing because He knows what is best for us. We don't need to pooh-pooh His advice or decide that something does not apply to us because we do not want to follow it. How would we feel if our own children did this to us? I don't believe that any of us would feel very good, because we have reasons for not wanting our own children to choose to walk in certain directions. God feels the same way about us, too.

If we do not want to do something that God has asked us to do, then we need to ask God to help us obey Him instead of fighting His command. God wants us to obey because He knows the proper way for us to maximize His blessing in our lives; *if we want to be happy and blessed, we need to listen to what He says!*

OBEYING THE FIRST COMMAND

Modern-day theologians have spent years analyzing the Bible and pointing out scriptural information pertinent to our understanding of the Word of God. We have bookstores filled with their commentaries, and churches regularly conduct Bible studies based on their findings. Pastors, rabbis, and priests also rely on their information for sermons, and many believers have benefited by listening to the opinions of theologians for years.

One thing that I do not understand, however, as I have been studying the subject of family planning in the Bible, is why the modern-day theologians, unlike past Church Fathers, have over-looked a very important *foundation stone* in God's plan for mankind.

In past centuries, church leaders, theologians, and church writers made many references to God's desire for obedience in the area of family planning. Throughout the ages many Godly men and women have voiced very strong, Biblically sound convictions on this subject. Yet today, there seems to be little emphasis by our leaders or theologians on this subject, even though it still is very important to God. I believe that this is because the enemy has found a clever way to bury this truth and make it seem archaic to modern generations.

I have been a believer since I was very small, and I can not recall ever hearing a sermon or reading a commentary about the significance of the very first statement that God said to mankind in Genesis 1:26-28.

If we go back to the beginning of the Scriptures to Genesis Chapter One, and read the first statement that God made to mankind, *we would see that GOD certainly thought that what He had to say was important when He said to man, "Be fruitful and multiply!"*

If we then read the Bible through to the end, we will see that people birthing new generations of people is a theme that runs throughout the Bible *from Genesis to Revelation...."Be fruitful and multiply"* (Genesis 1:28, 9:1, 9:7, 17:6)...."*Generations* will come from your loins" (Genesis 35:11)...."There was a man with *70 sons* (Judges 8:30),.... "...the son of..."(Luke 3:23-38)...."All *nations* will come and worship before you" (Revelation 15:4)....."Many *peoples, multitudes, languages,* and *nations*" (Revelation 17:15). The Bible shows us that there were nations of people being created at the beginning of time and there will be nations of people still here at the end of time. Within the first twenty eight verses of the Bible, God commands reproduction (Genesis 1:28) and He ends the Old Testament with the last verse emphasizing a warning to the parents, stating that their land would be struck with a curse if the hearts of the fathers turned against the hearts of their children (Malachi 4:6). Fathers create children, so here again we see an emphasis on *the family unit*.

To further emphasis the need for human reproduction and God's desire for families God then brilliantly opens the New Testament with a family geneology! Our God is NOT subtle. He continues pushing His idea of families. Several books later the third chapter of Luke re-emphasizes Jesus's family geneology again. Throughout the Bible God encourages the idea of families because the only way that any of these people throughout history can get here is to be conceived and be born on earth. God even shows us that until Christ Jesus returns and steps His foot down upon the Mount of Olives, there will be new babies being born! (Mathew 24:38). To continue along the same theme God ends the Bible by blessing the *people of God*, a people that must be created (Revelation 22:21).

God's story is a story of families.

I do not understand why church leaders today do not emphasize how important it is to God that people create more people. It is God's first statement to man! How could something *so important, so profound, and so pertinent to man have been overlooked by modern Biblical teachers?*

Is obeying God's first mandate no longer important to God? God certainly wants our obedience, or else He would not have made this bold command at the beginning of time and then re-emphasize it continuously throughout the entire Old and New Testament by beginning and ending the Bible on the same theme. I believe that Scripture indicates that right from the beginning He was trying to show us *how important* procreation was both to Himself and more importantly for us.

The Word of God says that in the beginning, God said, "Let us make man in our image, in our likeness, and let them rule...so God created man in His own image, in the image of God, He created him, male and female He created them" (Genesis 1:26-27).

God then blessed them and said to them, *"Be fruitful* and increase in number, *fill* the earth and subdue it. *Rule* over the fish of the sea, the birds of the air and over every living creature that moves on the ground" (Genesis 1:28).

Dear brothers and sisters, please stop and think about this for a minute:

God could have said ANYTHING to His new creation that He wanted to say because He was God and He was the creator.

He could have told man to always *love* each other, or He could have told them to always *be thankful* or not to forget to *worship Him.* These are the things that believers today feel are the most important things to know. But He did not start with any of these commands; instead He started with the thing that **He thought was most important** *for us to know:*

> *Be FRUITFUL*
> *(have sex which leads to reproduction)*
> *MULTIPLY*
> *(create many offspring)*
> *FILL the earth with people*
> *(until it is full)*
> *RULE and take charge of the earth*
> *Then man will have DOMINION*
> *and dominate the earth.*
> *(This would be achieved by creating more people!)*

If this was the *most important* thing for every man and every woman to know because *God announced it at the very beginning of creation,* then why aren't we still studying these verses and trying to make sure that we completely obey them? Why aren't there seminary courses on God's first statement to man? Why aren't our religious bookstores filled with books about one of the the most important things that God ever told mankind to do?

> *"Be fruitful and multiply" was the first thing that God said*
> *to the first couple, and He is still saying it to every*
> *married couple down through the ages.*

In marriage, God's mandate to every couple is: What God joins together let no man put asunder; now go and be fruitful and multiply and fill the earth with your family members. In times past, God's people continually did this, and generations were blessed because of their obedience. God's people today have unfortunately taken this commandment and changed its meaning to suit our understanding and to fit into our modern lifestyles. We have somehow decided that instead of allowing God to have His way and be in charge of our family planning during our entire marriage, that God must have *changed His mind* and forgotten this commandment. Modern believers think that what God *really meant* was for each Mom and Dad to decide how many children to have and when to have them, instead of leaving this decision up to Him. We dismiss the fact that married couples in past generations accepted this responsibility and carried on this task of creation willingly from their wedding night until God closed each woman's womb.

In today's world, most believers think that since modern medicine has created more options for controlling the number of children that we can be blessed with that we have been given *a new option* to make this choice ourselves, even though God's Word simply does not support this. This shift in our understanding of God's ancient truth has caused many Christian parents to be in marriages which lack God's intended balance for their families. When a couple makes the choice to *plan* the size of their family instead of allowing God to control it, they are not placing the *same value* upon their family that God would. How could they? Couples cannot see the future and do not have the wisdom to know what is in store for them as their married life unfolds. Only God knows the road ahead; the joys and defeats that each couple will encounter. Only God has the wisdom to know what will satisfy the inner needs of each man and woman.

God had a reason for why *the family* was to be at the center of the one-flesh union of marriage. There was a reason why He wanted couples to focus their efforts on bearing and raising their families. Unfortunately, because of lack of teaching in this area, couples today do not understand the reason why God had a plan nor do many seem to care, they simply want to be able to control their own situation.

GOD'S ONLY DESIRE IS TO BLESS PEOPLE!!

Most people in today's generations have not been taught that God's first statement to *"Be fruitful and multiply"* was anything of significance and certainly not that it is a commandment. This is because most people have never really looked at the choices they are now making in light of this statement. But when we actually take the time to study the Scripture, it is impossible to read this statement and see it as anything less than a commandment for every man and woman to follow—a commandment that His Word never withdrew.

God placed this commandment at *the very front* of our Bibles. He wanted people to realize that it holds a great deal of significance to Him. In fact, this statement was more than a simple commandment; this first statement made to man was a mandate to all people ever born, and it provides a beautiful picture of God's purposes for mankind.

Through this statement, God was saying to mankind:

From this time on—

Man and animals will reproduce and procreate! (Genesis 1:28)

Therefore God was saying, "I am finished with the responsibility of creating." (Genesis 2:2,3)

His part in creation was now ceasing, and He was

Passing the responsibility of continuing with creation over to man!

This great transference of *supernatural responsibility* indicated that He felt that mankind was capable of handling this great and awesome task. He was going to *allow mankind* to touch and participate in something *supernatural*. He was giving *the ability to create* to mankind *as a gift*. What a beautiful picture of the love of God!

Scripture shows us that this command to continue with creation was God's way of certifying that *creation* was a *good thing* and that man should continue with this *good thing* that God had started.

When we see that this command was placed at the beginning of the Bible, we can see that what God considered as *His first order of business* seems to be the *foundation* for everything else! All other truths of God build upon the principle of supernatural creation and its beautiful benefits. Creation introduces God's greater themes of love and the treatment of others; laying down our lives for others, serving others, helping others, etc.

This was why when God said:

"Man, reproduce yourself!".....He meant it!!

Reproduction was not intended to be optional.

But many couples today feel that God simply did not mean for them to be continually fruitful for their entire marriage. Once a couple has had one or two children, then the choice whether to continue having additional children becomes an option for their consideration. They will tell others, "We don't want any more children. We have a boy and a girl and we now feel complete," or "Our two children are more than we can handle," or "We do not want to be raising children forever; we want some time for ourselves." They have their reasons; they have their ideas about what they are supposed to be doing; and they look at children in light of how they will fit into their own plan for their marriage.

*If a couple reads God's Word from cover to cover, they will **never find** a discussion between God and man on this subject nor will they ever read a verse that will tell them to stop reproducing children once they had decided to be through.*

The reason why? Because God has always had a greater vision than man could ever possibly imagine and He stated His desire for man to create family members so that man could be blessed. *Creating families* has been His theme throughout time.

In Genesis, God revealed His plan for the world and set it into motion. We still see this same plan in motion all the way until the conclusion of time in the book of Revelation! Throughout every phase of history, every couple has assumed the task of continuously reproducing family heirs from their first night of marriage until they no longer were physically able to do so as old age approached. Reproduction was understood as the *basic purpose of every marriage*, because everywhere that we look in the Bible, we see the overwhelming emphasis that God places on *families.*

Every married person that we read about in the Bible
was reproducing families and not practicing
birth control, sterilization, or abortion!

The only Biblical characters that we see who were not producing a family were those who God specifically called to be single and to remain celibate or those whom He allowed to be barren. Many who were once barren also conceive at some point. To further stress the importance of the value God places on the family, geneologies are recorded in several books of the Bible. We see *family reproduction* emphasized everywhere that we read about the love of God. It is emphasized throughout both the Old and New Testaments! Family reproduction is one of God's Biblical themes.

The Bible is clear that throughout Biblical times, people desperately desired additional family members. Scripture makes one reference—a negative one—to people trying to control their reproduction in any way. Onan tried to use birth control by utilizing premature ejaculation, and God killed him for not wanting to see his family bloodline continue (Genesis 38:8-10). It is interesting to note: What does this story show us about using birth control? The birth control user certainly did not come away blessed. The Bible calls him a wicked man, and this sin was obviously one of the wicked things that Onan did. God may not have killed him for this particular act, but the Bible does tell us that he was evil and fails to mention the other evil things that he did. By using this story as an example and then calling him an evil person the Bible is inferring that God saw his "attempt to control his reproduction" as rebellion (1Samuel 15:23). God struck him dead on the spot for his wicked acts.

Some people *try to twist verses* by saying that after God said to "Be fruitful," He also told man that he needs to be responsible, which means not having more children than he can handle. Certainly being responsible is a major factor that needs to be considered. However, if this factor were part of God's commandment, then Genesis 1:29 (the next verse after this great mandate) would have told us to limit our obedience based on our circumstances. *But it doesn't say that!! Genesis 1:29 talks about eating green plants!*

God *never* tells man to place limits on creating family for *any reason*!! In fact He continously promised increase and specifically said **not to decrease**! (Jeremiah 29:6). The verses simply *are not there to refute what God was saying.* This is why today's believers need to consider making a change in this area. The only way that someone can *argue any* points to the contrary is simply to deny that God said this for today's generations. (Some may misrepresent or twist Scripture intentionally, but most believers are just misinformed about what Scripture says and do not understand God's motivation for asking for obedience in this specific area.)

God's way always proves to be the best for us!

God always has a good reason why He desires for His children to obey. It is *always* for our own good to bring about a blessing in our lives. There must be many good reasons why we need to continue reproducing, or else God would have told people *to stop reproducing when they encountered specific circumstances.* Since He did not do this anywhere in Scripture, then there must be a specific reason why couples need to be open to letting God have His way in this area. If we look at our world today, we can see that by our lack of producing needed people we have created practical problems that are beginning to affect our society.

In today's world, one reason that we need more people is for geological balance. When God put His creation into motion, He balanced His world. As the creator, He desired that this balance would continue, and this is why He commanded mankind to reproduce. This balance that He set forth is very important for the survival of creation and particularly for the survival of mankind. Everything revolves around a continuous progression that God started. In God's balance system, His desire was for new creation to continue reproducing itself over the centuries. Man, of course, having a *free will* to operate within that creation system could go against God and make choices that would affect the geophysical balance that God set forth at the beginning. Our culture pushes the idea that our choices with life do not affect the geophysical balance of God's world and they promote the idea that everything will eventually balance out. We saw this concept in the movie *The Lion King* where they beautifully used a song called "The Circle of Life" to encourage the New Age concepts based upon the Hindu beliefs about life and death. Hindus believe that all forms of life exist on a perpetual wheel of motion and that everything will eventually return to where it originally came from, creating a cycle throughout time which includes the lives of people as well. This idea goes totally against what Scripture says about life and death. However many children from Christian homes saw this movie and learned the song without realizing that they were being groomed to accept Hollywood's subtle interpretations of these godless beliefs. Parents need to point out these inconsistent ideas and educate our youth about what God's word says so that their generation can make the necessary changes to restore God's balance to our world. One of those changes will be to continue with family reproduction.

What if other forms of God's creation operated with the same *free will* that man has operated in?

For example, what if long ago, the oak tree had decided that it did not want to produce any more acorns? The oak tree would eventually have become an *extinct species* because the lack of acorns would have failed to reproduce more oak trees. What if birds refused to lay eggs or sing, or what if the sun did not want to shine? If every part of God's creation had been given a *free will like mankind's* and then operated according to its own whims and selfish impulses, then today we might not have the grass on the ground or the flowers blooming or the trees changing colors or certain species of animals existing, etc. It is the continued cooperation of God's creation that allows our ecosystem to continue.

Today, our world is suffering from the extinction of certain varieties of plants and animals. Through our careless behavior with pollutants and chemicals, man has caused these to exist no more. This has created an *imbalance*—called the *"Greenhouse Effect"*—that scientists are extremely concerned about. Imbalances are already changing our weather and other geological patterns. Our choices in the past are reaping us consequences now. There are consequences that God did not intend for our planet. God balanced things and put them into a forward motion for the survival of creation. Since mankind has moved away from God's balance, we are beginning to reap dire consequences.

In the area of human reproduction, consequences have become especially evident during the last few generations. Since the 1930s the idea has become popular in society that family planning is a matter of *"personal choice."* Today we are beginning to realize scientifically that this idea has created an imbalance. It fails to allow God to continue creation because *man chooses not to participate*. This is leading society into some very serious repercussions.

God knew *why* there needed to be a cycle of human reproduction and a balance for mankind to continue. He knew *why* we must continue with the task of birthing more people because He knew that for *mankind to survive as a species,* mankind needs to continue making new people. Just as with other forms of creation, this is very serious. It is possible that humans could *become extinct* if we keep altering God's plan.

"Oh," you say, "That sounds ridiculous!"

Really? Scientists are starting to think it's not so ridiculous.

Globally we are seeing the degeneration of our species. Because of the widespread use of birth control, sterilization, and chemical pollutants, sperm counts are going down and more and more women are having trouble conceiving because of problems within their own systems as well. In the future we may find a world where most wombs have to be artificially inseminated to get pregnant! This could lead to many forms of abuse. For instance, if the government did not like your political views or your religion, they might not allow you to reproduce.

In the first half of the twentieth century we saw generations of women having fewer children and beginning to go into the work force. In the second half of the twentieth century we saw many women not even being able to conceive. If we continue on our path, what will things look like fifty years from now?

If we stay on our charted course we will likely see more and more couples having trouble conceiving, children being birthed by surrogates or—if scientifically perfected—the widespread use of artificial wombs. Given the fact that mankind at this moment is debating human cloning, we might be heading for disaster! Our gross mishandling of God's creation will be our demise! *We need to turn back to His wisdom for our lives and obey Him once again!*

Another reason that God desired for mankind to be fruitful was because man is an eternal creature. He is different from the grass, the trees, the flowers, or inanimate objects, etc. Man is God's greatest creation because man was given a piece of eternity when God created him. God placed an eternal soul inside of man: this is what separates man from all other forms of creation.

Each person ever conceived is a *new creation* and will be given the choice to love and accept God, or to resist and reject Him. People are God's eternal fruit, and this is why He told us to fill the earth with more people—because *they are a reflection of the truth that God also is eternal!* God has promised mankind an eternal future in Heaven for those who are His friends and follow His commands (John 15:14). God has also made it clear that people who do not want to be His friends will not follow His commands (John 14:24).

Our decisions to contine disobeying God's system of balance cannot go unchecked much longer. Economists are beginning to worry that we are not replacing ourselves at a quick enough rate and that this could affect our global economy in the future.

Since our present society has begun to curtail birthing people, it has resulted in our nation not having the future workers needed to support our social welfare systems. Our choices to limit our birth numbers mean that future generations of people that would have been born will not be here to help run our country. This is serious!

Some of these people would have been future leaders of God's people, and many would have become believers! If we make choices that prevent God from having "friends," we may regret these choices. We forget that one day we will all stand before the Lord and give account for the lives that we lived on earth. I am afraid there may be many people from the twentieth and twenty-first centuries who may cry tears of loss (Revelation 21:4) as a result of their family planning choices. Praise God that there still is time left for many of God's dear people to repent and be restored.

> *How can we dismiss the first responsibility that*
> *He turned over to us?*

God has given man a free will. During the last several generations, medical advances have allowed people to exercise their free will to adopt society's *"pro-choice"* mentality. In God's infinite mercy, He is calling today's generations who have become entrapped in this mindset to begin to understand why His first commandment to "Be fruitful and multiply" needs to be followed continuously in marriage. When it is followed as God has outlined it, those living in today's generations will have *all* of the abundant blessings released upon them as His Word promises. Jesus said that He came to give *life* more abundantly (John 10:10), and He wants us to find that life by following His guidelines for our lives.

When I think about how good our loving heavenly Father is, I am thankful that He desires to show mercy to His people. Even though we have not been completely obedient in this area and have made our own choices, God has been patient and has been giving today's couples clues along the way to start the process of bringing them back to the way that He knows is best for their lives.

One way He is doing this, is through a little-known prayer that has been brought to the forefront in recent years by Bruce Wilkinson's book, *The Prayer of Jabez.* For several years this prayer has been causing quit a stir among believers everywhere. The prayer of Jabez says: "Oh God that you would bless me, and increase my territory..."(1 Chronicles 4:10). I believe that many people who are praying this prayer do not realize that this prayer comes into agreement with Genesis 1:27-28, "be fruitful and multiply."

One way in which God has always blessed His people, increased their territories and the wealth of their families was through birthing children, because it gave His people dominion and power to rule in the earth.

Most people who pray for God to increase their territory have not thought of *additional* children as an increase of their influence. Most are thinking, "Please make *me* have a greater impact on those around me by giving *me* blessings, giving *me* career advancement, giving *me* more money, giving *me* people to help, etc."—which are all good things to be blessed with.

But the way that God thinks is different from the way that man thinks. God says, *"Your ways are not my ways, your thoughts are not my thoughts"* (Isaiah 55:8). When God thinks about increasing our territory, He desires to give children as the first and greatest increase, then to send the blessings of material possessions and wealth as provision for the children that He has given. All of these blessings will *increase the territory* of one who is open to all that God has for him, especially the blessings of children. This increases the family's generational value and dominion on the earth and their realm of influence.

If some people today knew that God might send them additional children because they prayed the "Prayer of Jabez," some might not continue praying this! Unfortunately today's generations have little understanding of the powerful blessing of additional children. Thankfully the Lord is mercifully using a simple prayer to open our generational eyes and to bring today's couples back to His original intentions of what He will do if they will only ask and be open to His plan.

UNDERSTANDING GOD'S FOUNDATION

Scripture often refers to the *cornerstone*—the stone in the corner of two intersecting walls. The cornerstone was one of the most important stones in a building because *this one stone was the foundation* upon which the whole structure rested. This stone helped align the whole building and tie the structure together (Acts

4:11, Ephesians 2:20, 1 Peter 2:7).

Whenever we study *God's foundational truths* we must keep in mind the significance that each truth holds. We must also see how each truth fits into God's foundation for our lives. The cornerstone was laid *first* to ensure a good foundation.

God laid the cornerstone for marriage in the very beginning in Genesis 1:27 when He said, "Be fruitful and multiply." He said this to ensure that mankind understood the importance of why He put men and women together. The foundation for this relationship was being laid: the cornerstone of marriage was reproduction! This was what God intended. Obeying this would bring balance. This balance would be seen throughout the Old Testament covenant AND would also bring balance to the two New Testament truths of loving God with all of our hearts and loving mankind more than we love ourselves. Family reproduction takes the focus away from ourselves and places it on another person. Learning to be less selfish is foundational for loving God and for loving people. God was trying to help us out here by telling us to reproduce.

Many of today's married couples do not have *God's cornerstone* in the area of family planning. If they come back to what God desires in family planning, they will have a greater undertanding of the foundation that God intended for their marriages. The past several generations missed God's cornerstone because they adopted society's idea of *personal choice* in family planning. Because of this we see the breakdown of the family everywhere, even in our churches, and we can not look to very many in present leadership to lead us in something that they themselves are not following. Most of them cannot help it, though, because they have not been taught this *foundational truth* by their mentors either. Even though many denominational church fathers agreed with what I am stating here, this message has been lost to us and must be revived because it was God's original intention for marriages.

Instead believers in today's generations have a strong desire to know about two things.

> *#1: How God wants them to live in relation to Himself*
> *#2: How they should live in relation to others.*

Jesus emphasized these areas as being foundational truths of the New Testament, so we have Christian bookstores filled with books written on these two subjects!

The popularity of these two subjects among believers stems from Jesus' statement that the greatest commandment is to love God with all of our heart and to love our neighbor as we love ourselves(Matthew 22:37,38). Some believers think these two commandments supersede everything else ever written, and they want to throw out all of the rest of the Bible. This was not Jesus' intent. When He made this statement He was not throwing out the Old Testament but was in reality re-emphasizing the Ten Commandments.

The first four of the Ten Commandments talk to us about loving God with all of our heart and honoring what is important to Him; the last six of the Ten Commandments address our relationships to our neighbor. How does this relate to the area of family planning? Obedience to God's first great mandate of "Being fruitful and multiplying" is one way that we will love Him with all of our hearts. Showing God that we believe in what He says and then following His commands will be an expression of our love. Jesus went on to state that the other great command was to love our neighbor as we love ourselves. One way that we can love our neighbor or love another human being is by creating them (not blocking conception) or by allowing them to be born (not aborting them). Once they are born, we can teach them about the love of God so that they too can become God's friends. These are two ways that we can show God that we love Him and show our neighbor (our children) that we love them as we love ourselves.

BEGINNING TO UNDERSTAND OUR HEAVENLY FATHER'S LOVE

Why did God set things up this way? Because the concept of being fruitful and multiplying teaches humans about God by revealing His loving nature. This is a big key! When people enter into the marriage covenant and then have children, they gain a deeper, richer understanding of God's love, His heart for us, His gentleness, His forgiveness, and His goodness.

Through the creation of our *families,* God wanted man to experience *His heart* and begin to see Him as the ultimate creator, the ultimate author of everything that was good, and the ultimate God of love. *Through the beautiful experience of creating a child, a person can live the reality of love.* You could say that the experience of having children is like going to the school of God and taking His course on life: *LOVE 101: Understanding the Basics of Who Our Heavenly Father Is.* The birthing experience opens people up to experiencing the *Father's heart* because creating another human being is so magnificent that people experience the same emotions when they become parents that God feels for mankind. Once a couple submits to birthing their children, then they can go on to gain understanding of God's deeper truths. Parenthood itself then births a greater depth of the understanding of God's love because of the unselfish devotion that must come from parents in order to birth and raise their own children. Therefore, parenthood changes lives forever and teaches us the importance of understanding a part of who our Heavenly Father is.

What further reveals the *love* that God has for man is that this command to be fruitful was not just for believers to experience, or for those who He knew loved Him. *God allows anyone to participate with Him* in the joy of creating children so that *all* may partake of something *supernatural* and come to understand more about the knowledge and understanding of who He is. A person does not have to understand salvation, go to church or follow a certain religion in order to become a parent. Participating with God by allowing Him to bring forth individuals to earth is a *supernatural privilege* that He gave to *all* of mankind!

Since participating in the creation of new humans was the first thing that He wanted mankind to understand, *it can be viewed as the first act of love from God toward's mankind!* God so desired that man would experience *His heart* that He placed an innate desire to be parents inside people. They would desire to become parents whether they actually birthed a child or had the privilege of adoption. To become a parent is a privilege straight from the heart of God.

To our Heavenly Daddy, learning this *one foundational truth* is the basis for all our other relationships between God and man, and this is why it is the cornerstone! Can you grasp this? *The family unit helps us understand where God is coming from!*

The Bible shows us that God gave man thousands of years to grasp this first concept of God's love: *the gift of life.* There were thousands of years between the time that Adam and Eve lived in the garden until the time that God's people had grown to several million people living in bondage in Egypt. God had told mankind to be fruitful and multiply and increase in number as they became good stewards over all of creation. Reproduction in marriage acted as a *gateway* for God's creation by renewing His covenant with man to give life. Once God's people grew to know God as the author of all life and as the giver of sex and children, then they could move on to understand more about further serving this wonderful God who wanted a deeper relationship with them!

When the Israelites had already been serving God by birthing children for thousands of years, then God gave them an additional Ten Commandments in the desert of Mount Sinai. They already had a very clear understanding of servanthood by allowing God to plan their families and by joining Him in this *Covenant of Reproduction.* Having sex and creating children were a major part of their existence.

They clearly understood that the God of Abraham, Isaac and Jacob was a God who valued the gift of *the family* and that this gift represented *life.* They also knew that God despised those who worshipped *death.* They realized that their obedience was a covenant between themselves and their creator and that *the value of the family was the foundational truth that God began with. He then laid the Ten Commandments on this foundation.* By requiring servanthood in this first area, He could then build upon this concept and ask for servanthood in additional areas. In other words, it was obedience in family planning first (*sex and children*), then obedience to the Ten Commandments second, *(living morally),* then obedience to God's Laws given in the book of Leviticus third (*becoming a people who are set apart and holy*).

God was showing Israel how valuable this truth was for their lives because God had increased their birth rate and made them into a great and powerful nation by sheer numbers alone. *Exodus 1:12* states that "the Lord increased their numbers because the more they were oppressed, the more they *multiplied* and *spread.*" Through obeying God's commandment to "Be fruitful and multiply," God had made them into a great nation and they had gained *dominion* and *increased their territories*! In four hundred years their population went from seventy family members to approximately two million! (Exodus 1:5, Exodus 12:37) Their dominion and God's blessing of incresing their territories was threatening the takeover of the most powerful civilization on earth! This was why the Egyptians made them slaves—so that they could control over the emerging Hebrew nation before they became too powerful (Exodus 1:9-11).

Since the children of Israel had obeyed God and trusted Him with their family planning, this act of servanthood then opened the door for their deliverance out of Egypt and into the Promised Land! They were obedient even though Ancient Egypt practiced infanticide, birth control, and primitive forms of abortion. The Israelites obviously did not participate, as evidenced by their population numbers. Even when Pharoah feared the birth of a deliverer, the Hebrews continued to reproduce (Exodus 1:15-22).

It took 430 years, but God came and rescued them and brought them to the desert where *His people, after obedience with the Covenant of Reproduction (Genesis 1:26-28), were now ready to receive additional laws to live by.* The additional commands required servanthood to God in other areas such as learning to love God with all of their heart, having no other gods before Him, honoring their parents, etc. These were all commands that they could only grasp once they understood "being fruitful and multiplying." And this was the *foundation* that God intended for *all* marriages to be laid upon.

> *As a couple learned to obey, submit and TRUST Him*
> *with their family planning, then obeying Him in*
> *other areas became much easier.*

Why? Because trusting God with our family planning is a major issue for most people, even the ancient Israelites had to learn this trust. It always has been important since the beginning of time.

OBEYING REFLECTS OUR TOTAL COMMITMENT TO GOD

In today's world what most couples struggle with is surrendering control of the *husband's* paycheck, the *wife's* body, and the *couple's* plan for what they want to do with their lives. In reality when a couple submits this area to God, they are surrendering control and becoming God's servants in this area of their marriage.

This seems hard because most people tend to live for today, and the thought of actually allowing God to bring them a "surprise-child" that they were not planning makes them feel scared. God's motivation for blessing here is not fear. Children are meant to bring great joy, as well as spiritual and physical wealth. The decision to allow God to have control of this area of a person's walk with God is something that God required of people in the past because *it brought them to a place of complete surrender and trust.* Our society has chosen to no longer cooperate with God in this way and when we agree with society we are also no longer cooperating as well. This area is so out of order in today's society that the very idea of trusting God with family planning seems ridiculous. But if it is ridiculous and we have somehow "evolved" past it, then why do people have such a hard time trusting God with other areas of their lives? Maybe it is because we have walked away from how God wanted it! Couples are not allowing themselves to become His servants in this area anymore, and they are having a harder time trying to follow God's other commandments as well.

Unfortunately many of today's believers want everything to be easy and to require as little as possible from them. People do not want to make sacrifices if they can avoid them, and they certainly do not want to choose to be inconvenienced. Sadly many opt out of anything that requires too high of a commitment level, and they look at believers who choose to follow the Lord's way as being *too religious, too conservative or too radical.* They call obedience in other's lives their "personal convictions" or "their preferences" instead of recognizing committed believers trusting God with their lives as they walk a holy walk with Him.

When we look at the Ten Commandments and the reasons why God gave them to us, we see it was primarily so that His people could continue to be *holy and set apart* from the heathen societies that surrounded them. He told the Israelites, "I have called you to be a holy nation"(Exodus 22:31, Deuteronomy 7:6, 14:2). He wanted *his people* to be different from the unholy nations around them, and He also wanted His blessings evident upon His people. God wanted the other nations of the earth to be jealous of how the one true living God cared for His people as a whole, and as individuals. We see a good example of this with the Egyptians. They certainly saw God's blessing upon His people, because that blessing threatened the future of their civilization!

LOOKING AT THE TEN COMMANDMENTS IN LIGHT OF THIS FOUNDATIONAL TRUTH

Some believers today think that since the Ten Commandments appeared only in the Old Testament they are not relevant to our walk with God today, but this simply is not true. We are commanded to follow the wisdom of both the Old and New Testament teachings if we want to be completely blessed and happy. Jesus, the apostles, and the New Testament church followed *all* of these commandments. Jesus said, "I did not come to do away with the law but to fulfill it" (Matthew 5:17). If Jesus had thought that the Ten Commandments were not important, then He would not have followed them Himself or questioned the rich young ruler about following them (Luke 18:18-23). Following the Ten Commandments is the basic moral code for the believer's life; this was reinforced again in the New Testament when Jesus pointed out that we should love God first and then love our neighbor as ourselves (Mark 12:28-31).

Many couples today feel that it is *"their right"* to plan their families themselves and that this is their choice to control. But could this choice be the reason why so many believers today look down upon and have trouble understanding and obeying these simple, basic commands? Following the Ten Commandments involves our trust. Lack of trust in God may be the very reason why so many of God's people have struggled in this century with simply following His commands. In fact, we've seen the greatest moral decline since *the pill* was introduced in 1960. After this massive departure from surrendering to God's plan of creating a *family*, the moral code of our world has changed forever. Look at what has happened since unbelievers and then believers began to view the family as no longer being sacred. People used to at least save their marriages for the "sake of the children," but not anymore. The lack of children to protect may be why so many marriages end in divorce. Our society indicates the moral decline that has happened rapidly since people have adopted the "right to choose" and have stopped birthing children.

To whatever degree a person is able to trust God with their family planning, they may find the same degree of ease or difficulty in following the Ten Commandments.

Obedience to commandments is based on *trust*. Once we become ready to give God Lordship over our family plan, then we will be able to come even closer to understanding His additional Ten Commandments the way He intended. When we can trust God with *our* money, *our* physical bodies, and *our* plan for *our* future, then we will be ready for more. We also do not have to be married in order to turn our family planning over to God. We can commit our virginity and future family planning to God while we are waiting for the mate that God has chosen for us. Our heart's desire to submit to His principles when we are capable will help to allow us to grasp the deeper truths set forth in the Ten Commandments.

Let's look at each commandment to see how the way we handle our family planning could affect our obedience and outlook on every other command.

1. *God says have no other gods before me.*

The *trust* required to allow God to have our family planning helps us to be able to easily trust Him with other areas. Surrendering that trust will help to keep a person's heart free. Once people can trust Him with their physical bodies, their paychecks, and their own plans, that is a great step towards being free from other temptations. When people use birth control, sterilization, and abortion, they are not placing their trust in God but instead are trusting in their own ability to "control" their situation. By doing this they become more susceptible to idolatry and false gods because they do not understand *basic trust*.

2. *Do not make an idol.*

God does not want us *to place our trust* in anything except Him. God wants to be first in our lives because by putting Him first, we will not be consumed by idolatry. When we put false gods of greed (money), ambition (career), self-love (our desires), etc. before God, we find our time, our resources, and our love wrapped up in the pursuit of what does not satisfy.

3. *Do not take the name of the Lord your God in vain.*

God wants us to *honor His name* because His name is holy. We can honor His name by honoring how He loves. Reproduction honors His name because we take part in honoring His creation.

4. *Remember the Sabbath day and keep it holy.*

The Sabbath, besides being *a day of rest*, also represents God's transference of the gift of creation to man. When we obey by giving Him our family planning, we enter His rest.

5. *Honor your father and mother.*

Our parents are important because they are *the representation of*

God's love on earth. This is very special to God. Every time we create new life, we honor God. This also honors our parents. Therefore by creating new family members we honor our previous generations by giving them grandchildren, great-grandchildren, etc. thus continuing with the life-line of the family.

6. *Thou shalt not commit murder.*

The *value of life is precious* to God. This is why He wants us to value life and not to take the wasting of life casually. Murder steals God's precious gift of life. God does not want us to destroy the precious life that He has created by contraceptive use, sterilization, or abortion. If we clearly submit to God being in charge of our family planning, we will be allowing life to come, and this is in agreement with why God does not want us to murder. This trust will give us a strong sense of God's value of life.

7. *Thou shalt not commit adultery.*

The *sanctity of marriage* and *creating family* is precious to God. When a couple's family planning is submitted to God, then their goal for *family* will be in agreement with God's goals. This agreement is very strong because it is foundational for learning how to trust God with everything else in their lives. If a couple is not submitted here, then Satan can more easily tempt them towards other sins like pornography, sexual perversion, or adultery because they are not in agreement with the sanctity of the marriage vow.

8. *Thou shalt not steal.*

God wants us to *wait until He brings us the things that He has for us.* He does not want us to take what does not belong to us or is not intended for us. If we use contraception, sterilization or abortion, we are not waiting on His timing. His right to provide for and bless us is taken away from Him. This makes God sad because He wants to provide for us so that we can experience His love.

9. *Thou shalt not lie.*

Using contraception, sterilization, and abortion is largely about *lying to the outside world.* No one really knows what people are doing behind closed doors. A person may look one way to the outside world but in reality may be the opposite, living a lie. This eats away at a person; eventually the lie becomes visible and a person can no longer hide the truth. Many times this causes people to admit that they have had an abortion, been sterilized, or are using a contraceptive. Based on what they choose to believe about God's Word their admission may be casual or be because of conviction from the Holy Spirit.

10. *Thou shalt not covet any of thy neighbor's possessions.*

God wants us to be happy with what He has given us and trust Him for what He will give us. Coveting is about *being unhappy with what we have and wanting what others have* instead. Contraception, sterilization, and abortion can cause us to covet unconsciously because we see the children that others have and we may not be able to have them ourselves. This causes sadness and leads us into jealousy and envy because we experience the loss of what we could have had and now do not have.

See how giving God our family planning will help increase our level of trusting God in other areas? It is amazing how trusting God with our family plan will allow us to view these commandments in a different light.

What about those who are struggling with this concept of trust? Lack of trusting God with our family plan and ignorance of God's plan for the family may cause us to miss blessings. Many couples choose to block their own blessings because they do not completely understand the blessing of children. One of my friends told me about a Christian friend who lived in her neighborhood who was *with child.* Her friend had recently gotten a sonogram, which showed that her second child would be a boy. Her friend cried for days and was heartbroken because her first child was also a boy. She and her husband had both decided that they would only have two children, and now her plans to raise a daughter were shattered forever. When I first heard this, I felt sad and disappointed for this woman, but I did not understand why she did not just have a third child and try again. I asked my friend if there was a possibility that they could have a third child. Apparently this woman and her husband had always planned for only two children, and he would not agree to a third. In fact he was planning his vasectomy right after birth. Unfortunately for her, this would be it. I felt so very bad for her, but God certainly was not to blame. Giving this couple two boys was in His plan, but apparently not in theirs. Instead of rejoicing that God was blessing the first sibling with a brother and looking forward to whether a third child might be a girl, this poor woman was looking forward to birthing a disappointment. If God was planning to send them a third blessing, they were choosing never to see this child due to their own plan for their lives. This dear sweet woman may go unfulfilled the rest of her life because she and her husband chose to not allow any more blessings of children. Her unhappiness would come as the result of a choice that she agreed to make for her life, resulting in much self-inflicted pain and sorrow.

Misunderstanding God's idea of family planning may be why so many couples choose to block the further blessings of additional children. The blessing of provision is another area where couples may be blocking their own blessings simply because they do not want to welcome any more children into their lives. God will provide for the children that He blesses us with. I have watched the Lord's hand of provision upon the large families that I have known. Their children did not always get everything that they wanted—but who says that children *need* to get everthing that they want? These families were providing nicely and certainly were not starving. God provided their needs and many of their wants as well. There is a wealth of testimonies by many members of large families of how God always provided for their children the things that they needed even when the parents did not see how those needs might be met.

When we look at the patriarchs of the Bible, who Scripture indicates were obeying God with their family planning, we will see provision of possessions, wealth, servants, land, rulership of territories, etc. Their lives were blessed in *every area* when they obeyed

God. Christians should be blessed any time that they align themselves to completely following God's principles. It is promised in Scripture and should be expected as a benefit of knowing the Lord! Psalm 103:1-5 says to "Forget not all His benefits!"

AN ESSENTIAL KEY TO ENTERING GOD'S REST

We have looked at how God first told us to "Be fruitful and multiply" and how we need to completely obey this mandate and not partially obey it. We've also seen how our disobedience has thrown our world out of balance. We also talked about how trusting God here will help us to better understand and more easily obey His Ten Commandments, which leads to unlocking blessings. There is one more area that we need to understand to provide the foundation for why we need to continuously obey this first mandate of the Lord's. It is that by following God here, our lives and our marriages will rest in God's peace. I believe that this is something that most people want but do not know how to get.

When we look at Scripture, we will see that God uses the word *blessed* when referring to His creation of man. By using this particular word, it seems that He is trying to show us something amazing about His *blessing* at the beginning of time. He was giving us a clue to unlocking another wonderful truth.

The first time that the word *blessed* appears in the Bible is in Genesis 1:22. The Lord *blessed* the animals and declared that they should:

"Be fruitful and multiply and fill the earth."

The second time that the word *blessed* is used is in Genesis 1:28, where again God *blessed* mankind and told him to:

"Be fruitful and multiply and fill the earth" (with more people).

The third time that the Lord uses the word *blessed* in the Bible is in *Genesis 2:3:*

"God *blessed* the seventh day and made it holy, because on this day He rested from all the work of creating that He had done."

The fourth time that the Lord uses the word *blessed* is in Genesis 5:2 when He *blessed* both male and female as His creation and He named them "man."

The fifth time that the word *blessed* is used is in Genesis 9:1, when God told Noah and his sons after the flood to:

"Be fruitful and multiply and fill the earth."

The sixth time that the word *blessed* is used in the Bible is in Genesis 12:23, where God tells Abraham that:

"He will be *blessed* and God would make him into a great nation."

God continues to use the word *blessed* throughout the Bible when referring to the blessing of children.

The amazing thing about this is that the first time that God ever uses the word *blessed* in the Bible is when He is referring to the *blessing of reproduction* that He gave to the animals! He blessed their existence on the earth. The second, fifth, and sixth times He uses the word *blessed, He is referring to the gift of man's reproduction!*

The interesting thing is that the third and fourth time, He refers to *His own work being blessed and finished so He could rest.* He specifically *blesses* His creation of man and "*saw that it was good.*" With the gift of reproduction to both man and beast, *God could now be at rest.* "His work has been finished since the creation of the world" (Hebrews 4:3). Man and beast had been given the divine job of *continuing* with His creation!

Isn't it amazing that God passed on His
supernatural job to mere mortals!

It was God's plan that after He set the *balance* and put creation into forward *motion,* that man and beast would devote themselves to being obedient with the responsibility of reproduction by

71

continuing with His *"good work."* Man participates in the holy act of reproduction, thus touching something that is not of this world but is part of God's supernatural existence! With this in mind, we can easily come to the conclusion that to "be fruitful and multiply" is to enjoy holiness.

The *reason* why He *blessed* the seventh day was that He was *celebrating* that *His part* of creation was now completed and would be passed on to us. Since God rested from His work of creation, our continual agreement with allowing God to plan our family will *allow us to enter His rest!* (Hebrews 4:9-11)

Do you see this? God entered His rest when He passed the responsibility of creating over to us so that we could enter His rest when we obey in this area! Isn't that awesome?

We honor *His work* when we participate with Him! It's like saying to God, *"Lord we recognize that what you have made was good. Thank you for passing on to us the responsibility and the joy of continuing your creation by making more eternal creations. We want to honor Your name and Your holiness Lord, and we receive all the blessings of the Sabbath rest that come from cooperating with You in this area by ceasing from controlling it ourselves."*

"Therefore since the promise of entering His rest still stands, let us be careful that none of you be found to have fallen short of it"
(Hebrews 4:1).

Some of you may not care about entering God's rest because you do not understand what this means. In *each* and *every* area that you come to find His divine rest, your life will rest in His divine *peace* and be abundantly full of blessing; this is an important part of your walk with God. Throughout history those who found this rest were always filled and blessed. "Now we who have believed enter that rest just as God has said" (Hebrews 4:3a). Those who resist have to suffer the consequences, "So I declared an oath in my anger, that they will never enter my rest" (Hebrews 4:3b).

God said, "For *forty* years I was angry with that generation; I have said that they are a people whose hearts have gone astray, and they have *not known my* ways. So I declared an oath in my anger that 'They shall NEVER enter my rest'" (Psalm 95:10,11).

It has been a little more than *forty* years since the U.S. Food and Drug Administration's release of the birth control pill. If we look at the generation of people who have used birth control during this time, it is not too difficult to see that some of these people's lives and marriages today are not in a *state of rest* at all. Many are in a *state of unrest and turmoil* because they are suffering from the repercussions of their choices.

If doing it *our way* had been the *correct* way and God's way did not matter, then we would see the couples who are limiting their families being blessed beyond measure with lives of ease. But *we are not seeing this*. In fact, we are seeing just the opposite. Parents today are more stressed out than ever!

People with fewer children than us (usually they have two) sometimes ask my husband and me how we manage with so many children. He always says something like "Oh, we get by." He then adds, "Let me ask you a question. What do you do with all of your free time and leftover money?" They quickly respond with, "What free time and leftover money?" Their reponse always indicates to us that just because a person has fewer children, their life is not necessarily easier than that of a parent who has more children. The enemy wants people to think that the more children a person has, the more money they will need, the more time they will need, the more hassle they will go through, the more stress they will bring upon themselves. Wrong! Wrong! Wrong! If by choosing to have fewer children a person truly had more money and more time to be at leisure, then we would see parents of few being relaxed and walking in financial freedom. We do not see this at all. We do see some parents with greater material possessions and more leisure time. But they do not seem any less stressed out. In fact my husband and I feel like we are not nearly as stressed out as many parents that we meet with far fewer children. Maybe the choice to birth fewer children is not the least stressful choice.

Please let me pose a question to you: Who are we to think that during the twentieth century and now at the turn of the twenty-first century that we have suddenly gained independence from the roles set down at the beginning of time?

By desiring to become wise (and modern) we may have become fools (Romans 1:22). And Satan is laughing at our ignorance.

Some may be asking, *"Didn't that commandment, to be fruitful, apply at a certain time when the earth was new and needed people. Today aren't we overcrowded?"* God said, "Be fruitful (make love) and multiply (produce children) and fill the earth until you have dominion (keep having children until the earth is full)." He did not say, "Be fruitful and multiply until the world population reaches 6 billion." We are in the twenty-first century, and the earth is not yet full as far as Scripture is concerned, so we need to trust that God knew what He was asking of mankind and continue obeying. The earth still has plenty of space. We may have some serious food distribution problems in parts of the world, but the earth itself has plenty of usable space left. Careful research reveals much evidence that God did not leave us on a planet that cannot sufficiently meet the needs of a growing global population.

We must remember that if ancient peoples had decided not to obey this commandment and had quit reproducing, many of us would *not* be here today. Three thousand years ago the psalmist wrote, "That a people *not yet created* will praise Him!" (Psalm 102:18). That verse could apply to us living today or to any other group of people born throughout history. God's plan has always been for many, many people to have the wonderful, God-given privilege of coming to earth and knowing the Lord as Savior and friend.

When the people of God are not willing to bear the children that God has planned for their marriages and instead are using birth control, or are choosing to become barren through sterilization and or place little value upon their own abilities to give life, naturally the people of the world who do not know Him will allow this breakdown of the family in society. After all, they have no way to see God's truths unless His people live them out for them.

If we want our lives to be blessed personally and then corporately, *we must go back and completely obey God's first mandate:*Be fruitful and multiply. This is what God wants for mankind. Today, He is waiting for us to trust Him again so that He can release the blessings that have been ordained for us. Many are blessings of great possessions and wealth which the people of God need. Great wealth enables us to spread the gospel around the world and to do the work of the Lord: feeding and clothing the poor and nurturing the widows and orphans.

Being open to birthing children carries many promises of financial blessing. God promises to provide for His children. Unlocking this provision does require obedience in the area of finances as well as in the area of family planning, but when we do obey, the promises are there for us to claim. Scripture is full of promises of wealth, property ownership, and God's provisions of money!

Scripture says: *"If my people who are called by my name will humble themselves and pray and seek my face and turn from their wicked ways, then will I hear from Heaven and forgive their sin and will heal their land"* (2 Chronicles 7:14).

PRAYER for the wife:

Oh, God, I want to enter your rest! Even though having children does not sound restful, I know that your way is best. Help me to want this. I want your blessing on my life. Please forgive me for not valuing your first mandate to be fruitful and multiply. Forgive me for not knowing how important that this command is. Please help me begin to desire to obey and to get a proper perspective on obedience here and everywhere else.

PRAYER for the husband:

Heavenly Father, please forgive me for never stopping to understand the blessing of children. I didn't realize that my choices went against your mandates. Help me to be open to obey you in this area. I desire to understand how you view life. Please open my heart and forgive me for not following this first mandate.

CHAPTER 3

When Did Birthing Children Become A Choice?

The History of How We Arrived at Where We Are Today

"When SEVENTY years are completed for Babylon, I will come to you and fulfill my gracious promise to bring you back to this place. For I know the plans I have for you," declares the Lord, *"plans to prosper you and not to harm you, plans to give you hope and a future" (Jeremiah 29:10-11).*

For FORTY years I was angry with that generation; I said, "They are a people whose hearts go astray, and they have NOT known MY ways." So I declared on oath in my anger, "They shall NEVER enter my rest" (Psalm 95:10-11).

The bumper sticker on the back of my van reads, "Motherhood, changing society one diaper at a time." When I am out in public with my seven children, we seem to draw attention. Since most people in today's society do not have more than two children, I routinely have to listen to some pretty ridiculous comments. After a while I had to come up with clever responses because I just get tired of having to listen. When people ask me "How do you do it?" I say "The same way that you do it!" Some people comment, "You've surely got your hands full!" which I do not like, because it insinuates that I am doing an inadequate job. I usually respond by saying, "Our hands are not full yet! We plan to have a few more than this," which causes most people to gasp—as if we have no right to have more children if we want. But I do realize that most people make these comments primarily because they are shocked and not because they intend to be rude.

Sometimes people ask us, "Are you Catholic or Mormon?" I love the response that my husband has come up with. When asked if he is a Catholic, he says, "I am obviously one in my sex life!" Most people just laugh.

In reality we are people who believe Scripture, which says that children are a blessing from God. We also believe that Scripture is clear that we should be open to allow God to bring us all of the blessings that He is willing to give us. That is all. To others who do not understand this, we appear to be a bit off the wall. The people of the world cannot figure out why anyone would want to be raising a lot of children in today's society. It just makes no sense to their way of thinking.

This is very sad. Just *seventy* years ago the average person on the street would not have questioned a person having seven children, as there were many families with at least seven children and many had even more. For centuries people have had large families because all denominations agreed that Scripture was clear that it was a sin for people to have abortions, use birth control, or be sterilized. Only those who did not know God tried to control their fertility through these procedures. Let me repeat that: *only those who did not know God tried to control their fertility*—not those who knew anything about the ways of a loving and holy God.

God's people HAVE ALWAYS BEEN set apart in holiness in this area from the days of Adam and Eve until 1931!

Husbands and wives lived their spiritual lives accordingly. God's people followed Scripture and gladly received children as a gift. The views of God's people did not chnage until the beginning of the twentieth century, when for the first time in history, birth control methods became safe enough for users to prevent conception and not die from infection or other complications. Up until this time, when someone used birth control, tried to abort, or tried to be sterilized, they ran the risk of complications that many times led to infection or death—which also made it nearly impossible to keep it a secret if someone wanted to end a pregancy. Once safety was no longer the primary issue, *couples could decide behind closed doors whether they would choose to alter God's plan or not, and now the only people who would know would be themselves and God!*

Due to the numbers of believers who now choose to alter God's plan and use some form of birth control or sterilization method, one cannot look at God's people today and see a clear separation between their practices and those of the people who do not know God. God tells His people to "Come out and be separate" (2 Corinthians 6:17), but in this area we are making the exact same choices that everyone else is making. I believe this is what the Lord wants to change. He is calling His people to holiness in this area and to once again *come out and separate themselves from the world's ideas and practices!*

A BRIEF HISTORY OF BIRTH CONTROL

Most people are not familiar with the history surrounding the issues of family planning and birth control [2]; this brief review will help us to understand why God's people in the twentieth century and now into the twenty-first century have begun to receive less blessing in this area because of their choices. It is sad to say that as a group, God's people have gone from receiving the blessings of

God on their families for centuries to pretty close to a state of curse in the family planning area today.

We need to know what choices society in general and believers for centuries have made to get to where we are today. We need to look at how God's people have responded throughout history to the family planning practices of those surrounding them. Once we look at the history of birth control, then we can understand what God's people need to do in order to come back to God's Scriptural balance. When God's people return to the Lord in this area, they will be able to stand before the Lord in obedience as His people have done for generations. Then they will begin to receive the blessings in this area as families did in centuries past.

What most people do not realize is that throughout history, beginning with Adam and Eve, *God's people were never instructed to use contraceptives!* Many church fathers of the Christian faith spoke out against its use. In fact, Catholics, Jews, and Protestants were *in complete agreement that Scripture was clear* on this issue until 1931. As already stated, prior to that time recorded sources indicate that it was only those outside of Christianity and Judaism who tried to curtail their reproduction.

One of the patterns that we see in Scripture is that God operates in generational time periods. One way that God makes distinctions is in *seventy-year* time periods, and then another way is with *forty-year* time periods. These are considered Scriptural generations by theologians. What is interesting with this particular observation is that if we look at this subject from the standpoint of Scriptural generations, we will find that there have been distinct events where God's people in today's generations fell away from the truth at both the seventy-year mark and then fell even deeper away at the forty-year mark.

About seventy years ago the first event ushered in the *"permission" to change what God's people had been doing in family planning for almost 6,000 years!* Then thirty years after the first event, which was about forty years ago, a second event further gave "permission" to make changes in family planning ideas, confusing the issue even more. This "permission to change things" was not given to God's people *by God*, but by man's secular ideals being expressed through the medical fields which were beginning to revolutionize contraceptive ideas and sterilization methods.

I found both of these distinctions very interesting especially since the Scriptures that God led me to (found at the beginning of this chapter) spoke of how God's people who had left His ways and were disobedient *would never enter His rest* because of their compromise. Then after seventy years that He would call them back to a place of righteousness. And this seems to be exactly what is happening right now, seventy years after some of God's people initially left their previous place of obedience on this issue.

A little more than seventy years ago, in 1931, the Anglican church held a conference in Lambeth, England, and decided to change their doctrinal stance on family planning. Just one year prior in mid-1930, the Central Council of American Rabbis had voted to change their doctrinal stance on family planning as well. During this time, America and much of the rest of the world were suffering from the Great Depression. Many people were out of work and experiencing much poverty. Due to economic and other pressures, the Anglican Church ruled that birth control was acceptable in rare cases, especially if the life of the mother was at risk. This gave people the initial permission and reasoning that they needed to begin to stop obeying God's Word.

If God's people had even stuck with the original ruling—which was very strict and applied only in extreme circumstances such as life-threatening illnesses—we would not be seeing all of the problems that we are seeing today. But this is not what happened. This decision opened the door for compromise of God's principles and led additional Protestant denominations to follow with similar rulings. Couples in all denominations, including some Catholics, began to make their own choices based on personal circumstances and what they desired "for the good of their own life" and not on what the Word of God showed that God desired for people. Once this pattern was established, God's people—especially the Protestants who compromised first—were ripe for the next thing that Satan planned for them.

Thirty years after the Lambeth Conference, approximately

forty years ago in 1960, the FDA (Food and Drug Administration) introduced the birth control pill, and things really began to get out of balance. Suddenly women were given a form of birth control that was supposed to be 99.99% effective and they *were told that it could not harm them.* The other huge benefit was that now *no one would really know if anyone used birth control or not* because the risk of death and serious illness was being removed—or at least this is what they were led to believe about the pill. Couples rejoiced everywhere because this was the answer that they had been looking for: unlimited sex without the worry of pregnancy!!

The pill was so readily accepted by society,and unquestionably by believers as well, that people acted as if GOD had introduced the pill Himself and had given it to them as the answer to their problem!

In 1961, just one year after the pill's approval, the National Council of Churches declared a liberal policy of birth control use, subject to *mutual consent* between partners. After this ruling couples could pretty much decide to do whatever they wanted. By the mid-1970s the only denominations who were still teaching any sort of Scripturally accurate view on the subject of family planning were the Amish, the Roman Catholics, some of the reformed Presbyterians, Orthodox Jews, and a handful of other Protestant congregations where the pastor held to a personal conviction. The Mormons have a similar position. Everyone else (Baptist, Lutherans, Methodists, most Presbyterians, non-denominational, Fundamentalists, Charismatics, Assemblies of God, Church of God, Church of Christ, Seventh-Day Adventists, Missionary Alliance, Word of Faith, Bible-based, Jewish synagogues, etc.) had abandoned the Scriptural stance. *This "falling away" has led the people of God into a great deal of physical and emotional suffering due to turning from God's plan and choosing to make their own choices.*

"There is a way that seems right to a man, but in the end it leads to *death*"(Proverbs 14:12).

Since 1931 and 1960, many Godly people have suffered *death* both physically and emotionally as the result of these choices.

Infertility, miscarriages, breast cancer, hysterectomies, prostate cancer, impotence, and even autoimmune diseases have been brought on by choices that alter God's plan. Emotionally, they have reaped the sorrow of barrenness as they have watched others around them having the children that they would have liked to have. They try and convince themselves that they have good reasons for not wanting additional children but their denial causes them a great deal of *fear* and *rejection* as well as many other emotional scars.

Their pain was not part of God's original plan. From the beginning of time, one of His goals for people was that they would make more people. God wanted to see people filling the earth with more people so that *some day individuals and entire families would all love Him and become His friends.* He made procreation easy and fun for mankind by designing the male and female bodies for this purpose and by making sex something that would be exciting and would bring mutual pleasure.

God has never withdrawn the commandment to be fruitful and multiply. This was *His special plan* that He put into place. He wanted to *see man enjoying children* the way that God enjoys His children. In this *God-inspired network,* God planned for each man and woman to create for themselves something that they could look forward to with great anticipation. God considered it a *high honor to be chosen to parent children,* and one of the earthly rewards for doing this was to hopefully live long enough to see the blessing of the generations passing before their very eyes. Jacob told Joseph that God had given him the greatest honor. He had thought that he would never see Joseph's face again, but God had not only reunited him with Joseph, but had also allowed Jacob (Israel) the privilege of seeing his grandchildren and speaking a patriarchal blessing over them (Genesis 48:11). This is a picture of the beauty of God's blessing!

God's way will leave people *happier* as they age into grandparenthood. The more children that they are blessed with, the more grandchildren they will likely be blessed with, giving them a greater desire to hold onto life. As the blessing continues their children should be happy to have them around because Scripture says that children are proud of their parents simply because they are *their* parents and their grandchildren will be their crowns. The Bible says, "Grandchildren are the crown to the aged and parents are the pride of their children" (Proverbs 17:6).

As people age, God wants them to be looking forward as they age to a future of warmth, happiness, and a celebration of wisdom. "They will still bear fruit in their old age" (Psalm 92:14). God's plan was for people to enjoy family reunions with their grandchildren and to have happy memories of their children's days spent in their household. As they age they are to be *guiding the next generations* with the help of the Lord and with the wealth of His wisdom.

The Lord intended for dinner tables (especially during feast times at the holidays) to be filled with happy families—relatives who have all grown up together and who are continuing the family tree by having their own families. He wants His people to be able to train their own children to love Him and then inspire their grandchildren to love Him as well. *"Even when I am old and gray, do not forsake me, oh God, until I declare your power to the next generation, your might to all who come!" (Psalm 71:18).* This wisdom was not meant to *fall by the wayside* but to be a blessing for future generations!

God intended for children always to be in people's lives from the beginning of their marriages until their final days on earth. His desire was for people to be surrounded by the innocence, tenderness, and love that only a little child can bring. If possible, it is God's best plan for childbearing to be started when people are young (Psalm 127:4, Proverbs 5:18, Malachi 2:14, Joel 1:8, Isaiah 54:6) and completed when they are old: "They shall still bring forth fruit in old age" (Psalm 92:14)..

Surprisingly, Hollywood gave a beautiful picture of this a few years ago in a movie called *Father of the Bride 2* which embraced a theme that is rarely seen in America. Both the mother and the daughter were pregnant at the same time. At the end of the movie, the father (played by Steve Martin) holds his new daughter and his new grandson in his arms at the same time. As he's standing there rocking the two generations he says, "Life doesn't get any better than this." He is right! The beauty of God is being revealed at this moment. What could give a person a greater honor than to be able to see the birth of their own child at the same time that their grandchild is also being born. The old with the new, the experienced with the inexperienced, the elder enjoying this *pleasure* (Genesis 18:12) one more time.

Birthing your own child at the same time that your grandchild is being born appears *odd* to our culture. But this idea is not strange to the Lord. He intended for this to be the norm, as it was from Biblical days up until the 1930s. When people marry young, have children, and allow the womb to stay open until menopause, their childbearing years may overlap those of their children. It is simple math. It may seem odd or strange to us, but God created our bodies with lasting fertility so we can have the necessary opportunities to grow our families.

WHERE HAS SOCIETY BEEN?

Since time began, a demonic force has been working against man trying to keep him from doing things God's way. Men and women who were not believers have tried to do things their *own way*. They wanted to have all the sex that they could possibly have without producing children. Deep inside, they desired to *rebel* against what their bodies were created for; they wanted to *control* their family planning and reproduction.

History has proven that choices always have consequences. Throughout the ages, many women have contracted serious infections or even lost their lives by trying to end their pregnancies by crude methods.

As previously stated, Scripture provides a good example of a man who tried to use a method of birth control to control his situation. In Genesis 38, we can read the story of a man named Onan who practiced coitus interruptus (withdrawal) and spilled his seed on the ground. This was his attempt at stopping his dead brother's family and family name from being passed on. The Lord saw this act as so wicked that *God struck Onan dead* for doing this! Onan cheated himself out of receiving the blessing of helping his family bloodline continue, and he lost his life because of his disobedience. This is the only Biblical story that happens to mention the use of any form of birth control. In this case Onan practiced withdrawal.

The Lord was not pleased with Onan's actions, and God killed him. We do not know if God killed him specifically because he used withdrawal, but this passage is clear that he was not blessed by his actions. Instead he was struck dead for them.

Archaeologists have found evidence that ancient man tried to hinder the process of procreation. Papyrus texts from ancient Egypt dating back to 1850 B.C. indicate that upper-class women put various substances into their vaginas to block or kill sperm. These included crocodile dung pessaries; different gums mixed with sodium bicarbonate; and a mixture of ground dates, honey, and acacia (tree bark) ground into a paste and dipped in a lint tampon made from seed wool. These unusual mixtures actually had scientific properties. When fermented, acacia turns into lactic acid, a well-known ingredient in spermicide. Crocodile dung (later elephant dung was used) is slightly acidic like modern-day spermicides.

We know from Scripture that the Israelites were not engaging in these practices; Exodus 1:12 tells us that God was increasing their numbers. The more that the Egyptians oppressed them with hard tasks of slavery, the more their numbers of children increased! Their high birth numbers are clear evidence that they were not using birth control.

The ancient Greeks experimented with birth control as did the Egyptians. They used juniper berries on the penis, which was said to provide temporary sterility. They also placed oil of cedar on the tip of the cervix, and ointments of lead or frankincense mixed with olive oil into the vagina, to prevent sperm from surviving. Hippocratic texts advised women to drink copper in various forms to avoid pregnancy for up to one year. Upper-class Greek women even used rolls of wool as a form of diaphragm.

These methods were not safe, and people suffered serious illness or death as a result.

Throughout history, women have been advised to try an assortment of techniques, oral potions, and vaginal substances. They've been told to try sneezing to expel sperm, to drink cold water, and to avoid orgasm, all with the goal of preventing pregnancy. Ancient texts from India recommended salt-water douches and eating carrot seeds. Islamic doctors of the fourteenth century advised the use of rock salt, tar, onion juice, and oil of balsam on the penis; or tampons mixed with pomegranate pulp for women. Lemon juice has also been widely used in many cultures because of its acidic properties. Four thousand years ago, Chinese woman were encouraged to drink mercury. Women in New Brunswick, Canada, were said to have drunk a brew of beaver testicles.

Condoms date back to ancient Egypt when male sheaths were made of animal intestine. Archaeological digs show many drawings and documented finding of males wearing various sheaths. Even the Egyptian god Bes has been shown in statuettes wearing the birth control sheath. Upper-class women in first-century Rome are believed to have used a goat's bladder as a form of condom or diaphragm.

During the time of Rome and the beginning of the New Testament Church, Scripture indicates in many places the importance of family reproduction. The entire book of Numbers is an example of how important God felt reproduction was! We see family geneologies recorded throughout this entire book and in the Old Testament in too many places to list. We see family reproduction again at the very beginning of the New Testament as well! As in the beginning of Genesis we see the opening of the New Testament stating the same important concept: family reproduction and its importance down through the ages. What is God trying to tell us? Family reproduction is both an Old and New Testament concept and very, very important to God! These geneologies are further proof that God's people were not engaging in modern birth control customs as God was blessing their lives with increase and increasing their territories in the earth.

In the New Testament we also see the concept of family reproduction encouraged as Paul advising Timothy and Titus to encourage the women to stay home and be the caretakers of their homes, raising up Godly children (Titus 2:4,5, 1 Timothy 5:14). Paul further advised couples to not deprive each other of sexual relations except for a time of rest for prayer and fasting (1 Corinthians 7:5). Their advice coincides with Old Testament principles of being fruitful and multiplying as God blesses. We have no evidence of God's people as a global group engaging in the use of birth control anywhere throughout history until the twentieth century.

Despite the testimony of God's people, pagans continued using various forms of birth control methods. The invention of the condom—to prevent the spread of syphilis—came about around 1504, when an Italian inventor named Fallopius sewed strips of linen together to create a device which fit over the tip of the penis and was held in place by the foreskin. Condoms didn't come to America until 1840, and rubber condoms became available in 1880 but were not used widely until the 1930s (when the Protestant church began to allow the use of contraceptives).

Both men and woman have used various forms of condoms. Japanese men in 1870s wore a form of hard condom made from tortoise shell, horn, and leather. Japanese women used balls of bamboo tissue paper as diaphragms. Tribal women in Africa used seed pods as a form of female condom and plugs of chopped seed or grass as diaphragms.

Coastal women at various times in history have been said to dip sea sponges in lemon juice and place them into the vagina as a sort of contraceptive sponge. The Victorians were said to have invented a wooden block with a carved-out dome on one edge which women would insert into the vagina as a diaphragm; it was later outlawed because it was said to be an instrument of torture.

Throughout history, *upper-class women* were the ones who used many of these methods. This may be because it was common for them to give their children over to wet-nurses instead of nursing their own children. We see this happening in the story of Moses in Exodus 2:7, where Pharaoh's daughter hires Moses's mother to nurse him for her.

Breastfeeding an infant has been known to be a "natural method of birth control." Women who breastfed were more likely to be able to space their pregnancies naturally. Full-time breastfeeding causes the woman's body to put off regular ovulation for a period of time or at least to keep it from coming back immediately after the delivery of a baby. Since upper-class women tended not to breastfeed, they may have been likelier to become pregnant more often than their lower-class counterparts. This may be one reason why throughout history the upper class resorted to risky, life-threatening methods.

Isn't it amazing that every time that people wander from the way that God intended for things to be, they *always* lose? By choosing not to breastfeed, these women put themselves in difficult positions. If they had breastfed, they might have been able to space their pregnancies and not have resorted to life-threatening methods.

As America was founded on Godly principles and a firm commitment to follow God's ways, God's people were trying to make sure that birth control practices from pagan influences did not invade American society. Despite the fact that America was founded on religious principles, some people were still engaging in unScriptural family-planning practices in the newly founded country. Abortion, although extremely rare, was not regulated; and abortions did occasionally occur in America. During the Great Awakening, the country re-evaluated moral issues and wanted to stop allowing procedures such as this to degrade society. Congress passed legislation defining and banning abortion.

In 1873 a man named *Anthony Comstock* successfully passed a law through Congress that defined contraceptive information as obscene. It became a criminal offense to advertise birth control devices in the newspaper or to pass out literature discussing birth control choices. The new legislation stated that "The moment of conception was the beginning of life and therefore the life of the baby began at conception." These new abortion laws and the Comstock Laws changed things in America. (Some of these laws were on the books until 1970 and the widespread use of the birth control pill. The moral decline of that time caused Congress to let go of laws made during the Great Awakening and allow birth control devices to be imported into our country from foreign countries. This was when Germany brought us the IUD and the diaphram, and now we have the French abortion pill RU486 being marketed here as well.)

My research indicates that pro-abortion advocate groups today claim that Congress passed pro-life laws such as the Comstock Laws because the government was encouraging population growth. America was booming economically and financially and needed workers for farms and factories. They dismiss the fact that a God-fearing Congress cared about social morality and that the killing of innocent life through abortion indicates the moral degradation of society.

The turn of the twentieth century brought new breakthroughs in contraceptive technology. For the first time in history, safer choices were available and people could have sex without the fear of pregnancy. Male and female sterilization was pioneered. For the first time in history, people could become completely sterile by choice and still remain sexually active. Prior to this time people either died or could not successfully have sex anymore due to the complications caused by crude hysterectomy and sterilization operations.

In the early 1900s, President *Teddy Roosevelt* (the father of six children) attacked birth control use and saw the trend towards smaller families as a "moral disease." At the same time, the Women's Suffrage Movement was gaining ground, and feminists proclaimed that they no longer wanted to spend their whole lives bearing and raising children. Using birth control for them was a way to revolt against the notion that motherhood is a woman's primary role on earth. (In many ways this was a battle against God and His ways.)

From 1914 to1937, a radical feminist named *Margaret Sanger* worked hard to remove the stigmas attached to family planning. In 1916, she opened the first Birth Control Clinic in Brooklyn, New York. Hundreds of women came, but Sanger was arrested within a month for distributing birth control literature, which was against the Comstock Laws which were still in effect. From 1921 to 1930, she worked vigorously to repeal the Comstock Laws, but her efforts were rejected.

What were God's people doing during this time? Churches were still teaching their people to choose what the Bible says and to be fruitful and multiply. Large families were still being produced. But as God blessed America and technology increased, what did God's people do with that blessing? Unfortunately they began to jump on the bandwagon and move away from God's Word and God's plan.

By 1930, latex technology brought better condoms and the introduction in Europe of the modern-day IUD, which was first used in Germany. These items were illegal in America but people could get them because they were routinely smuggled in and sold on the black market. Objects used as IUDs had probably been placed in the uterus for years, but these modern inventions made this choice somewhat safer. Also around 1930-1931, the Anglicans and the Jewish leaders began making doctrinal compromises on family planning. Around this time, Margaret Sanger successfully convinced a few doctors in the medical community to help her. In 1933, the medical community began to support her cause. In 1936, she managed to get a bill through that supported a woman's choice to kill her baby if her own health was in jeopardy. This was to apply to rare medical cases and very isolated incidents. The Senate approved this but had blocked all previous legislation.

Utilizing the change in popular opinion that was occurring from feminists and world population organizations, as well as the Protestants and Jews adoption of modern beliefs, Margaret Sanger was gaining success. She was on a mission to see a world where women could control their reproductive cycles and choose to do things their *own way* instead of *God's way*. She felt this was the greatest way to help women. She set up the organization that became known as *Planned Parenthood*. (Today, Planned Parenthood is the number-one group that supports and financially benefits from abortion on demand in our country. After they have killed the babies, they sell these aborted body parts to be used in various industries. Planned Parenthood clearly sees abortion as a business to profit from financially.)

Margaret Sanger's greatest dreams came into fruition during the 1950s, when scientists successfully developed *synthetic hormones* which could dislodge a newly formed embryo from the uterine walls. While in her eighties, she raised $150,000 for the research necessary to produce a human birth control pill. The creation of the world's first birth control pill in 1960 meant that all women could have absolute control over their reproduction. This was exactly what she had envisioned. *The pill* was approved by the U.S. Food and Drug Administration even though there was no long-term research on the possible side effects. Women and their reproductive lives became the guinea pigs.

The birth control pill was advertised by feminists as the

answer to freeing women from the drudgery of bearing unwanted children. *Women could now be free, and couples could now choose to stop being open to God's plan without anyone knowing, except themselves...and God!*

After *the pill* was introduced, a trend toward smaller families began. No longer concerned about possible pregnancies, many women went out into the work force and brought in a second income, which—along with fewer children to clothe and feed—increased the standard of living for many families.

In "The Green Revolution," P. Scott describes what happens when countries see an increase in the standard of living of residents. Couples will *voluntarily limit their family size* to gain more material goods and more dollars to spend. "Our evidence shows us that there is a proportionately larger falling birthrate in nations touched by increased standards of living." [3]

This is one thing that the birth control pill did for American society.....less children....more material possessions!

How far things have deteriorated at the turn of the twenty-first century may be seen by analyzing the beliefs of religious leaders. Most pastors today counsel young couples to decide before they are married what form of contraception they will use. The Early Church Fathers, on the other hand, condemned both contraception in general and particular forms of it (such as abortion, sterilization, and oral contraceptives). Their writings speak of the value of children and the value of families. One of the most famous Christian leaders in Protestant church history, Martin Luther, considered birth control and contraceptive use to "be sins worse than adultery or incest." They called birth control "an inherent evil." Other Protestants such as Calvin, Wesley, Spurgeon, and the Pilgrims all condemned the use of all forms of birth control. Many Catholic popes and church writers also condemned birth control. Church leaders, both Catholic and Protestant, were all in agreement that children should be received from God with great joy. Most modern day believers would be shocked to know that their choices in family planning are in opposition to their founding church Father's or

God's ways. This concept is far from present day teachings of the scriptures.

On the other hand many believe abortion is wrong and have it in a totally separate category from birth control, but is it?

> *Birth control*: the regulation of child bearing, especially by contraceptives.
>
> *Contraception*: artificial prevention of the fertilization of the human ovum.
>
> *Abortion:* the termination of a pregnancy after, accompanied by, resulting in, or closely followed by the death of the embryo or fetus.

Anything that keeps a baby from being conceived or born is birth control. *Abortion* is thus a form of birth control because it seeks to regulate childbearing by preventing a new person from being born. Abortion clearly violates the sixth commandment: "You shall not murder"(Exodus 20:13). Most contraceptives are designed to prevent conception before the egg and sperm meet and begin new life and people use this idea as a justification for various forms of contraceptive use. They feel they are harming nothing if they prevent the conception from occuring yet in their action they are blocking God from the privilege to give life if He so chooses. The birth control pill on the other hand may be an exception, as there is evidence that the pill many times may act as an abortifacient in a woman's body (abortifacient is something which causes abortion). If this is true, then the women who use *the pill* may be guilty of murdering their unborn children.

There is much controversy surrounding *the pill*. There are many different kinds of pills and pill formulas, yet the *Physician's Desk Reference* documents that the main objective of all forms of *the pill* is to act as an abortifacient in a woman's body, with the primary purpose of preventing implantation and the secondary purpose of preventing fertilization. Most women do not understand these facts, and many believe *the pill* is working in the opposite way. In reality conception may occur, but *the pill* will prevent the fertilized egg from successfully implanting in the uterine wall, causing the new child being formed to die. This process occurs very early after conception, and the woman could have what appeared to be a regular monthly cycle but could in fact have aborted her child without knowing it. Unfortunately many Christian women today are using *the pill* and could be guilty of murdering their unborn children. Of course this is something that few want to talk about or recognize as fact even when medical science tells us that it is true.

In recent years new evidence has proved that the IUD is an abortifacient. Once proven facts about how the IUD really works became clear to God's people, many pro-life women went to their doctors and had their IUDs removed, only to be given *the pill,* which they did not realize was acting as an abortifacient as well.

Sadly many are suffering from their lack of knowlege.

Before abortion became popular and somewhat safer, many cultures practiced *infanticide*—killing a child after birth. Especially in times of shortage and famine, female infants were killed to make room for male babies, who would grow up and be eligible to fight in the armies. When the Hebrews lived in Egypt, after the time of Joseph, the pharaoh had male Hebrew babies killed because he feared of a Hebrew deliverer. Later, King Herod in Jerusalem had the same fear of a coming Jewish Messiah (deliverer) which caused him to kill the male babies. Throughout history infants have been sacrificed to idols as well. Church leaders spoke out against such practices. Tertullian, a famous second-century Catholic, said, "It does not matter whether you take away a life that is born, or destroy one that is coming to the birth. In both instances, the destruction is murder."[4] Sixteenth-century reformer John Calvin said, "The fetus, though enclosed in the womb of its mother, is already a human being and it is a most monstrous crime to rob it of its life, which it has not yet begun to enjoy."[5]

Many do not realize that there was a time when even America, "Land of the Free," forced sterilization on its people. Between 1907 and 1917, sixteen states adopted laws advocating the *forced sterilization* of socially dependent poor, criminals, retarded people, and others the government saw as allegedly unfit to have children. By 1937, twenty-seven states had adopted such laws, but thankfully after twelve thousand people were sterilized on the basis of these laws, Congress stopped this practice.[6]

This is where society has come from....

WHERE IS SOCIETY TODAY?

We are reflecting the ideas that feminism and the pill brought us.

Did feminism work? For centuries, women have been looked upon as sub-humans instead of equals to men. The feminist movement's goal of helping women did have some validity. The feminist movement helped women be able to vote, get college degrees, and train for meaningful careers. It earned women equal pay for equal work and set them free to be something in addition to motherhood if they chose to pursue their own interests. However, the problem that feminists created was that in their goals to liberate women, they sought to downplay God's primary role for women, which is mothering children. The feminist movement told women a lie: "Women can have it all—the career, the money, and, if they want, a few children too." *Their goals were to change the thinking of women* so that women would stop desiring to sit at home with ten babies and instead go out into society and "make a greater difference."

These choices created a *new form of womanhood* and intended to do away with God's order. The feminist's movement at times was subtle in their ideas as they did not tell women to completely forget motherhood (because they would have been perceived as being to anti-feminine) instead they approached the subject from the angle of establishing a career first *before* considering motherhood. While establishing their careers, many young women's mothering opportunites were passing them by. This has brought countless women pain and suffering, for when they were finally "ready" to bear children, their bodies would not cooperate. Many women have had trouble conceiving due to long-term use of *the pill*, abortions of children that would have messed up their career plans, as well as aging factors.

The feminists movement sold women a bill of goods and many are suffering from the consequences of leaving God's ways!

THE PILL REVOLUTION HAS CAUSED MUCH CONFUSION

The changes of the last seventy years have devalued one of the most important marital decisions: whether a couple should be open to receiving children from God.

Not all decisions that a couple will be faced with in marriage are of equal importance. The enemy has deceived us into thinking that we have a choice, and then that this choice is "no big deal." This causes confusion because *the enemy has successfully clouded the issues.* Today's couples think that having a child is the same type of decision as "What color paint should we paint the kitchen?", "Where should we spend our summer vacation?", or "What should we fix for dinner?"

By confusing the issues, the enemy has been allowed to take a *holy* and *precious eternal decision* and confuse potential parents into thinking that it is the equivalent of a materialistic decision. The decision to have a child affects eternity. Whether our kitchen should be painted yellow or blue does not. Unfortunately today's couples have not been taught the value of such decisions. People are told by their church leaders that the decision to follow God is an eternal one, but they rarely taught that the decision of creating a child is also one that will have an eternal outcome. Out of the one-flesh union of husband and wife comes an eternal being.

Did the birth control pill fulfill ALL of its promises? The pill was advertised in the late 1950s as being "the answer for society." It was supposed to relieve society of overpopulation, large families, poverty, unwanted children, child abuse, and marital stress, as well as to eliminate the "need" for abortion by preventing the baby from growing in the first place. Parents could now choose what they wanted and would therefore be happy! But in reality, instead of eliminating the need for abortion, widespread use of *the pill* set a moral tone for our world that opened the door for *legalized abortion.* When man does not value the beginning of life, then all forms of life become vulnerable.

The birth control pill has done much to promote the breakdown of the family during the last forty years.

Forty years later, we are seeing the results. A 1996 in *U.S. News and World Report* stated, "Since the early 1960s we've seen a whole new class of poverty caused by the widespread use of *the pill*: broken homes, male irresponsibility, legalized abortions, single moms, deep resentment and alienation between men and women." [7] *The pill* has halted population growth in the U.S. and Europe. It threatens the future of our Social Security system. In 1994, the U.S. had four million births and 1.4 million abortions. *Twenty-five percent of the children conceived were aborted!*

At the same time that *the pill* was changing attitudes toward reproduction, America began to face a multitude of other problems. In the 1960s, the divorce rate increased; prayer left public schools; both parents began working, thus taking the woman away from the home; alcohol and drug abuse soared, as well as pornography sales. By the 1970s, free sex/free love was expressed everywhere, and one-night stands were the rage. Teen pregnancies became an epidemic (mostly because moms and dads weren't around). The venereal disease herpes was on the rise, and by the early 1980s, AIDS began to spread and take lives as the result of a "free sex/no responsibility" lie to our culture.

Children known as latch-key kids were everywhere, and one-parent households became common. Many children saw their parents get married more than once, sometimes enduring several divorces. They also spent weekends being juggled between parents, always having to adapt to a new situation, leaving them without the security that children need in order to feel loved. One in three children were from a divorced family. The saddest result is that it has created a generation of emotionally wounded, insecure people, who are now very disillusioned about life in general.

Now, at the turn of another century, the pill is a *3.5 billion-dollar-per-year business* with a *75% profit margin*! Abortion kills 4,000 babies per day. Many couples can't conceive anymore. Many must resort to in vitro fertilization to conceive, and some never conceive. Many women have died from breast cancer. Ovarian, endometrial, and cervical cancers are on the rise; men have prostate cancer or are impotent, and many need the drug Viagra just to function in their sex lives.

Are ladies better off because of *the pill*? Some would argue that in the sense that a woman has gained control over pregnancy, the answer may be yes. But at what price? For many women, the price may be their precious health. Is that choice worth it?

If a woman begins to use the birth control pill in her teens or twenties, she may develop health problems by the time that she is in her forties. After twenty years of being on the unnatural hormones in *the pill*, her body may be so depleted of its nutrients that she may look older than she should, and she may feel tired most of the time. Because of unnatural hormone abuse, she may not be able to conceive, may have developed breast cancer, may have gained unnecessary weight, or may need antidepressants just to cope. She may feel awful most of the time, may have symptoms of pre-menopause, or may be suffering from unnatural bleeding; or her health may be failing in some other way. When she then reaches menopause, her body begins to break down due to damage that twenty or more years on contraceptives has incurred. *She pays a high price for her freedom. The price is her precious health!* How many young woman would choose *the pill* if they knew that maybe in twenty years or less that they would suffer tremendously from its effects? Most would tell the men to put on a condom! Woman do not want to suffer such complications while trying to work a full-time job or while trying to raise little children.

The pill did not even solve the problem of abortion! "Abortion both legal and illegal has become the most widespread fertility control method in use in the world today."[8] We are also now dealing with the harvesting and selling of dead babies' body parts so that we can use their tissue to develop medicines and vaccines. (Several vaccines are already made from human cell lines and grown on the body parts of aborted babies. In the future there may be even more vaccines created from aborted body parts. These are well known facts throughout the vaccine industry.) On top of all of this, Congress is deciding on the morality of human cloning; pro-life organizations predict human tissue farms emerging if cloning is legalized. These farms would use leftover embryos from in vitro fertilization to grow until a specific developmental stage, when the usable tissue would be cultivated and harvested. The newly formed life (person) in the petri dish would then be discarded.

The pill has caused a lot more harm than good. The enemy has won because a little more than forty years after the beginning of its widespread use, *the breakdown of the family is seen everywhere!*

Do you see how this verse can apply to our situations today? "For forty years I was angry with that generation; I said, 'They are a people whose hearts go astray, and they have not known my ways.' So I declared on oath in my anger, 'They shall never enter my rest!'" (Psalm 95:10-11). Society is definitely in a state of unrest due to their decisions.

Society has redefined what a family is, and believers have agreed with popular thinking. In 1860, the average number of children in a family was 6. In 1970, the average number of children was 2.4.[9] Then during the next thirty years the birth rate declined to fewer than two children per couple—a rate insufficient to replace the population. In 2004, couples are encouraged to bear between one and two children. If a couple has more than three children, they are usually perceived as being stupid or irresponsible. The birth rate in 2000 was 2.1 children per family.[10]

One reason why there are so many divorces may be because there are not many large families anymore. People used to stay together "for the sake of the children," but not any more. Today, there are not many children to stay together for the sake of. People do think differently about divorce when they have one child instead of six or eight children still at home to raise. When couples had larger families, marriages stayed together more often and society looked down upon the men who *abandoned their families* and judged them as being *rascals and scoundrals*. Today because there are so few children in the average family, it has become quite acceptable for a man to leave the woman and society no longer looks at this as abandonment. This lack of children to stay for, the unhappiness of mothers and fathers and the acceptance of behavior may be one of the greatest reasons for casual divorce!

Because of contraceptive use, some couples are choosing to live their adult lives without bearing any children at all so that they may pursue education, career, and so on. Sometimes these people are labeled as DINKS (double income no kids). Many of these adults were born in the "baby boomer" generation—the generation after World War II when young couples were happily putting worries of war behind them and birthing children.

I am from a suburb of Washington, D.C., where many couples would be considered DINKS. Most live in upscale neighborhoods in and around Washington. They have expendable cash. Because of their large salaries and lack of children to spend money on, they use their expendable cash to live the lifestyles of the rich and famous. Some jet to the islands for weekend getaways or fly to New York City for shopping and Broadway. They have lots of material wealth, but without the investment in a family, there is a strong probability that many of them are lonely. Due to the lack of children in their lives, many are destined for futures as elderly people without any family to care for them. The end of their lives may be spent alone.

Most of these DINKS would probably have had the opportunity to have families, but because of widespread use of abortions, contraception and sterilization, their choices may have made this an impossibility. Without children, they will have no one to whom to leave their legacies. It is sad to think that they will have missed out on one of God's greatest blessings—to birth and raise children and to have someone care for them as they age.

Everywhere that we turn we see the *breakdown of the family* being reflected in the actions of a society suffering from the *ideas of feminism* and the acceptance of *the pill*. Believers who have compromised and blended with these ideas are also suffering and many have no idea why because their denomination is not leading them to answers.

HOW WORLD RELIGIONS VIEW CONTRACEPTIVE USE TODAY

Scripture describes sex as a beautiful act between a man and a woman. Adam knew Eve and she conceived (Genesis 4:1); the two were naked and not ashamed (Genesis 2:25). God compares our relationship to Christ as being that of a bridegroom and his beloved bride (Revelation 21:2). Proverbs tells a man to "Rejoice in the wife of your youth....let her breasts satisfy you always" (Proverbs 5:18-19). Due to the stigmas attached to sex by various popes and religious leaders, many believers ceased to see the beauty of sex and began to see it more as having the primary goal of creating children.

In the **Roman Catholic Church**, these rulings are what confused people about the joys and pleasures of sex:

In 600 A. D., Pope Gregory said all sexual desire was sinful

In the 1600s, the Council of Trent said celibacy and virginity were to superior to marriage.

In 1950 Pope Pius XII broke with tradition and allowed the rhythm method of birth control. (Prior to 1950, the Catholic Church held the position that every form of family planning was sinful.)

In 1960, Pope Paul VI tried to provide theological backing for unity in marriage outside of procreation.

Today, the Roman Catholic Church, which claims to be the largest religious institution with over one billion converts world-wide, universally supports the sanctity of life. *They hold to the belief that all life is sacred* and therefore should not be taken by abortion or blocked by contraceptives. They have upheld this stance amidst global criticism.

The **Mormons** (Church of Jesus Christ of Latter-Day Saints) believe that the command given to Adam and Eve to be fruitful took precedence over eating the fruit, because God said it first. That is why they oppose abortions and strongly discourage birth control. Large families are seen as creating spirit children occupying human bodies. They believe that Adam acted in unity with Eve when eating the fruit because his unity kept the commandment of procreation.

The **Moslems** believe that birth control is permissible, and they welcome sexual pleasure. Even ultraconservatives say that Mohammed allowed birth control. However some sects are choosing not to use birth control and are having larger families so that the Moslem population will increase.

In **Buddhism,** monks are celibate. Lay Buddhists are encouraged to live the "middle way" between the extremes of sensuality and the denial of pleasure. Sex is not limited to procreation, but can bring pleasure too.

Presbyterians support birth control and abortion. They believe that sex is God's gift to be enjoyed, but not abused. Some congregations of **Reformed Presbyterians** believe all forms of birth control, sterilization, and abortion are wrong and preach the Biblical stance on this issue.

Most forms of **Judaism** believe in the use of birth control. **Orthodox Jews** believe that Scripture is clear that children are a gift from God, and they do not use birth control.

In 1999, the **Seventh-Day Adventist**s reaffirmed their views at their annual conference. They believe that it is important for a couple *to be responsible* with their time and talents and not have more children than they can physically and emotionally handle. They believe that sex is for procreation and unity in marriage and that God gives each couple the responsibility to exercise wisdom when making decisions concerning family planning. Both partners need to consider each other's needs and life's goals. Parents should first consider their finances; the physical, spiritual and mental needs of the mother; along with the social and political circumstances globally at the time. As stewards of God's creation, couples need to look past their own "selfish desires" for more children and consider the needs of others and the effect that children might have on themselves and the world in general. Seventh-Day Adventists accept *the pill* and IUD as being practical because the majority of fertilized ova fail to implant or are lost after implantation. For the IUD, morning-after pill, injections, and implants, they advise letting a doctor help with the decision. They do not believe in abortion or sex outside of marriage.

After reviewing the guidelines of the Seventh-Day Adventists, I would say that their beliefs are similar to those that most of the other Protestant denominations are currently following. I was brought up Southern Baptist, and these doctrines represent what I was taught. My husband and I were told that we needed to be *"responsible and careful stewards."* This was the idea that was pushed on us during the time that we began our marriage. The idea that "God gave me a brain and therefore I should not have more children than I could handle" was the idea that was taught the most.

We never had a pastor or Bible study teacher even attempt to teach us what God had to say in Scripture about the subject. Birth control was expected to be practiced, and it wasn't until we were married for five years and began visiting other types of churches that we first met people who had more than two or three children because they felt that God wanted them to. Even then, we had been so indoctrinated and did not know what Scripture said that we could not see the need to be open to having more than one or two children. God had to open our eyes supernaturally.

Now that we have seen the history of where society has been and understand the state of unrest that we are in at the present time,

WHERE ARE GOD'S PEOPLE HEADED IN THE FUTURE?

What does God have in mind for His people as we step into the first years of the 21st century?

Because God is a merciful God He wants to *heal* the pain and suffering that birth control and all of its deceptions have caused His people. He want to *deliver* us, and to *bring us back* to His pure way of welcoming little family members into our lives once again! Remember the verse that I started off with? It reminds us that we chose our own way. We followed after society and fell into rebellion and now after seventy years of pain and suffering, God is calling us back. Will we respond to His call?

> "When seventy years are completed for Babylon, I will come to you and fulfill my gracious promise to bring you back to this place. For I know the plans I have for you," declares the Lord, "plans to prosper you and not to harm you, plans to give you hope and a future" (Jeremiah 29:10-11)

Can we afford to keep rebelling? People are tired and fed up with the lack of blessings in their lives and are looking for answers. They are willing to make changes to gain greater joy. God is calling to us from the scriptures to remind us that His plan when followed brings great blessings.

There is a growing movement among God's people to begin to review this whole subject once again. It seems the Holy Spirit is inspiring young couples everywhere to re-examine this subject and *not* to use birth control. Young couples that I have talked with want to trust God in all areas of their lives and see using birth control as a lack of trust. They tell me, "I love Jesus so much that I have to trust Him because He knows what's best for my life!" It excites me to see this openness and willingness in these younger generations.

I believe that God wants to change our leader's hearts so that they will be good examples once again in this area. In the past, couples have heard teaching on every other aspect of raising Godly children except in the area of family planning. Then the pulpit was silent, and the couples were to make *their own choices* in the same way that the pastor and his wife had done. I believe that this silence is something that God is going to root out of His church and that we will see *future leaders emerge* who will trust God with this area once again and preach about it while being the example for their parishioners to follow.

We have taken something holy into our own hands that was NEVER ours to control! We have come far from what Scripture says and the Lord wants to lead us back to His way because it is always the best way for our lives.

"You say, 'I am rich; I have acquired wealth and do not need a thing.' But you do not realize that you are wretched, pitiful, poor, blind and naked. I counsel you to buy from me gold refined in the fire, so you can become rich; and white clothes to wear, so you can cover your shameful nakedness; and salve to put on your eyes, so you can see" (Revelation 3:17-18).

To come back to a balance in this area we will need understanding, conviction and repentance. The Lord is calling us back. He wants us to be a bride that is clean, pure, without spot or wrinkle. "Those whom I love I rebuke and discipline, so be earnest and repent!" (Revelation 3:19). We need to be earnest and repent. God is also speaking to those of you who just *didn't know* and compromised. Many of you may be past your childbearing years yet it is possible for you to repent for your decisions to control your family size so that your future generations will not fall into the same trap.

God can use your repentance to open up your children's abilities to regain what may have been stolen from your family tree.

Birth control decisions have brought us pain and sorrow. "My people are destroyed from lack of knowledge" (Hosea 4:6). God wants us to return this area to Him. He wants to heal us and make us whole again. Great is the mercy of our God.

PRAYER for the wife:

Lord, please open my eyes. I submit to you. There is so much that I do not know, but Lord, I desire to be open. Please open my heart and my mind so that I can come closer to these truths. I am scared. This could mean great changes for my body and my goals and what I want to do with my life. I am not sure how I feel about this. Lord, I give you these fears. Please work in my life and help me to realize these truths. I want to know You more and desire to place my trust in You. Please help me, Lord.

PRAYER for the husband:

Lord, please open my eyes. I submit my heart to You. There is so much that I do not know, but Lord, I desire to learn and be open. Please open my heart and mind to receive new understanding about this subject. This is something that I have not spent a lot of time examining, but I believe that You want to show me a new way. I receive that. Lord, show me how You will provide if I trust You here. I need to have faith to believe; for this I ask right now. Please help me to submit my fears to You and be open to what You want to say to me.

CHAPTER 4

What Is Really
Going On Here?

Exposing "Politically Correct" Thinking

*When the Lord first started opening up His truths to me
concerning what Scripture teaches about birthing children,
it was a really painful message for me to grasp because I
have been raised in the humanistic culture of the United States.
I had a lot of resistance to even considering what He was
showing me because it was so foreign to my way of thinking.
I had been subtly brainwashed to believe that I should look
out for myself first and be concerned with how this revelation
could affect me and my personal plans for my future. God had
to open my eyes to show me how our society has changed right
and wrong and replaced it with preference and how He intended
to bless me if I would yield my choices to Him.*

POLITICALLY CORRECT BELIEVERS

My high school biology teacher once told our class that the easiest way to kill a frog is to slowly boil him to death. This could be accomplished by putting the frog into a pot of room-temperature water; as it slowly heated up on the stove, the frog would not realize that the temperature was increasing until it was too late.

Many of us do not realize how much we are like this frog. Our thought processes have slowly been boiled to death by media spin, cultural norms, and the opinions of the individuals who surround us. Our society has subtly brainwashed us into believing that it is very important for our self-esteem to care about ourselves first and not to be concerned much with the needs of others, except maybe during the holidays or other special occasions. The rest of the time, society tells us, we should concentrate our efforts on our *own* lives, our *own* goals, and our *own* personal dreams for the future. We do not realize when we do this that we become hearers of the Word of God, but not doers (James 1:22).

We become perfectly comfortable knowing that God wants us to live our lives for others and yet living our lives to please ourselves; this happens often in the area of family planning. Many believers have never been made aware that God has a specific plan for them in this area. They do not realize that God desires to bless their lives and marriages with the children that He intends for them to raise. They have accepted the cultural norm that parents should *choose* the size of their family based on what will best suit *their* needs and *their* goals for *their* futures, never even considering that God may want to bless them differently from what they may have expected. Believers seem to forget that they are called by God to *make an impact on society* and not to blend with the culture that surrounds them. But in today's world, the enemy has successfully deceived believers into accepting the politically correct attitude that parents should *never* have to raise children that they do not want.

What defines a child as being un-wanted? Society wants
us to believe that it is the fact that they are un-planned.
Our world equates un-planned with un-wanted and has

> *convinced us that only those children that are planned*
> *will be those that their parents will love.*

Many believers accept this concept of society and believe that God would not want them to raise a child that they do not want meaning that God would not want them to raise a child that they have not planned to have. They do not have any scripture to back up this idea but many believers feel that God would only want them to raise children that they wanted. They have also accepted the idea that the perfect family consists of two parents and one, two and hardly ever more than three children. This is consistently reflected in United States census reports. For several decades now the average American family (both believers and nonbelievers) has consisted of 2.3 children.

> *Believers have come to accept society's ideas about family*
> *planning and to participate in birth control and sterilization*
> *without even questioning whether they should or not.*

This may be because most believers do not know that Scripture says anything about this subject. Because of this they cannot combat the lies that they are hearing from the society around them. Being unaware of God's truths is robbing many couples of their God-given inheritance, and most do not even care because they do not know the great blessings that they are missing. Scripture says that, "The man without the Spirit does not accept the things that come from the Spirit of God, for they are foolishness to him, and he cannot understand them, because they are spiritually discerned" (1 Corinthians 2:14). Believers cannot fight against the lies of the enemy until they understand who and what they are fighting against. "We have not received the spirit of the world but the Spirit who is from God, that we may understand what God has freely given us" (1 Corinthians 2:12).

God is calling His people to *submit* to His ways. To gain His perspective we must first understand which worldly ideas have infiltrated our thinking and caused us to accept lifestyles that do not go along with Scripture. Actually there are three terms that we need to understand: *humanism, hedonism,* and *self-worship.* All three describe the culture that we encounter on TV, in our movies, in books and newspapers, at our jobs and schools, and even in many of our churches. Everywhere believers turn, these ideas form the foundations for the thoughts and actions of our society; they are the filters through which so many of us make our decisions.

Humanism — any system of thought or action which is concerned with merely human interests or those with the human race in general. (In this belief system, *man is first,* instead of God or other humans.)

Hedonism — the doctrine that *pleasure* is the principal good and should be the aim of all actions. (In this belief system, *seeking pleasure* is a way of life.)

Self-worship — the state of caring only for oneself; regarding one's own personal needs and interests; viewing all decisions for the sake of personal advantage or gain. (This belief system promotes *a self-centered lifestyle.*)

The religion of secular humanism — Humanism is actually a religious thought process. In humanism, the *glory of man* is elevated above the *glory of God.* (In this religious belief system, *man accomplishes great things* without the aid of a Higher Power.)

There are national organizations and false religions devoted to the teaching and indoctrination of these ideas of secular humanism. They have successfully infiltrated our thinking and our lives, and they push their agenda in many different cultural sectors. We see the most influence in the realms of education, books, magazines, television, and movies. Humanism was especially noticeable in recent Hollywood movies that portrayed natural events: *Twister* (about a killer tornado), *Dante's Peak* (about a volcanic eruption), *A Perfect Storm* (about a group of fisherman who tragically lose their lives to a killer storm), and *Apollo 13* (about a group of astronauts who almost die in space). In each of these movies the characters are facing life and death situations, but not even one of them makes any reference to God, calls out to God for help, prays to God in any way, or leans upon *any form* of higher power.

What people do not realize is that all of these secular humanistic ideas cause people—even believers—to sidetrack themselves from viewing God as superior to man. Instead humanism subtly convinces people to see *themselves as being superior to God* and to concentrate on elevating themselves and what they have accomplished. It becomes easy for people to begin to think, "Everything I have I have worked hard for; therefore I deserve to enjoy my life and my things." People dismiss the fact that a gracious Heavenly Father has allowed their great accomplishments to exist or that He helped to bring these accomplishments into being.

One aspect of secular humanism is a belief that *everything that man needs to do to accomplish his own personal goals can be justified if he has a **good reason** for his decision.* We call this *situational ethics.* In situational ethics a person must make a choice that goes against a *moral* absolute. For example, Scripture says, "You shall not murder" (Exodus 20:13). But in situational ethics, a person must decide whether it is OK to murder, based on their particular circumstances. They are not concerned with the fact that God's Word says that it is morally wrong in every case. The situation justifies the reasoning, offering no other solution than going against the moral absolute.

When we analyze the situation, it is easy for our own decision-making process to become clouded; we are tempted to say to ourselves, "Well, I guess in that situation, it was correct to murder because that person had no other choice."

But is it OK? God did not tell us to follow His commandments based on circumstances. God's Word presents us with an absolute command, but secular humanism blurs the lines.

Unfortunately for believers, situational ethics gave birth to something I call *situational Christianity.* In situational Christianity, a person's Christianity is no longer based upon the written Word of God but instead depends entirely upon *his personal situation* and how *he feels* about it. Situational Christianity is an offshoot of an unholy alliance with secular humanism, and it is trapping millions of believers today. Since many of us have been influenced by situational ethics in our media, our society, and our classrooms, we are not quite sure whether God really meant for His Scripture to be taken literally. Our thinking has become so clouded that I believe that the majority of believers in churches across the country today follow a form of situational Christianity. They have come to believe that "Whatever I do is OK with God as long as it is the best decision for my life and my set of circumstances."

This may sound acceptable to our culture, but is this true spiritually? Is it up to us to interpret God's moral absolutes based on our lives and our own set of circumstances? Should we live as we see best for ourselves? Too often, believers feel that because they have been given a free will, God really does not care what they decide for their lives as long as it makes them happy.

Certainly God does want for believers to be happy, but what people feel will bring them happiness many times turns out to not bring them long-term happiness because people look at things from a far different perspective from the God of the Universe.

Situational Christianity does not acknowledge that choosing to ignore God's Word brings consequences. Many of our preachers and teachers have begun to promote the idea that God's New Testament grace supersedes the penalties outlined in the Old Testament for sinful behavior. Most believers today are not being taught that even after the death of Jesus on the cross, the concept of a person reaping what he has sown still applies.

In the New Testament we read, "Do not be deceived: God cannot be mocked. A man reaps what he sows" (Galatians 6:7). Despite the grace of the cross, believers may still suffer painful consequences (though not loss of salvation) for disobedience.

If we are being taught that the Old Testament does not apply to today's world, then we may end up like many of the believers that we see today. They are living their lives wondering why they are not happier, why they cannot pay their bills, why their marriages are not successful, why they are sick, why they do not have better relationships, etc. Some are being taught to *accept this lack and suffering as something sent by God* and rarely as the result of anything that they have chosen to do. This is because they have come to believe that their Christianity is situational and based upon their particular situation for which the Word of God simply does not apply. Some do not realize that they like it when teachers tell them what they want to hear instead of what they *need* to hear. "Soft-sell Christianity" helps them hide behind the notion that the grace of God means that every decision works out for their good and that no one should ever tell them that their decisions could be wrong. Unfortunately these are false ideas about what it really means to live the spiritual life and multitudes of believers in the Body of Christ have been misled about what it means to truly surrender and walk a life with Christ.

The introduction of grace was never meant to do away with God's wisdom contained in the Old Testament laws. During the Old Testament era, God was revealing to His people many of *the secrets for how to live the abundant life.*

God's goal for all believers is that they will have *life* and *live it more abundantly* (John 10:10). Believers do not realize that they will produce painfully bad fruit in their lives when they make choices that go against the wisdom of the Ten Commandments, the command to be fruitful and multiply, the laws of Leviticus, God's dietary laws, etc. If we ignore how God told us to live, then it is not God's fault when we produce unhappiness. God put these principles in the Old Testament to be our guidelines for life and to help us be able to choose the path of wisdom. God told His people how to make good choices when handling their money, for enjoying their marriages, for raising their families, for prosperous business practices, and for their health. These truths were God's *wisdom,* and many are still applicable today. When people ignore God and produce bad fruit, sometimes they reap so many negative consequences that they could spend the rest of their lives trying to undo the mess that their choices have created. New Testament grace does not do away with the blessings that come when we apply God's wisdom to our lives in these areas. Too many times believers today are trying to completely ignore the commandments in the Old Testament and are missing blessings because of it!

The area of family planning is one of those areas where believers have completely missed out on what God intended, and many are reaping *bad fruit* due to their ignorance of God's wisdom. Believers are operating in free will while ignoring God's ideals. All of us have the right to do as we choose but not without consequences. Because of free will, believers can choose to have as large or small a family as they want. They can choose to use birth control and become sterilized when they are finished with childbearing. These decisions will not affect their salvation, and they will still go to Heaven because they have Jesus as their Savior. They can still be with Him in glory. But, if believers make these choices and do not allow the Lord to have *His say* in this area of their lives, they will more than likely not reap entirely what God intended for them. Their marriages and relationships may suffer and they may even reap bad fruit in their physical bodies as a result. They also may get to Heaven and find out that there was so much more planned for their lives and their generations that they missed out on (1 Corinthians 3:12-15, Revelation 21:4). *This is their choice.* Believers have been given liberty, but it carries a responsibility and a price tag.

Another thing that secular humanism brought to us besides situational ethics and situational Christianity was that it paved the way for us to embrace the ideals of feminism. The feminist movement did benefit women by opening doors for women to vote, to drive cars, and to become educated. It also brought equal money for equal work. But one of the bad things that it did was to bring about *gender confusion.*

Once feminism was embraced by society, men and women were considered complete equals. Therefore a man was no longer expected to open doors for women or give up his seat on a bus, not even for a pregnant woman. Women have also become confused about what they are supposed to be trying to accomplish. *Who am I?* has become a question that many young women have been asking themselves.

Society tells a young woman that she should not be *just a wife and mother, but also should have a career.* Giving in to society's pressures, women head off to college and out into the career world looking for fulfillment. The fulfillment they find is there, but at what cost? Who must suffer for the woman to find this fulfillment? The innocent children have been the ones bearing this burden for several generations now.

Fulfillment in the world's workplace more than likely is not where God intended for women to find the majority of their happiness—at least not during the same years in which their bodies are capable of childbearing. As women have become confused about the differences between male and female roles, their lives have become increasingly unhappy. Gender confusion has tried to make women become like men and men become like women. The women must go out into the work force and "bring home the bacon" as well as be able to care for the children. The men must stay home and "help out with the housework and be sensitive to the family's needs." Even though these role reversals did bring some needed changes, for the most part they have left men and women feeling confused. Many are weary because they are trying to make themselves fit into new roles that society constantly redefines and changes.

Often when a woman gives up her opportunities to be a mother in exchange for career advancement, she usually loses out somewhere else in her life. As she seeks fulfillment in the workplace, she loses out on fulfillment achieved by mothering a family. Many times her loss is irreplaceable because her body really does have a biological clock and it really is ticking.

In 1987 Hollywood produced a wonderful movie that addressed this very subject. In *Baby Boom* Diane Keaton plays a career woman who had risen to the top of her career. She had a degree from Harvard and made a six-figure income at a prestigious ad agency. She was very happy with her life and totally career-oriented until one day she was given charge of an orphan. At first she wanted to give the child up for adoption, but she eventually realized that she should parent the little girl herself. Seemingly overnight she was transformed into a caring mother with a strong desire to be the best parent that she possibly could be. It is a lovely story of one woman's transformation from "having it all" to the realization that *having it all leaves a void*. In the end, her life is very blessed for the choices that she has made, and she realizes that true happiness is *not* what she originally had envisioned. Being a mother was what made her truly happy. Being a mother also did not stop her from fulfilling her career ambitions; she just had to learn how to accomplish her goals differently from when she was not a mother.

An idea that always amazes me—one that this movie rein-forces—is that when people are given a child they can be trans-formed into warm and caring people simply because a person smaller than themselves needs them. When this happens it is a beautiful picture of our Heavenly Father's love.

POPULAR CULTURE INFLUENCES US MORE THAN WE REALIZE

I believe that in today's society, many churchgoing people base their value of a human being on what they see in our popular culture and not on the Word of God. In fact, it is rare to find a Bible-believing person who knows what the Word of God says about the subject of birth control and what it might mean to trust God with this area of their lives. At the same time, many of these same people know the latest trends in pop culture, TV, and Hollywood movies!

For example, if we consider the effect that television and movies have had on our beliefs, we may find some reasons why God's people and society in general do not want children.

I noticed that from the time that I was leaving high school in 1978, TV shows like *The Brady Bunch* with their six kids were long gone, and the new mindset was that fewer kids was better. Holly-wood followed suit and started producing movies in which families had only one or two children.

In 1980 the movie *Kramer vs. Kramer* introduced a new idea about parenthood. In the film, the couple only had one child and then divorced. The new idea was that the father instead of the mother was the better parent. This movie did a lot to change popu-lar views on the nuclear family and the role of motherhood. It was a big hit at the box office, indicating that people liked this movie and wanted more like it.

Hollywood followed with a whole series of movies during the next twenty years where the ideals of marriage were changed. Also the ideal family was portrayed as having only one or two children: one child per family in *The Champ*, *Fatal Attraction*, *Pay it Forward*, *Sleepless in Seattle*, *Jingle all the Way*, *Richie Rich*, and

The Princess Diaries; two children (one boy and one girl) per family: *What about Bob?, Father of the Bride, Spy Kids* and *Honey, I Shrunk the Kids.*

Hollywood has been pushing the idea of smaller families for years! Even in the 1930s, when many families were quite large, the Shirley Temple movies always placed Shirley in a family where she had no siblings. We always saw Shirley all alone as an orphan or with only one parent. One movie, *Our Little Girl,* even tackled the idea of divorce which was almost unheard of in those days.

In the 1950s, when TV became popular, shows such as *Ozzie and Harriet* and *Leave It to Beaver* had only two children, and *I Love Lucy, The Andy Griffith Show,* and *Dennis the Menace* had only one child. None of these shows ever portrayed the friends of any of the main characters as being from large families either. Yet all of these shows became very popular even though there were still many children in the Thirties, Forties, and Fifties that were being raised in families with three or more children! Fortunately, the movie studios were still producing a few films during that time that featured large families, such as *Cheaper by the Dozen* (a family with twelve children) and *Spencer's Mountain* (nine children).

By the 1960s, Hollywood began to make a real switch. (Remember the birth control pill was now being used by millions of couples and the idea of a large nuclear family was quickly disappearing). Films about large families were still produced, but it was clear that they were Roman Catholic families (which was to indicate somehow that these were the only people who still desired large families).

Films such as *The Sound of Music* (seven children) and *Yours, Mine and Ours!* (a blended family of nineteen children) portray the family in a positive way, but this was no longer the norm, so Hollywood also produced films such as *Chitty-Chitty Bang-Bang* (two children), *Charlie and the Chocolate Factory,* and *Winnie the Pooh* (one child).

We also saw for the first time the popularity of new themes in American movies. *Mary Poppins* added a new mommy figure, a nanny! Nannies had been popular in England for years, but for Americans this was a new concept. Instead of the mother and father caring for the two children, now the children had a better caretaker, a nanny who could do a more efficient job than either parent. This film must have done a good job of convincing people that nannies were adequate caregivers because by the 1980s it had become quite popular for working mothers to hire a nanny for their children. These 1980s parents were the same people who saw *Mary Poppins* as children and maybe dreamed themselves of having someone to play with them as good as Mary Poppins.

During the 1970s only a few TV shows depicted large families: *The Waltons* (a Depression-era poverty-stricken family whose grandparents lived with them), *Eight Is Enough* (a blended family), and the *Little House on the Prairie* (the family grew as the series continued).

Small families continued to be the norm on TV in the 1980s. However, in the late 1980s one TV show that portrayed a very positive pro-family view came forth. *The Cosby Show* positively portrayed an African-American family of working professionals with five children. Dr. and Mrs. Huxtable were happily married, highly educated, financially successful, and very good parents. This popular program changed public perception of African-American families.

In the 1990s families began to be portrayed as being extremely dysfunctional in shows such as *Roseanne, The Simpsons, Married with Children,* and *The Osbournes.* Some of the themes that these shows tackle were unheard of on TV even a decade earlier: poor manners, making rude and disgusting remarks, kids talking back to parents and rebelling, disrespect, sexual undertones, and poor relationships. These types of shows convince viewers that *all* families are dysfunctional and that children cannot be controlled, disciplined, or taught any form of manners.

Movies rarely portray large families; when they do, the families are usually depicted as poor because they are raising more children than they can afford. In *National Lampoon's Vacation,* the Griswalds (a two-child nuclear family with a boy and a girl), visit their home schooling, poverty-stricken cousins who live on a farm and are raising immorally impure children. The couple appears uneducated and clearly overwhelmed with more children than they seem to be able to handle—a portrayal which brainwashes viewers into believing that all large families have these kinds of problems. People seeing this on the big screen aren't going to want this hardship for themselves, so naturally they will agree with the subtle message that children are not necessary unless they are wanted, and parents *should* be able to afford them.

Hollywood's messages are subtle. They put across ideas that over time convince us that since we are not seeing things portrayed any other way, this must be the norm for everyone. We are hypnotized into thinking that all families are small, large families are impoverished, and the parents of many children are just irresponsible morons. It is hard even for God's people to realize that this is *a mirage* because it is so convincing. After a while we begin to think that in every circumstance, life is the way that we are seeing it portrayed by Hollywood.

Everywhere in pop culture, the focus is on not getting ourselves into circumstances that would hurt us or cause unnecessary hardships. This *SELFish outlook* is influencing all of our choices as it reminds us that *we are important* and that things should be for *our enjoyment* and *our pleasure.* We are told that if something will not give us great pleasure, then we should not have to put up with it. This is the influence of hedonism on our culture. Our culture always focuses on our self. Even our TV commercials tell us to "Be all that you can be" and "Have it your way." Our magazines have titles such as *SELF* and *Me.* We are told that *everything* is for our good, especially when seeking pleasure.

This emphasis on putting self first also stresses that *sex is for pleasure and not childbearing.* Pregnancy is seen primarily as the messy consequence of a pleasurable act. Society and Bible-believing clergy encourage couples to use birth control to avoid *unwanted children* while searching for sexual fulfillment in marriage.

When we trade God's mindset for society's, we will *only want children when we want them and see no reason to have them if we do not want them.* This way we will never have to suffer an "oops" baby or create the kid that was a "mistake." Our society and churchgoing believers have come to think that unless a child is planned, the child has no value (thus the reason to use birth control), therefore the child should not be allowed to be born (the practical reasoning for abortion). I would hope that in the event of contraceptive failure, most churchgoers would at least opt to go ahead and have an "oops" baby rather than an abortion.

Where did we get the idea that children should be wanted in order to be born? The American people are constantly being bombarded with stories of unwanted children in the news and on TV shows such as *20/20, 48 Hours,* and *60 Minutes.* They use media spin to create stories that push the mindset of our self-absorbed world. They tell us of the tragic tales of unwanted children who are victims of poverty and broken homes. Of course these stories are true for a very small percentage of the population, but that point is not stressed. They tell us that the worst thing that could possibly happen to a woman is to be made to birth and to raise an unwanted child. What we are not guarding against in our minds is that these sad depictions of poverty and broken homes subtly cause us to reason who has value and who doesn't. We find ourselves wondering why these parents would have a child if they did not want him.

You see? We get trapped into believing that people should not have to conceive, birth, or raise unwanted children. This is so subtle that we do not even realize that *we are in agreement with the ideas of society and not the ideas of our Lord.*

The Lord says that *every child is a gift* (James 1:17). In God's eyes there is no such thing as an unwanted child because to God *each child is sent to be a blessing* (Psalm 127:5).

The media never show us the other side of the unwanted-child scenario. They never show stories about women who were initially shocked or displeased to be pregnant but who either during pregnancy or at birth decided to accept the child. If these women could do it all over again they would still decide to keep the child. They also do not show parents who were initially shocked or dismayed about a pregnancy yet found that the child brings great happiness. Instead we are led to believe that once a person is conceived in an unwanted circumstance, he will be unwanted for the rest of his life and that his parents will never love him. This is simply not true! Unfortunately these types of portrayals mislead and convince people—even God's people—that they should hesitate before conceiving a child that they do not think that they want because the decision to have a child should always be carefully planned by the parents.

Once we are indoctrinated into a *politically correct mindset* in the area of family planning, we will have trouble discerning truth from lies. Politically correct words influence us more than we realize. One way that we are deceived is when society uses politically correct words to describe medical procedures that alter God's plan. Word choices can make people feel more comfortable and soften the effect of surgical procedures that steal the inheritance of God's people. We should be outraged, but instead we begin to actually accept this terminology into our own vocabularies:

> *Pro-Choice* instead of PRO-ABORTION
> *Infertile* instead of BARREN
> *Vasectomy* or *tubes tied* instead of STERILIZATION

Most people do not want to hear the words *abortion* or *sterilized* because they bring a sorrowful picture to their minds. When they hear the word *abortion* instead of *pro-choice,* they think of the abortive medical procedure. When they hear the word *sterilized*, they think of the forced sterilization done by the Nazis in Hitler's Germany, by Communists in Red China, and here in the United States in the thirties, forties, and fifties to innocent mentally ill, retarded, and epileptic people. These are ugly reminders. Sterilization is also a word that we use to refer to control animal population. Softer words such as vasectomy and tubal-ligation help them to forget that we are sterilizing people as well as animals. For comfort's sake, we use politically correct phrases to dull the senses and appease the conscience. Even clergy now use these phrases from the pulpit.

What would happen if we heard the words *pro-death* or *pro-killing-of-innocent-babies* instead of *pro-choice*? It might evoke a different reaction in us. How about *destroying your God-given rights to ever bear children again* instead of *getting your tubes tied,* or *blocking God's plan* instead of *birth control*? If we were fed a diet of TRUTH every once in a while, we might be making other choices!

Society's attitudes have successfully influenced everyone, including God's people.

By following society's lead, God's dear people have surrendered to the idea that children should be *wanted and planned* by parents. God's people will argue with intensity trying to defend their personal reasons for why they should *always have the right* to plan their own families instead of trusting God to do it. The anger that can be expressed when the subject is brought up amazes me.

Since secular humanism is in reality the worship of man and his accomplishments without God, when engrossed in humanism, man forgets God and forgets to thank Him for the ability to accomplish great things. *His focus and his attention are placed upon HIMSELF.* It is almost hypnotic. Everything becomes focused upon individual gain, which is the opposite of the love expressed in Christianity. Christianity teaches love and sacrifice that does not benefit us. Jesus said, "Whoever wants to become great among you must be your servant" (Matthew 20:26). The greatest LOVE is to lay down your life for your friend, child, spouse, or neighbor (John 15:13).

But even though Christianity teaches a lifestyle of servanthood and sacrifice, the Apostle Paul told us that in the last days we would see the opposite from those who are religious. "There will be terrible times in the last days. People will be lovers of themselves...having a form of godliness but denying its power" (2 Timothy 3:1-2, 5). When it comes to the excuses that people give for why they could never be open to having more children, they are in a sense denying that God has the power to help them, although they do not realize that this is what they are doing. Deception is ingrained into their thinking.

People want to believe that the things that they are doing with their lives are good things. Many believe if they had more children they could not do these good things. They cannot see if God gave them more children that they would still be able to do practically everything they already do. They have become so trapped in their own beliefs concerning what they should be doing with their lives that they cannot conceive of doing even greater things. They get ideas in their heads about *how things should be* and *what they want* and *what they should be doing*, and then they cannot conceive of things happening any differently. People feel that adding more children is unnecessary and may distract them from the good things that they desire to do. These good things may be good, but they also might not be the *best* things that God has for them.

Many of these ideas that God's people have actually line up with the agenda of the pro-choice movement. One of Planned Parenthood's very successful anti-family mottos sounds very much like the attitude of today's believers:

Our Lives—Our Bodies—Our Choices!!

This slogan means that no one should tell people that they have to do anything that they are not comfortable doing, including becoming parents. It is *our* life, *our* body, and *our* choice. This idea about personal rights may be something that we can expect from people who do not know God; but when God's people go around boasting about *their* rights, then this is sin. We must remember that we have been bought with a price! When God's people want to argue with God about their rights, then they have missed a major understanding of what it means to walk in servanthood to Christ. When a believer tells God, "It is MY LIFE, it is MY BODY, and it is MY CHOICE," God will allow them to have their way because He has given each person a free will and will reap blessings or lose them according to their own choices.

Many of the family planning choices that God's people are making today are in agreement with the founder of Planned Parenthood, Margaret Sanger. As described in Chapter 3, she spent her whole life working in opposition to the Word of God and the Christian lifestyle. She was so successful with her family planning campaign that today there is seldom a difference of opinion between believers and nonbelievers in this area. Current statistics indicate that by age forty-five, *70% of men and woman have voluntarily been sterilized!!* (Many of these are God's people!) That's more than two-thirds of the people over forty-five years old!

I have found these statistics to be true in my own life because I just turned forty two and almost every girlfriend that I have, whether they are believers or not, can no longer have children because they had their tubes tied or their spouse had a vasectomy or they have been on *the pill* for so long that they are no longer fertile.

Some are suffering from repeated miscarriages. Many of these friends are believers in their late thirties and early to mid forties!

Since God's people and those who do not know Him think exactly alike on this subject, God's people are not being a testimony to our society. Instead, society can see our Heavenly Father's judgment on us and our families for this sin. The world is watching, and they are finding God's people to be in the same unhealthy, sinful state that they are in! Instead of finding Godly examples to follow, they even see pastors whose wives have their tubes tied, resulting in multiple hormonal problems, female complications, or full hysterectomies. Or they see pastors who have had vasectomies themselves and because this decision caused their immune system to break down, now their health is failing them. They also see miscarriage rates in our churches that are higher than those in their own neighborhoods and they see cancer of the reproductive organs (breasts, ovaries, cervix, and prostate) in the lives of believers to be at the same epidemic proportions as society. Society also can not look to us and find very many large families living out glorious testimonies of the Lord's provision in a materialistic world.

When society cannot see a difference between themselves and God's people, then there definitely is a problem that God's people need to deal with.

This is what we are seeing today. Both Christian and non-Christian women are saying, "I want my freedom! I don't want to spend my life just raising kids." Both Christian and non-Christian men say, "I do not want to be raising kids when I am fifty-five! I want to play golf, travel, and enjoy a few luxuries for myself." When the people of God are living in agreement with the goals of those who do not know God, then they will reap the fruit of their wrong choices.

Recently I visited a church where the pastor and his wife had just had their first baby. The pastor's wife said that she only wanted one more child and after that, "I want them to burn, cut, tie, and seal my tubes off so I do not ever have to go through this again!" Unfortunately this Godly woman was not informed about trusting God with the number of children that He wanted to bring her. She too is an example of someone who may love the Lord but who has also been deceived by the selfish ideas of our society in this area of her life.

One hundred years ago when families were larger, parents did not use birth control or become sterilized and did not experience these complications in people's lives that we see today. Cancers of the reproductive organs were rare; miscarriages were rare; autoimmune diseases were rare; divorce was rare; impotence was rare; female problems were rare; and infertility was rare. Today, however, almost everyone uses some form of birth control or becomes sterilized. The bad fruit that we see so many suffering from today only proves that *the enemy has won the battle for the family in this area.* Those who live their lives in agreement with the world's beliefs will sadly reap sorrow somewhere for their choices.

THE BATTLE BETWEEN GOD'S WORD AND SECULAR HUMANISM

In our society today a battle is raging between the ideas of the secular humanist and the Word of God.

On one side, secular humanism is changing our views about children.

On the other side, God has a Biblical plan that most believers have not been taught.

Many of God's people do not realize that they do not believe God. Often they lean towards the world's agenda strictly because they are bombarded with secular ideas everywhere they turn, and their church does not teach them what Scripture says about this. Let's compare the two and see what God's Word says.

1. God says: Children are His gracious gifts. The Bible says, "Every good and perfect gift comes down from the Father of Lights" (James 1:17). Children are what God graciously gives us. "These are the children which the Lord has graciously given your servant" (Genesis 33:5). Children are a glorious marital gift and the fruit of intimacy. "Sons are a heritage from the Lord, children a reward from Him" (Psalm 127:3). "I will surely bless you and make your descendants as *numerous* as the stars in the sky" (Genesis 22:17). "May you *increase* to thousands upon thousands" (Genesis 24:60).

Secular humanists do not see children as gracious gifts, but rather as financial burdens. Economists at the United States Department of Agriculture tell us that a child born today will cost a parent $250,000 to raise through college. The economists figure in typical expenses of clothes, food, braces, college tuition, etc. Most parents look at these figures and then think about their own futures. They might ask themselves, "Do I want to waste my life raising children who will drain that kind of money from me and who may grow up and not even love me?" A fearful and practical parent may decide to limit his family size so that he can retire some day and not be broke. Once the believer who has been influenced by humanism looks at the figures he may wonder whether the statistician added in the cost of private church school tuition; private Christian college; church camps; and religious books, tapes, and videos. The believer then realizes that if he wants all the things he thinks are necessary to provide the best religious environment for his child, he will have to have more than $250,000! The believer is really convinced that he must limit his number of children so that he can pay for the added expenses often involved in raising a child as a Christian. Whatever happened to the idea of trusting God for the things that we cannot see? Isn't this what Faith is supposed to be all about?

2. God says: Children multiply your wealth both spiritually and financially. "*Prosperity* will be yours" (Psalm 128:2). "I was young and now I am old, yet I have never seen the righteous forsaken or their children begging bread" (Psalm 37:25). Scripture says that if you have children, other people will recognize you as being blessed. "All who see them will acknowledge that they are a people the Lord has *blessed*" (Isaiah 61:9). The promise of God is that our children will grow up to love us and exalt our family blessing (Psalm 128).

Secular humanists do not see children as making a person rich, but rather as being a burden for working parents and an imposition on their mommy's career. In our society children are pushed into daycare at birth so their mothers can return to their careers. Of course some women do have to work just to get by, but there are women who pursue careers because they do not want to be home dealing with their children. Women in our society are told that they will not be fulfilled unless they have a few children *and* a career. Many women try to juggle both, usually feeling guilty the whole time. Women in our churches battle the ideas that humanism has brought into organized religion. They are told that they will not be fulfilled unless they contribute to the work of Lord and volunteer in some way. This desire for God to use them sometimes takes the emphasis away from their homes and redirects their energy into the church. Unfortunately, few churches emphasize what a ministry raising Godly, obedient children is, except on Mother's Day. The rest of the year we tend to forget the mothers. We seem to ignore the little mommy sitting on the back row holding her infant and quieting her toddler. In God's eyes, she is just as important as the women who volunteer in the various ministries, because she is focusing her efforts on raising the next generation.

3. God **says***: Children are our future! They are our Godly seed to take our place when we die.* "Your sons will take the place of your fathers; you will make them princes throughout the land" (Psalm 45:16). Children are our heirs (Jeremiah 49:1) and are the result of following God's Scriptural mandate to be fruitful and multiply (Genesis 1:22, 28). God desires that we fill the earth with people to praise His holy name (Psalm 102:18). The more people who are born, the more people have the opportunity to choose to be His friends.

Secular humanists do not see children as our future. Humanists tell us that instead of birthing children to have a future, we should curtail reproduction and control population growth, or else in the future our planet will be overcrowded without enough resources for ourselves or our children. On any given day, we can turn on the cable TV, read in *USA Today* or any other secular newspaper, read in school textbooks, or hear a news report about social problems in our world that come from overpopulation. We hear about people starving in other parts of the world and overcrowding in places like China. Environmentalists give us figures on how we will run out of food and water if we continue to overpopulate the planet with people. These facts are simply untrue and can be scientifically disproven. Our world has plenty of resources; God did not leave us on a planet that cannot meet the needs of a growing population. However those who shape our world want us to believe that we have a problem and if they tell us about it long enough, then we will finally believe it. Pastors are not speaking out against the idea that our planet is running out of resources and most fail to challenge parents with the commandment to be fruitful and multiply. This has led to the attitude in America that the average Christian family should be small. In most churches when couples choose to have more than three children, people start to ridicule them. Usually they are labeled as being irresponsible, especially if they look like they are unable to care for more children in some way.

4. God says: Children are power! They are arrows in the hand of a mighty warrior to mold for God and aim at the lies and agenda of the enemy! Children can make you powerful when you raise them be friends of the Lord and aim their lives in the right direction (Psalm 123:4-5). Your children will be mighty in the land (Psalm 112:1-2). God planned for us to fill the earth with people so that even children yet to be born can have the opportunity to know Him. Believers have failed to see that our children are our future. They can possess the gates of the enemy and take back spiritual land that was stolen from our family bloodlines. "If you are righteous and walk in God's ways: your descendants will take possession of the cities of their enemies" (Genesis 22:17, 24:60).

Secular humanists do not view children as people who can know God. Instead they view each child as someone who is entitled to life, liberty, and the pursuit of the best of everything that his parents can afford to give him. Children are given the power to control their parents because parents believe that kids somehow deserve this entitlement and then they parent accordingly. Since most people believe that no one should have to raise an *unwanted child*, their attitude sometimes changes to the opposite extreme once they conceive their *wanted* child. Many act like they believe that a child who is wanted should lack nothing! Even before birth, the wanted child is tended to with special care. Sonograms and tests are administered to make sure that the wanted child has all of its body parts so that it can keep being wanted. Once assured that all is fine, the parents search for the perfect birth experience.

Once the child is born, many parents seek to provide the best that their salaries can provide with the attitude of "nothing but the best for this much-wanted child." As the child grows, opportunities abound. In some cases the wanted child gets to wear designer clothes and sneakers, take gym classes, and learn to use a computer before he is one! Then the specialty lessons, the expensive private school, the extravagant birthday parties, and so on. Parents in our society really believe that children deserve to have things, so parents make sure that their wanted children do not miss out on all of the good things that a parent's income can provide.

Much of this behavior may be motivated by a parent's guilt. When parents choose to have the wanted child instead of having a much larger family, they overspend on and overindulge their wanted children. There is more money to go around, and they can hide their guilt by appearing as if they are doing a much better job than if they were raising more children. The wanted child gets more of everything, and the parents look like excellent parents all at the same time! Things get harder as the wanted child grows because as the child is raised with the best that his parents can provide, the parents live with the constant pressure of having to create a perfect world that revolves around the wants and needs of the child. In a sense, the *wanted child* becomes the *worshipped child with the power to control his parents.*

As the child grows up he is sadly disillusioned when he finds that he actually has to serve other people because the world does not reflect around him. Many marriages result in divorce because the partners want to take and be given to but do not want to give. Those who were spoiled as children also have trouble in the work place when they find that the workplace does not revolve around them as well. This form of parenting produces selfish people who cannot give because they want the world to serve them. Even a believer can produce a selfish child who lacks the understanding idea of servanthood because of parental worship motivated by guilt.

5. *God says: Children help us to praise the Lord and take the focus off ourselves.* Children help us to be a blessing to others. God's Word says that life is not about what can benefit us, but how we can be a blessing to others. "Through your offspring all nations of the earth will be blessed" (Genesis 22:18). Together with our children we can be a blessing to God by offering praise and worship to His holy name. "From the lips of children and infants you have ordained praise because of your enemies to silence the foe and the avenger" (Psalm 8:2). "It is not the dead who praise the Lord, those who go down to silence. It is we who extol the Lord, both now and forevermore" (Psalm 115:17-18). The focus is on praising the Lord and blessing Him and not ourselves.

Secular humanists do not understand what it means to focus our lives on others instead of ourselves. They believe that everything people do should be done to push their own personal agenda forward, focusing on their own pursuits. We are told to "Go for the gusto because we only go around once!" Genesis 11:1-9 records the story of the Tower of Babel. The people wanted to build a tower to Heaven to "make a name for themselves." This goal angered the living God, who came down to see the tower that they were building. He confused the languages of the people and scattered man to the ends of the earth. Making a name for oneself and being successful seem to be huge goals for many people in today's society. People focus on *their* career, their retirement, *their* vacations, *their* financial portfolios—all seeking success and life's pleasures.

6. *God says: Children are workers for the harvest.* "The harvest is plentiful, but the [spiritual] workers are few. Beg the Lord of the Harvest to send more [spiritual] workers into His field" (Matthew 9:37). "Open your eyes and look at the fields! They are ripe for harvest" (John 4:35). One of the greatest purposes for birthing children is so that they can be mighty spiritual workers in God's harvest field. Wherever that harvest field is for them and at whatever point in history that they arrive, children can participate with God in helping others find the love of God. Even from the time that they are little children, they can lead their friends in their neighborhoods and at school to God. A child has to be born before he can be brought up to be a spiritual worker.

Secular humanists do not believe that children are spiritual workers for God, but rather that they are people who will not be fulfilled as adults unless they grow up to make a lot of money. Our society places a *huge* emphasis on educating children so that they will grow up to make a lot of money. Some people worry from the time their children are born about them getting into a good college. They feel that the child must choose a lucrative career or else they will be a failure at life. There is nothing wrong with choosing a financially successful career in the secular world. God sends most people into the secular world as spiritual lights in darkness. This is one way that a person can be a spiritual worker in God's harvest field. Making a good salary is a nice thing for a believer, but it is not the ultimate goal of life. For the humanists it is extremely important because they have nothing more to live for than pleasure. These sad pleasure-seekers are often left feeling empty at the end of their lives; they discover that, as the writer of Ecclesiastes describes, it is all "meaningless" (Ecclesiastes 1:2).

7. *God says: Children are Godly offspring—the fruit of the one-flesh union of marriage.* "Has not the Lord made them one? In flesh and spirit they are His. And why one? Because He was seeking Godly offspring" (Malachi 2:15).

Secular humanists say that children are simply what you produce from sex. They are a problem and should be prevented unless wanted. Thus the reasoning for using birth control is to prevent and keep children from resulting from the pleasurable act of making love.

8. God says: Children are not really ours; they are just on loan to us from God. This is why Jesus said, "Let the little children come to me, and do not hinder them, for the Kingdom of God belongs to such as these" (Luke 18:16).

Secular humanists do not see children as God's, but as something a parent should control and make decisions about. God and His choice are left completely out of the equation.

9. God says: "Be fruitful and multiply and fill the earth with children," *then your children can carry the Lord's purposes into future generations, even to those yet to be born!* "They will proclaim His righteousness to a people yet unborn" (Psalm 22:31). "Posterity will serve him and future generations will be told about the Lord" (Psalm 22:30). "So the next generation would know them, even the children *yet to be born*, and they in turn would tell their children" (Psalm 78:6). "Let this be written for a future generation, that a people not yet created may praise the Lord" (Psalm 102:18). *Children pass the torch from one generation to the next. Parents teach them the ways of God throughout the generations.* "Tell it to your children and let your children tell it to their children and their children to the next generation" (Joel 1:3). "Impress [these commandments] on your children. Talk about them when you sit at home and when you walk along the road, when you lie down and when you get up" (Deuteronomy 6:7). "Teach them to your children, talking about them when you sit at home and when you walk along the road, when you lie down and when you get up"(Deuteronomy 11:19). "Come, my children, listen to me; I will teach you the fear of the Lord" (Psalm 34:11). "What we have heard and known, what our fathers have told us. We will not hide from our children; we will tell the next generation the praiseworthy deeds of the Lord, His power, and the wonders He has done. He decreed statutes for Jacob and established the law in Israel, which he commanded our forefathers to teach their children" (Psalm 78:3-5). *Children are our descendants who will receive these promises.* In the last days, "I will pour out my spirit on all flesh; your sons and daughters will prophesy and see visions"

(Joel 2:28).

Secular humanists do not believe that there is a life after this one; therefore they are not looking to the future. Humanists and atheists do not believe in eternity. They believe in living life as if things will be over at death. God has not given them spiritual eyes to see the blessing that children can bring to the future generations.

10. God says: Children establish the work of our hands. "May the favor of God rest upon us and establish the work of our hands" (Psalm 90:17). God tells us that the next generation should produce even greater things. They should pick up where we left off. Smart people make decisions based upon how they will affect the future.

Secular humanists do not see a child as establishing anything. They see children as burdens, not establishers. Instead they say that, "I will establish the work of my own hands." They see themselves making all of their own choices and decisions. They choose everything to satisfy their own lives, and they live for today and *not* for tomorrow.

11. God says: Children keep us from shame. "Blessed is the man whose quiver is full of them. They will not be put to shame when they contend with their enemies in the gate" (Psalm 127:5).

Secular humanists do not see children as keeping us from shame. They see children as shameful. They do not realize that they are being blessed by God with children. Instead humanists focus on the negative aspects of children and how they can shame their parents through poor behaviors, such as; drugs, sex, alcohol abuse, suicide, teen age pregnancy, drunk driving, etc. Children are not seen as a blessing but a burden.

12. God says: Children are our ammunition in the spiritual realm to whip the enemy! Scripture says that one of God's people can chase 1,000 enemies, and two can put 10,000 to flight (Deuteronomy 32:30). When I found this Scripture, my excitement was unbearable. *God also says that there is power in numbers!*

When God's people are plentiful, we can come up against society going in the wrong direction, against wicked political systems, against immoral laws and anti-family legislation, and make them back down! I believe that this is one of the greatest reasons why the enemy wants us to limit our number: *Satan knows the power of God's people more than we do!*

For example, I have nine people in my family. If one person can put 1,000 of the God's enemy to flight, then nine people could scatter 9,000 demons. That is a lot of demons! Right now, when my family gets together in unity and prays in agreement for the safety of the President of the United States or for the healing of a child who is deathly ill, our prayers of unity could put 9,000 demons of the enemy away from the situation. These prayers can also protect our family as well. *This is true spiritual power!*

Here is a second way that this verse might be interpreted. What if God did the math by tens instead of by simple multiplication? Then this verse would mean that one believer could put 1,000 demons away, two believers could put 10,000 demons away, three family members who are believers could put 100,000 demons away, and four could put 1,000,000 demons away! A family of my size when praying in unity could put billions of the enemy away!

God says, "For my thoughts are not your thoughts, neither are your ways my ways" (Isaiah 55:8). Yes, because God is far bigger than anything we can imagine, either way that we interpret the numbers, what God wants us to see is that *there is power in numbers*, especially when they are in agreement. A large Godly family or groups of large Godly families can accomplish much in prayer based on this one factor alone.

This is why Satan so desperately wants us to limit our numbers—he knows the power that we have to fight against him better than we do. If we would only trust the Lord, what greatness we would accomplish for Him! As future generations grasp hold of this concept, the world will see power being released like never before!

The incredible value that our children have in the eyes of God is amazing! The secular humanist fails to see the incredible benefits of this awesome gift to mankind.

COULD YOU BE INFLUENCED BY HUMANISM?

Quiz yourself to see if you have subtly adopted some of their ideals:

1. I believe that parents should decide how many children to have so that they do not have more children then they can handle.

2. I believe that children should be *wanted* before they are allowed to be born.

3. I especially do not understand why a mother would really want to have a severely handicapped child.

4. I believe that parents should not have more children than they can financially afford.

5. It does not bother me when I hear politically correct words like pro-choice, vasectomy, or tubal ligation. These words are just keeping up with our times.

6. I think that children should have the best of everything if I can provide it.

7. I believe that serving God in some way outside of my family is very important, and if I had too many children I might not be able to give my time to God.

8. I believe that the worst thing that could happen to a woman would be to bear and to raise a child that she does not want.

How did you score? If you answered yes to one or more questions, you have been influenced by the secular humanist ideas that affect our culture.

Let us not forget that secular humanism devalues all of us because it causes us to look to ourselves for our own salvation and to become a selfish person instead of one who gives to others. We must remember that scripture warns us that in the last days even God's people would be lovers of themselves more than lovers of God! (2 Timothy 3:2-5). Selfishness never brings anyone true happiness. Only a life poured out for others will bring true happiness.

Now that I have presented the facts about what we have come to believe, I believe that the Holy Spirit would like to begin to cut away these lies and bring His people into a new understanding about the powerful blessing of children.

God wants us to see that children are not expensive burdens, but something that He will provide for. He wants us to see that they are the future generation, the royal heirs of God and valuable participants in His work on earth. They are people made in the image of God to show forth His praises in a dark and depraved world, and we all need them!

PRAYER of repentance for the wife:

Lord, I have had wrong ideas about children and I did not realize it. Please cut away the lies of secular humanism from around my heart and mind so that I can see children the way you see them. I repent of wanting to choose the number of children to have. Please help me to allow you to move me closer to being open to your plan for the family. Please help me to see that raising Godly children is a high goal and needs my full attention. Please call me back to my most important role as a woman, which is to birth a family. Help me to hold my head up high when humanism tries to devalue me for not choosing to do things the way that society expects me too. Please show me the joy and lifetime fulfillment that I can attain from this choice.

PRAYER of repentance for the husband:

Oh, Lord, I repent of my humanistic ideas. I did not realize how far that I have come from what your Word teaches. Many of my ideas about being a father have been focused on what I want instead of what you want to give me. I repent. I do not want to see my children as a burden, and I repent of thinking that I should only want to have children if they are wanted. If children come from you then I should always want them. Please change my old thinking so that I can accept You as Lord and the one who plans my family. Help me to surrender my control over this area of my life.

CHAPTER 5

What Will You Leave Behind When You Die?

"Here am I and the children that God has given me"
(Hebrews 2:13).

A GENERATIONAL HERITAGE

My grandfather was a pastor for fifty-five years. When I was a child, he and my grandmother heard about a missionary family that their church wanted to begin supporting, and when my parents heard about this family they wanted to support their missionary work as well. One day our family invited the missionaries over for dinner when they were in the States on furlough. Even though I was probably only five or six years old at the time, I remember that when they walked in, I knew that I was in the presence of people who really loved the Lord. They had dedicated their lives to God's service in the remote jungles of South America. They were very humble and gracious. Something else about this family made a lasting impression on me: when they walked into my parents' house, they were followed by their ten children!

Our family had never met anyone with ten children before, and we did not know what to think. I recall that their children were polite and friendly. They visited our home several more times over the years, and their visits were the only time I was ever exposed to a family as large as theirs.

What these missionaries did was very clever. Besides choosing to serve God as full-time missionaries, their birthing of five girls and five boys created a spiritual heritage that is still being used by God today. My family met them almost thirty-five years ago. Today, most of their children have grown up, married, and returned with their spouses to the jungle to minister alongside their parents.

Now, at the turn of a new millennium, their children and grand-children are carrying on with the work that they started more than fifty years ago. These missionaries have three generations of family members all working together to win the lost to Christ!

By the grace of God they have now *replaced themselves* with ten children and many more grandchildren to continue their legacy as these grandchildren grow up in the jungles of South America or minister to others in the States. When the grandchildren get married, they too may return to help teach the natives about God as their grandparents did or continue taking part in God's work in some other capacity. The *family mantle of devotion to God* is being passed down through these generations.

". . . Fathers tell their children about your faithfulness" (Isaiah 38:19).

"Tell it to your children and let your children tell it to their children, and their children to the next generation" (Joel 1:3).

This story is a beautiful example of the amazing spiritual heritage that is available for families. Because this couple was obedient to Biblical principles, God has blessed their life's work and family bloodline. Think of the spiritual blessings that have come from one man and one woman deciding to trust God with their family planning! These blessings have come upon their children and grandchildren and can continue past these generations all the way until the Lord returns.

"One generation shall praise thy works to another, and shall declare thy Mighty acts" (Psalm 145:4).

Passing the fruit of our lives on to our children and then our grandchildren and then on to our great-grandchildren is what a Godly heritage is all about. This is what the Psalmist meant when he asked God to *establish the work of his hands* (Psalm 90:17). He was asking God to give him a personal contribution of eternal value that could be established for generations. This is why Scripture says, "Generations come and go" (Ecclesiastes 1:4).

WHOSE IDEA WAS IT FOR FAMILIES TO GROW TO BE LARGE?

It was God's idea from the beginning. This is why the Scriptures are full of genealogies. God wanted to show the passing of the generations and how each person fits in. When we look at the issue of what a *heritage* is and also explore the subject of *fruit,* we will see that God put an amazing plan in place for us so that He could give us something of great eternal value: *a large group of offspring who love God who can make an impact on this world for Him!*

"I will perpetuate your memory through all generations: therefore the nations will praise You forever and ever" (Psalm 45:17).

Would you like to make *an investment* in this lifetime that will produce spiritual fruit for many generations? According to God's Word, that investment could very easily be the wonderful children with whom God has graciously blessed you. *Each child is an eternal creation* designed by God with an eternal soul. Each is a person whom you can influence for Christ. Your children can grow up to love the Lord and become the friends of God.

"So the next generation will know them, even the children yet to be born" (Psalm 78:6).

This is what the Lord desires for every person ever created, and each of your children can fulfill this purpose just by being born and by being raised in the training and instruction of the Lord (Ephesians 6:4). "Let this be written for a future generation that a people not yet created may praise the Lord" (Psalm 102:18).

It is amazing that throughout the Scriptures, God uses the word *blessing* to describe the birth of a child. Your seed will be blessed and your descendants will be a blessing (Psalm 37:26). This is where the expression "blessed event" comes from. Children are one of the most valuable blessings and opportunities for success that we could ever receive from the Lord. One of the things God does through our children is that He uses their lives to establish the value of our lives and to solidify our life's work. They show what our hands have been doing—caring for and raising a family. "May the favor of the Lord God rest upon us, establish the work of our hands for us—yes, establish the work of our hands" (Psalm 90:17). "Whatever your hand finds to do, do it with all of your might" (Ecclesiastes 9:10a).

When God was establishing His covenant with Abraham, he told him that his *descendants* would be more numerous than the stars and the sand on the seashore (Genesis 22:17). God's covenant with Abraham involved his *offspring*. God was planning to bless Abraham by giving him a heritage of people that would come from his loins. These people would *establish* Abraham and they would prove God's validation of his life. God fulfilled His promise and birthed a great nation of people in the hope that these descendants would love Him. God gave Abraham a *future* inheritance. He desires to give the same inheritance to each of us through our offspring.

"It is through Isaac that your *offspring* will be reckoned" (Genesis 21:12).

"I will look on you with favor and make you fruitful and *increase* your numbers" (Leviticus 26:9).

"May the Lord make you *increase*, both you and your children" (Psalm 115:14).

Scripture also tells us this about children:

Children are a *heritage* (Psalm 127:3).
Children are a *treasure* (2 Corinthians 4:7).
Children are a *sign of strength* (Deuteronomy 21:17).
Children are a *sign of blessing* (Psalm 128:5a).
Children are a *sign of wealth* (Psalm 128:5b).
Children are *God's reward* (Psalm 127:3).
Children are a *perfect gift* from God (James 1:17).
Children are *power* (Psalm 127:4, II Corinthians 4:7).
Children are *God's way* of saying, "I love you!" (Job 42:12-17, 1 Samuel 2:21).

AN OPPORTUNITY FOR SUCCESS IN LIFE

Did you know that God considers a person to be *rich* if that person has many children? For many of today's believers, that does not sound right. It certainly is not part of the American Dream. Today's Americans believe that children will *keep them from* achieving wealth. They believe that children are so expensive that if they had too many of them, they would not be able to have the American Dreams of home ownership and financial success. Most people believe that the only thing that children will do for them is make them poor! But this is false thinking according to God's Word. God perceives a man who has many children as being truly rich.

Children are a sign of God's wealth and a symbol of God's approval on a man's life. They are a sign of prosperity and productivity. These are facts that our culture does not understand about children, but *ancient peoples* understood them and knew why children were important. Even ancient people who were not believers in the true God understood the great wealth that children could produce; this is why there was such an emphasis on fertility in ancient cultures. These people groups understood the wealth that children represented for both families and societies. They realized that in order for their civilizations to go on, their people must reproduce children who would grow up, fill their armies, and replace the aged.

Ancient cultures such as the Egyptians, the Greeks, and the

Romans all had goddesses of fertility. Society encouraged vast world advancement through reproduction in allegiance to these fertility goddesses. Human sacrifices were often offered to these goddesses as a request for *more* children. These people groups desired more children and abundance in crops and cattle. People were encouraged to birth children because these civilizations knew the great potential of producing more people *of their own kind.* But events did take place to undermine population growth and extinguish various people groups even within civilizations. Famines, hostile takeovers, wars, infanticide, prevention of population explosion, death by diseases and plagues were all factors that worked against specific people groups taking over or ruling the world through reproducing people after their own kind.

The Children of Israel were blessed when they were slaves in Egypt. "The more that they were oppressed by the Egyptians the more they multiplied and spread" (Exodus 1:12). The Jews were taking over Egypt! (This was Abraham's inheritance). This aroused great fear among the Egyptians. They recognized a population explosion taking place right in their land and they wanted to stop it. But how can one stop God when His people are in agreement with Him? God was blessing the Hebrews in their oppression. He was multiplying their seed on the earth. He was fulfilling the promise that He had made to Abraham: "I will make you into a great nation and I will bless you. I will make your name great and you will be a blessing" (Genesis 12:2).

Because of God's promise to Abraham, the Israelite families who were creating families during Biblical times were much more aware of the *wealth* that each child could potentially represent for that family. Biblical families understood the value of children; throughout the history of God's people, *large families have been greatly envied.* God's people have always been encouraged to reproduce and to not hinder bringing forth the blessing of children.

In Biblical families children were seen as being especially valuable. Often the patriarch in the family received the child into his arms *at birth* (meaning he was present at the birth). He then would speak a blessing over the child as soon as the child was born. We see this happening with Manasseh being placed on Joseph's knees at birth (Genesis 50:23). This was family tradition! Biblical families recognized the *value* of each new family member to the survival of the clan. They believed that *children made them wealthy and were a sign that God approved of their existence.* The more children one had, the more wealth the family could possess! These families saw the death of a child as a loss of wealth for the entire bloodline. They understood how important family representatives were for the continuation of what that particular family set out to accomplish!!

Couples in today's world do not seem to understand God's awesome concept of gaining wealth through bearing children.

Couples today seem to be busy pouring their lives into things that may not be useful to future generations or to themselves in eternity. When we give birth today, we are not focusing on how our children will affect our bloodline, nor do we worry about the survival of our family clan or even the survival of the family's name. Things like this do not seem important to us anymore. Instead, we are worried about issues of material wealth. Will we have enough *money* to raise this child? Can we give our children the *things* that we want them to have? Material possessions have taken over our focus.

We have failed to understand what it means to get rich from receiving a heritage of children. Instead many people in today's world seek to be *rich with money.* Most people who live in America know someone who is focusing their entire life on gaining material wealth. God's Word asks us why we would spend your days pursuing the things that will not bring happiness: "Why toil for what does not satisfy?" (Isaiah 55:2). When people die, they can not take any of their material possessions with them.

PEOPLE ARE TRUE WEALTH

Creating a heritage is even richer than just being open to bearing children. God allows us to give them *an inheritance!* Through our children God allows us to pass along the gifts and blessings that we receive through our faithfulness to God in our lifetime. God will pass this spiritual wealth along in the form of blessings to our future generations of children, grandchildren, great-grandchildren, and so on. God says He will *bless a thousand generations of* those who love Him (Exodus 20:6). This Biblical concept of passing owner-ship from parent to child will continue as it already has, from our ancestors to us to our children, grandchildren, great-grandchildren and all through our family generations until the end of time passing into eternity! Wow!

If we leave behind the investment of children instead of the gaining of material possessions, we will be leaving behind some-thing of great eternal value. Children are people with eternal souls who can become God's friends. They also can reproduce more chil-dren with eternal souls who can also become God's friends as well. According to God, *people are true wealth!*

Accumulating M-O-N-E-Y is not God's idea of true wealth.
God spells true wealth as C-H-I-L-D-R-E-N!

The miracle of wealth for individuals is to see their family increase with people because this increases their spiritual effective-ness. This can happen by adoption too. All of these promises of passing on generational wealth can apply to the Godly person who chooses to adopt a child and to add them into their family bloodline. When parents die and goes to be with the Lord, a piece of them will still live on in their children, grandchildren, and great-grandchil-dren, etc. Through the next generation, the ways of the Lord can live on and on, *thus replacing the previous person.* This is the phys-ical and spiritual goal: to replace oneself with another person who can continue with the spiritual gifts of the previous generation and the lifelong desire to love God for another generation. *The more ancestors following in one's footsteps, the more that God multiplies the spiritual wealth of that person's life.*

When each new generation grows up and gets married and continues the process of producing heirs who love God, then the spiritual wealth continues for another generation. We hope that this will continue on and on, just like in the example of the missionary family. This is considered *true wealth* in the eyes of God, and this is one reason why He is desperately trying to give us children to bless us. We need to let Him!

A famous family has utilized the same principle as my missionary friends. In my lifetime, Billy Graham has introduced more people to Christ than probably anyone else has. God graciously blessed him and his wife with five children and nineteen grandchildren. Several of his children have followed in the Graham family footsteps of serving the Lord. Franklin Graham has been a wonderful help to his father and also runs an organization that gives to the poor and needy. Anne Graham Lotz authors books and Bible studies and speaks internationally. Gigi Graham Tchividjian has also authored many books, some co-authored with her mother. We can already see the influence that Billy Graham and his wife Ruth have had in the lives of their children and grandchildren. With God's blessing, their influence will continue to be passed down through the future grandchildren and great-grandchildren. I wouldn't be surprised if someday we see amazing things from more of Billy Graham's descendants.

A VOICE INTO THE FUTURE

Your heritage is a spiritual opportunity to have a *voice into the future* and to pass on the *spiritual gifts* and *family blessings* with which God has blessed you to another generation, so that these things can continue long after you are gone from earth.

"We will not hide them from our children, we will tell *the next generation* the praiseworthy deeds of the LORD, his power and the wonders he has done" (Psalm 78:4).

Teach God's ways to your children and to *their children after them* (Deuteronomy 4:9).

"Tell it to your children and let your children tell it to their children, and their children to the *next generation*" (Joel 3:1).

"So that you, your children, and their *children after them* may fear the Lord their God…" (Deuteronomy 6:2).

"So that it may always go well with you and *your children after you*" (Deuteronomy 12:28).

"So the next generation will know them, even the *children yet to be born*, and they in turn will tell their children" (Psalm 78:6).

"Keep his decrees and commands which I am giving you today so that it may go well with *you and your children…*" (Deuteronomy 4:40).

Your Heavenly investments will continue to accumulate because of the fruit of the blessings of God. Your offspring will continue to be blessed because *they came from you!*

Once we understand this concept, we can think about how many children we are leaving behind and what kind of spiritual inheritance we can bless them with.

A HERITAGE CAN GET REALLY BIG!

The issue of a Godly heritage may not seem very important to you if you are a new believer. You may be assuming that you are the *first* person to come to God in your family. This may not be the case, however. I believe that most people who become believers today had someone praying for them and that if they could trace their family roots, they would find God's people in their bloodline somewhere. We really have no idea who our ancient relatives were. We could be related to famous Biblical people and not even know it! Only God knows where everyone came from and by what means we have come to know Him. One reason why we must be open to children at this time in history is because we do not know whose ancestral wealth that we represent.

Another picture of generational heritage is the preservation of the Jewish people. To be a people group that is still somewhat intact almost six thousand years after God made a covenant with Abraham is truly amazing. God has helped preserve a rich heritage. *Millions of*

Jewish people are the descendants (offspring) of Abraham. These descendants have been faithfully passing on their family faith from generation to generation. This is a remarkable thing to observe. It is a living picture of the fulfillment of Deuteronomy 4:9: "Teach God's ways to your children and to their children after them." This is exactly what the Jews have done, thus keeping alive the traditions of their faith. Whether one agrees with all of their ceremonies is not the most important part to note here. It is the obedience in passing the information from father to son that is so meaningful to observe. This can clearly be seen in their tenacity as a race and as a people group.

Personally, I love the concept of having a family heritage and it is very important to me. The recent movie *My Big Fat Greek Wedding* reminded me not only of the riches that come from having parents, brothers, and sisters; but also the joy that comes from the extended family of aunts, uncles, and cousins that makes a heritage so beautiful to enjoy. The similarities among family members are amazing to observe!

God blessed me with a "Big Fat, Italian" heritage. As I have aged, I have been able to see the beauty in it. My father's parents immigrated to America from Italy in 1927, settling in Washington, D.C. God has blessed them with six children, seventeen grandchildren, twenty-seven great-grandchildren, and two great-great grandchildren so far. They are no longer living, but they started a family tradition that we are still continuing. Every Thanksgiving it is tradition for the Giove offspring to get together and celebrate. Every family contributes to the meal in some way. Different aunts bring their specialties, many of which are family recipes cherished over the years.

I have always enjoyed this day because everyone in the family is there. Thanksgiving just does not seem as special for me unless I get to attend. Most of my cousins are believers, as my grandparents were, and it is neat to see the similarities in our families. I believe that the Lord smiles over the Giove family on that day because we are acting out one of His traditions: coming together and enjoying the unity of our family.

I feel richly blessed because both sides of my family have passed along a Godly heritage to me. From what we can trace in our family history my great-great-grandparents on two sides of the family and my great-grandparents on the other two sides all knew the Lord, as have all of their offspring ever since. Our family has experienced many generational blessings and gifts because of this heritage. The torch has been passed on from great-great-grandparent to great-grandchild to grandchild and so on, all the way down until it has reached me. I am trying to teach my own children how to love the Lord so that they will also continue on. We have had pastors, missionaries, evangelists, writers, Christian songwriters, and Godly business people come through our family's bloodline and dedicate their lives to the purposes of God.

It is a wonderful thing to be living with a heritage of blessings. The rich spiritual wealth that is available to me has allowed me to possess spiritual gifts that may have come as the results of Godliness in previous generations. Their actions and Godly lives brought blessings down on themselves, and because of God's faithfulness, I am still enjoying these blessings generations later! This fulfills the promise: "I will show love to a thousand generations to those who love me and keep my commandments" (Exodus 20:6). If we follow God, He will continue to pass these things on to my grandchildren and great-grandchildren and so on until the Lord returns for us.

"The righteous stand firm forever" (Proverbs 10:25b).

"The righteous will never be uprooted" (Proverbs 10:30 a).

"Prosperity is the reward of the righteous" (Proverbs 13:21b).

"In the way of righteousness there is life; along the path is immortality" (Proverbs 12:28).

I owe it to my ancestors who laid the foundation for me that today I can still build upon. Jesus is our family's cornerstone (Ephesians 2:20). My family heritage is still speaking many generations later, and if I obey and train my children correctly, we will send our family's love for God far into the future. *Before it is all over, some from our family may be participants in the end-time army of the living God!*

Along with our descendants, we can change the world if we ask God for this opportunity. Nineteenth-century theologian Jonathan Edwards and his wife Sarah loved the Lord; God blessed their union with Godly offspring (Malachi 2:15). In 1900 A. E. Winship did a study (a summary was published in a booklet on motherhood distributed by Focus on the Family) listing some of the accomplishments of the 1,400 descendants that came from one man and one woman.

The Edwards family produced:
13 college presidents
65 college professors
100 lawyers and a dean of a law school
30 judges
66 physicians and a dean of a medical school
80 public officials
3 United States senators
3 mayors of large cities
3 state governors
1 vice-president of the United States
1 comptroller of the U. S. Treasury

Fourteen hundred people coming from the union of just two people who were more than likely trusting God with their family planning! This is *incredible fruit*! Their agreement with God fulfilled the verse, "Their descendants will be known among the nations and their offspring among the people" (Isaiah 61:9) his children after him" (Proverbs 20:7).

THE FRUIT OF THE WOMB IS HIS REWARD

Because I live in central Florida, one of the citrus capitals of the world, I have grown in my understanding of the subject of fruit production. On the property where my house is located there used to be an orange grove, and there are still many groves around us. Most of my neighbors have several fruit trees in their yards; on any given day during harvest time, they can go out and pick fruit right from their own trees. Fruit trees and groves line our local roads, and the abundance of citrus is overwhelming at certain times of the year.

Almost everybody enjoys fruit. Before sugar abuse became so prevalent in our society, fruit was one of the sweetest tastes that most people ever enjoyed. It was a blessing to enjoy fruit and its pleasant flavors.

Scripture talks a great length about fruit. In fact, the pleasure of eating fruit was part of the temptation that lured Adam and Eve to sin. I find it interesting that God calls our children the *fruit of the womb* and the *fruit of our bodies.* They are the sweet pleasantries of life brought to earth for our enjoyment.

"…..He will bless the *fruit* of the womb" (Deuteronomy 7:13).

"The *fruit* of your womb will be blessed" (Deuteronomy 28:4).

The child is called fruit in Luke 1:42: "The angel said to Mary, 'Blessed is the *fruit* of your womb.'"

Webster's Dictionary says *fruit* is "the plant's ability to reproduce itself; the reproductive element of a healthy plant; something to feast on and enjoy."[11]

Song of Solomon 2:3 and 4:6 say that *fruit* is a blessing, pleasant and sweet.

If you know a little child, you know what *sweetness* is. Little children are sweet and innocent and pure. God calls our children fruit because He wants us to experience *His sweetness* through children! They are to be as a *pleasant and sweet fruit* dwelling in our household who help us experience the *sweet love* that comes from our wonderful Heavenly Father.

Scripture continually lets us know that fruit is a good thing and something to be desired. The Bible says *fruit is valuable*! (James 5:7). "A wife is a fruitful vine" (Psalm 128:3). The goal for those who love God is fruitfulness! To still be bearing fruit even when we're old is considered to be a blessing because we are staying "fresh and green" (Psalm 92:14). "…Leaves always green, never fails to bear fruit…" (Jeremiah 17:8).

PRODUCING FRUIT IS THE WEALTH OF OUR INHERITANCE

There is much being said by God's people today about produc-ing fruit. People seem to be *desperate* to produce fruit for the Lord and to make their lives count for eternity! One of the biggest desires amongst believers today is to *be productive* for God. People are desperately trying to figure out what it is that God wants them to do with their lives so that their lives will *count for the Lord.* People want to produce good fruit for God. When Jesus told His disciples to go and bear fruit that would last (John 15:16), most New Testament believers have been taught that this meant *go convert* new believers. Surely Jesus did mean that but it also could have meant do this in addition to *birthing* new believers. All of God's people back then allowed God to plan their families, so the people to whom this command was spoken were already allowing children to come into their families who could become new converts. It was not until the last century, since birth control use infiltrated God's people, that believers have dismissed the value of *birthing* new converts and instead have gone out into the world to seek new converts. What an awesome opportunity is being passed by. We should be doing both things: *seeking* new converts by preaching the gospel to the world and *birthing* new converts and raising them in our Godly families.

What is ironic in today's world is that as believers desperately seek to produce good fruit for God, few are telling parents that the greatest ministry calling that God has given them is to birth and train up the next generation of believers in God. Their lack of understand-ing this role causes many of them to be upset. They tell others, "I do not know what God wants me to do with my life." The answer is right in the word. God says that He wants us to "go and bear fruit"; then He can give us whatever we ask in His name (John 15:16). That fruit can be children. We are to be open to receive as many as God has planned for our lives. Then God can give us whatever we ask in His name because of our obedience. What a nice bonus!

God set things up so that we would be *fruit-bearers.* Maybe you have never thought about this, but your children represent *you.* If you have two children, then you have two representatives to carry on in your footsteps after you are gone. If you have ten children, then you have ten family members who can carry on in your footsteps after you are gone. When we trust God with our family planning, we will produce the needed heirs to continue for us, and *only God knows that number for each family.*

Children are the fruit that represents reproduction in a person's life. When people say, "That's my boy!" or "He's just like his Daddy" or name the child *Junior*, they are acknowledging that their children are a reproduction of themselves. People name a child after the father in hopes that the child will grow up to be like his father, and they also pass on the family surname so that it can be continued through the pages of history.

My family made a big deal of this. My Italian grandparents had six children, and my father was named after his father. My parents decided that when they had children, they would pass on the family name because it was very important to my grandfather. Before I was born, my parents planned to name me Joseph Giove III, but I turned out to be a girl, so they picked the name Rachel out of the Bible. Then when my sister was born, she was supposed to be Joseph Giove III, but she also turned out to be a girl. Nine years later they had a son, and he finally got the name Joseph Giove III. My Italian grandfather died at age eight-nine, three weeks after my brother's birth, happily leaving earth with another heir named after him. My brother plans someday to name his son Joseph Giove IV in honor of the family.

This is an example of legacy. My brother never knew the man that he will someday name his son after, but he will name him in honor of this grandfather who passed on the family name. That's pretty amazing! How much more does our Heavenly Father want to honor us by giving us a spiritual legacy through our family heritage that can live on long after we are gone?

GENERATIONAL WEALTH IS YOURS FOR THE ASKING

Many believers do not realize that there is *wealth* that has been laid up in *God's Heavenly vaults,* just waiting to be released upon the faithful who will ask for it (Proverbs 28:10, Proverbs 2:7-8).

This is *generational wealth* that came from the passing on from father to son and son to grandson (Psalm 48:13b, Psalm 112:2b), yet stopped somewhere by sin (Proverbs 2:10b-15) and put on hold, until a man of faith comes along and asks God to release it to him.

The *fruit of our family trees* may have been held up somewhere due to disobedience in previous generations. Remember Exodus 20:6 says, "I will bless a thousand generations who obey me and curse a thousand generations to those who are idolaters" (Exodus 20:5). In the area of family planning, if the family ancestors did not value their fertility or did something to alter God's plan, then the blessing of the generations promised by God may not have been received due to shameful living. Since God does not forget the faithfulness of the previous generations, these blessings are still due to this family bloodline. God has allowed these blessings and not taken them away, so they still exist in the realm of the Heavenlies. These blessings are waiting for a family descendant to right the wrong through repentance so that God can release the wealth back to the family after repentance for these sins.

God will then release *the fruitful blessings of your family tree that may have been held up.* The kinds of blessings related to families are: wealth, wisdom, money, property, healthy and peaceful family relationships, salvation, spiritual gifts, etc. These blessings could all be released to those family members who will obey God with their family planning once again. *This is why repenting for disobedience and making a change can bring forth blessings.*

Jabez prayed, "Oh Lord that you would bless me and enlarge my territory" (1 Chronicles 4:10). God's greatest desire is to bless us and enlarge our territory in every area, but He cannot do this if we will not obey! He desires to *enlarge many families* and restore much of the territorial wealth both spiritually and physically that has been laid up for generations. There are children planned for those families *who must be born in order for that wealth to be released to them.* The right individuals must be here to govern that family's *spiritual wealth!*

Unfortunately, there are many believers who do not see the riches of *being open* to the possibility of a large family. I have heard many believers argue that "We do not have to have *physical fruit* (children). God can bless us with *spiritual children* birthed through our participation in church-related activities." This may be true, because God wants us to produce all kinds of eternal fruit. I believe, however, that *our goal* should be to be open to producing *both* physical and spiritual children because this is what God told Abraham to do. God likes *both kinds* of fruit—both physical children and spiritual children. God's desire is that our *physical children* become believers, and then they can become our spiritual children as well. If we limit our fruit to only the kind that we want to produce, we will not be following *God's system of balance, especially if He wants to give us physical children as part of the fruit of our life's work.*

This is why God calls "the *fruit* of the womb His *reward*" (Psalm 127:3*).* God is saying that children are a *great reward* in this lifetime; the birth of each child is like winning the *grand prize* in a big contest!

Everyone likes to get prizes. This is why every spring millions of people send in their Publishers Clearing House entries so that they might be picked as one of the lucky million-dollar winners. This is also why state lotteries make so much money, and why shows like *Who Wants to Be a Millionaire* and reality shows where people win a lot of money are so popular: winning make us feel good. Even little children love to get prizes. They can't wait to get to the bottom of the cereal box or to open up their fast-food meal just to get the prize. Everyone loves prizes and rewards, yet when God calls children *a prize* and *a good reward*, modern people and many believers say, "No thank you! We don't want *that kind* of prize."

God says that these prizes are a living example of God's blessing on a man's life and "blessed is the man whose quiver [home] is full of them!" (Psalm 127:5). It is proof that God is expressing His love for that man by rewarding him with God's *ultimate prize* and *reward* in life—the gift of children.

People do not realize the degree to which they are cheating themselves when they opt not to receive children from the Lord. It is as if God says to us, "I have *one hundred billion dollars* that I cannot wait to give you" and we reply, "I will be happy with just *ten thousand dollars* instead." By not being open to receiving the *one hundred billion* we miss out on the greater blessing that God offered. It is the same way with children. God knows what to give each person. We sin when we dictate to God *what we want* and use birth control and sterilization to control our situation instead of leaving it up to God to bless us with more than we could have ever asked for or imagined.

Children are a great opportunity from the Lord. He will bless the fruit of your womb (Deuteronomy 7:13 and 28:4). Fruit represents the productivity level of a plant; it also measures the productivity level of a person's life. When people find out how many children we have, sometimes they say, "Well, I know what you have been doing!" They have figured out one thing that we have been doing, which is having a wonderful and fruitful sex life. We are both proud to admit that this is something that we are enjoying, and our children are the beautiful fruit of the joy that we share in the bedroom.

God promised Abraham that He would bless him and make him into a mighty nation. This was the greatest promise that God could give to Abraham. By creating a nation of people from his loins, God did just that. Abraham's people are *still here* today.

This is what God wants to do for each of us! He wants to give us a *prize* far greater than any prize that mankind could come up with. He wants to give us *wealth* that does not stop in a single lifetime. God's wealth goes on and on and on . . . down through our generations. This is a wonderful opportunity for success, if we will grab it!

"He will spend his days in prosperity and his descendants will inherit the land" (Psalm 25:13).

"Then we would claim: 'I will make you into a great nation and will bless you. I will make your name great and you will be a blessing'" (Genesis 12:2).

"Through your offspring all nations will be blessed because you obeyed me" (Genesis 22:18).

If we will stay open to receiving the heritage of people that God planned for us, then one day in eternity, we can say to God: ***Here I*** *am Lord, with ALL of the children that you have graciously blessed me with . . . and my descendants*. (Hebrews 2:13)

"Thou O Lord remainest forever; thy throne from generation to generation" (Lamentations 5:19).

PRAYER for the husband:

Lord, I had no idea that you were trying to bless me with a heritage. I have never understood it quite like this before. Now that it is clear, I desire to receive a greater heritage for myself and my family. I repent of my lack of understanding and ask You to help me to begin to be open to receiving all of the children that You've ordained for my bloodline. I want future generations to enjoy the fruit of my Godly actions today.

PRAYER for the wife:

Lord, I want to have the children that are supposed to come into my family. I want to stand in Heaven with all of the children that You intend for me to raise. Please help me to be open to receiving these children and open to being pregnant when necessary. I desire to be a part of a great heritage. I repent of my hesitations and look forward to being blessed now and in eternity.

CHAPTER 6

The Destiny of Your Seed

"Children are arrows in the hand of a mighty warrior. They are His reward. They are like sharp arrows to defend him. Happy and blessed is the man who has a quiver full, for that man will have help when he goes to speak with his enemies at the gate."
Psalm 127:4-5 (paraphrase)

It seems like every day since the dawn of the new millennium, I have heard someone mention the word *destiny*. This word has become the defining theme for this new season on planet Earth. It seems that people everywhere feel that we have come into a "new time" and that this new season is releasing people to discover their destinies. I even felt led to name my new daughter Destiny. The word "destiny" evokes the idea of fulfilling your calling and realizing your dream in God. For those of us who are passionate lovers of Jesus Christ, this is our ultimate heart's desire. We want to leave earth knowing that we discovered God's destiny for our lives and lived it to its fullest potential.

ARROWS IN THE HAND OF THE MIGHTY WARRIOR

One of the most important themes of the Bible is that believers are fighting in a constant spiritual war against the Prince of Darkness. God wants to make us keenly aware that this fight is for our very souls. One thing that I found fascinating as I researched family planning in Scripture was that God sees our children as instruments of war. Psalm 127:4 says that children are a man's arrows. When God referred to people's children in this way, He was recognizing their need for ammunition to fight against the enemy to defeat him. By using this metaphor, He wanted to indicate to His people that their lives hold a much deeper purpose than they could have imagined.

In ancient times an arrow was as an instrument of war. When a warrior was about to go to battle, he would fill his carrying case or quiver with many arrows so that he would have enough ammunition to use when his enemies attacked him. These special arrows were handcrafted by the warrior himself and were carefully fashioned to achieve the purpose of annihilating the enemy. At the time of battle, the arrow would be shot carefully towards the enemy, hitting the target and rendering the enemy powerless.

Without the arrows the warrior would be a dead man. Every arrow counted and was critical to his survival. The warrior was especially careful to not waste any of his arrows!

When God called our children arrows, He was showing our desire to win the spiritual war. Scripture says that our children can possess the gates of our enemies which means that they can take back the spiritual ground that has been stolen from our families (Genesis 22:17b, 24:60). This means that they can go to spiritual war to conquer, take back, and possess what the enemy has stolen. As conquerors they will rule, govern, and possess their inheritance. Godly parents who carefully mold and fashion their children to strategically point them in a righteous direction will be winners in life. God can then use their children to defeat His enemies. Each parent has the opportunity to raise his children to be mighty warriors on the battlefield of life and to become victorious.

> *If you had been a warrior on the battlefields of the past,*
> *how many arrows would you have wanted to help*
> *defend you against your enemies?*

Another use for an arrow is to achieve forward motion. An arrow, when shot, moves in a forward direction. It starts at one point and then moves far beyond its point of origin to hit the enemy target. The *destiny* of each arrow is to serve the purpose of hitting and killing the enemy. The warrior stays in a stationary place and the arrow is the thing that moves beyond the warrior to accomplish this purpose. In a sense, *the arrow works for the warrior.*

This is what God was trying to convey to us about our own quivers full of arrows. Some day, they will move away from us to accomplish the purposes for which they have been sent, one of which is to *move past us into a future time and a future place.* Because we are mortal, we are limited by time and space. We each have potentially 120 years to be on earth (Genesis 6:3), and then we die. In this illustration of the warrior with his arrows, God is trying to point out to us how we can spiritually overcome this physical limitation.

By giving us children God is giving us an opportunity to overcome our lifespan limitations and continue to bear fruit. Our children will be granted opportunities that we will not, one of which is to be able to live in the future. Children born today could still be living 120 years from now, long after their parents have left the earth. These children will live in a future time where their parents will not be able to live but where the children could be their spiritual representatives.

In a sense, because we have children, a part of us stays alive on earth. This is a spiritual principle that very few people realize. This was what Job understood when he complained to God about why the wicked were blessed with children and questioned why his own children were no more (Job 21:8). Children are living proof that their parents once existed on earth and they carry the family fruit with them. When people meet our children and grandchildren in the future, they are in a sense meeting a special part of those who created them and fashioned their lives. When we raise our children to be God fearing people, then those who meet them in the future will find them to be a blessing. Through our children we can pass along our legacy, and they will benefit from our family blessings on the future battlefields of life.

> *How many arrows would you like to have representing you on the spiritual battlefields of the future?*

Our children basically pick up where we leave off. If our children birth children and raise them up to be righteous, then our grandchildren can also be arrows in the hands of our children, but originating from our loins. Our grandchildren will then go that much further into the future—another 80, 90, or 120 years. Most of us will die before the end of this century, but our grandchildren could be here well into the next century, and so on. We could birth a child now, and the fruit coming from that one child could go on until the Lord's return. The family arrows never stop until they land in eternity. This is another great truth that the Psalmist is trying to communicate to us when he says that our children are arrows in the hands of a mighty warrior. *Once created, the lives of these family arrows are eternal.*

This concept of arrows holds significance for me. When I get to Heaven some day, besides seeing Jesus, the people that I want to see will be my great-grandparents from both my father's side and my mother's side. They all died before I was born, but my life was impacted greatly because of their choices. I am especially curious to meet the parents of my mother's mother. Even though I never met them, somehow I feel that I do know them. They left five of their six children on earth when they died; and I had the wonderful privilege of meeting four of those children, one of whom was my maternal grandmother. These four children were some of the finest people that I have ever known. They were simply wonderful people: sweet, kind, gentle, compassionate, friendly, unpretentious, giving, lovers of the Lord. Meeting their lovely children indicates what fine people my great-grandparents must have been. Their daughter, my grandmother, made a huge contribution to my life. I am so very thankful to them that they raised my grandmother to love God because she impacted my life forever for the Lord. Their example compels me to want to meet the parents who fashioned these soldiers of God and to desire to raise my own children to continue to follow in their footsteps of righteousness.

GOLDEN LOINS: THE MIRACLE OF A MAN'S SEED

We are living in a time when the *vasectomy* has become quite popular. Its widespread acceptance by society has caused most men not to realize the spiritual value of their own fertility. Sperm is something that is joked about in movies such as *Look Who's Talking*. At the beginning of the movie, we see the male sperms all racing each other to unite with the sexy female egg. Our society jokes about something that is holy and precious to God. Most men have never even given this subject a second thought. It is not a subject typically discussed in Bible studies or Sunday School lessons, yet the Bible speaks about a man's sperm many times. God refers to this sperm as *seed,* and He considers seed to be *holy.*

Because of our lack of understanding and teaching about this, few men realize that they *have a holy and precious force inside of their bodies.* This *force is greater* than every war that was ever won, every Super Bowl or World Series, every stock-market high, every accomplishment of material wealth! *The sperm of a man is one of the most precious commodities on earth because it houses the ability to create as God created and as God intended.*

Sperm has the ability to change the outcome of the history of the earth!

The loins are the first area that develops in a tiny human; they could be considered the beginning of man. The loins house a person's reproductive organs and are covered by the intestines. When Ezekiel saw God in a vision, God had *FIRE emanating from His loins.* (Ezekiel 1:27). Daniel saw *GOLD covering God's loins* (Daniel 10:5). When we find out that God has fire and gold covering and protecting His loins, isn't this a clue for us that this must be an area of significance? Obviously God values the loin area in a far greater way than we may have grasped.

Ancient cultures placed great value upon their loins. Pagan societies worshipped their reproductive organs and set up altars and phallic obelisks to fertility gods, symbolizing the worship of their genitalia. The ancient Babylonians and Egyptians believed that eternal life was somehow connected to the sexual act. These people groups did not know God, yet they were still able to understand that there was significance in these body parts, and this was why they worshipped them. Some of these beliefs are still followed today by pagans. Eastern Laya yoga, which embraces the New Age idea of energy chakra, refers to this area as the Swadhisthana chakra, from which they believe eternal light emanates.

Loins are very powerful because they contain a person's heritage. Our loins are not to be worshipped, but they are something that we should *value dearly* because God values them dearly. This area of our anatomy is sacred unto the Lord because the loins can produce mighty warriors for God and for our own benefit. These organs are God's and should be dedicated to Him. This is why it is not a good idea to tamper with or physically alter these organs when they are in good working order. Our whole body is a temple and should be used for God's holy purposes. *We are not our own; we have been bought with a price:*

"Do you not know that your body is a temple of the Holy Spirit, who is in you, whom you have received from God? You are not your own; you were bought with a price. Therefore honor God with your body" (1 Corinthians 6:19-20).

"Therefore do not let sin reign in your mortal body so that you obey its evil desires. Do not offer up the parts of your body to sin, as instruments of wickedness" (Romans 6:12-13a).

SCRIPTURE HAS A LOT TO SAY ABOUT LOINS

Besides being holy, *loins* can represent a place of readiness and preparedness.

Be ready for Passover having your *loins* girded, your shoes on and the staff in your hand (Exodus 12:11).

Be ready. Keep your *loins* girded about and your lamps burning (Luke 12:35).

Stand firm (against the enemy) having your *loins* girded with truth (Ephesians 6:14).

Loins can represent the strength of a woman: "She girded up her *loins* with strength" (Proverbs 31:7).

When Isaiah prophesied about the Messiah, he said that he would have "righteousness over his *loins*" (Isaiah 11:5). If the Messiah had righteousness covering His loins, shouldn't we also seek righteousness covering our own loins as well?

Throughout Scripture, God places *a high value upon every man's loins* because they contain his heritage. Heritage is the ability to change history through the creation of human beings!

God told Abraham, "A son coming *from your own body* will be your heir" (Genesis 15:4).

God said to Jacob, "Be fruitful and increase in number. A nation and a community of nations *will come from you and* kings will come from your body [loins]" (Genesis 35:11).

"All those who went to Egypt with Jacob, those who *came out of his loins* were 70 persons" (Exodus 1:5).

God told David, "Thy son that shall come forth *out of thy loins*, he shall build the house unto my name" (1 Kings 8:19, KJV; see also 2 Chronicles 6:9).

"If *your children* keep my commands they will sit on the throne forever" (Psalm 123:12).

SACRED SEED

Scripture says that the "fruit of the womb (children) is his reward" (Psalm 127:3). We have already established that children are the fruit that comes from the sperm. In God's creation, in order to have fruit, a person must first have adequate *seed*. Scripture says that "God gives *seed* to the sower" (Isaiah 55:10, 2 Corinthians 9:10).

Seed is power.

Throughout history, farmers have counted on seed to produce an adequate crop of food. Seed was considered very valuable. *If we do not have seed, we cannot grow new life.* In the New Testament, Jesus talked about the parable of the seed. Even He recognized the need for seed and its purpose of blessing.

Seed is the essence of life.

Webster's Dictionary defines *seed* as: the source, origin, or beginning of anything; the part of a plant that contains the embryo and will develop into a new living organism; sperm; semen; ancestry.

Man's seed (sperm) is needed to produce children. Without seed, a person can no longer continue with the balance of creation that was put into place by God at the very beginning of time. God said, "Let the land produce vegetation, seed-bearing plants, and trees that bear fruit with seed in it, according to their own kinds" (Genesis 1:11). Then God told man "Be fruitful and multiply" (Genesis 1:27). Then God told Noah, "Take a male and a female animal *to keep SEED alive on the earth*" (Genesis 7:3).

If the seed of the plants and animals was sacred to God, how much more sacred and holy is the seed of humans to God? When Onan purposefully spilled his seed on the ground God judged him by killing him! (Genesis 38:9). Onan did not recognize the holiness of his own seed! Obviously *God valued* the seed (sperm) that Onan so easily discarded (Genesis 38).

Men are the ones that God chose to give the seed to. Their sperm is actually human seed and when united with the female's egg it becomes a *new spiritual family heir* who can receive all of the promises of God. This was why *God told Abraham amazing things about his seed:*

Look at the stars; so shall *your seed* be (Genesis 15:5).

I will establish my covenant with you and with your descendants for generations to come (Genesis 17:7).

"The promises were spoken to Abraham and to *his seed.* The Scripture does not say 'and to seeds,' meaning many people but 'and to *your seed,*' meaning one person, who is Christ" (Galatians 3:16).
"...until *the seed* to whom the promise referred had come" (Galatians 3:19).

If you belong to Christ, then you are *Abraham's seed*, and heirs according to Christ (Galatians 3:29).

God says that a *man's inheritance comes from his sperm.* Because so few men realize this power, it has been easy for Satan to disguise himself in this area by successfully clouding the issues.

Every day, Godly men who know the Word and who study
the Scriptures submit to the severing of their precious
ability to create new lives simply because they do
not understand what they are really doing.

Every time that God is doing something great on earth, Satan works vigorously to destroy the children, therefore stealing the blessing of family inheritances. During the time of Moses when God was sending a deliverer, the Egyptians slaughtered the male babies to try to kill the deliverer. Then when Jesus was born, Herod slaughtered the babies to prevent the Messiah from coming. Now we are approaching the final events of earth and once again Satan is working vigorously trying to prevent the births of necessary children by utilizing medical knowledge and societies' choices. Even children seem to sense when it is time for another family member:

"Mommy and Daddy, can we have another baby? I want a little sister!" How unfortunate for many families that the parents have already made sure that the little brother or sister will never be born.

What if the first man on earth had done what is popular in today's world and had gotten a vasectomy?

Adam and Eve could easily have justified this choice. After all, they were living in a beautiful garden *alone.* They could have said, "You know, it is kind of nice living here on earth with just the two of us; let us not have any children." If they had opted out of birthing children, history certainly would have been different.

After giving birth to Cain and Abel they could have said, "Two children are way more than we can handle. We had better do something quick to make sure that this does not happen again!" This is another excuse that people use *today* in favor of choosing sterilization. But if Adam or Eve had casually been sterilized after the birth of their first two children, then when Cain killed Abel, they could not have had another son to restore their loss. Through Seth, Adam and Eve were in the direct bloodline of Christ. If Seth had not been born, they would have missed out on being used in this special way.

What about Noah? What if he or his children had been sterilized? They would not have been able to replenish the earth after the great flood.

Then there is the great patriarch Abraham. *What if Abraham had had a vasectomy?* Scripture often refers to Abraham and Sarah as the ones who gave Israel birth (Isaiah 51:2).

The following passages explain how God views the *power of loins.* Genesis 14:20 tells us that Abraham tithed one-tenth of his wealth to Melchizedek, King of Salem. Hebrews 7:9-10 explains, "One might even say that Levi, who collects the tenth, paid the tenth through Abraham, because when Melchizedek met Abraham, *Levi was STILL IN THE LOINS of his ancestor.*"

Scriptures proves this powerful principle! God looked *four generations ahead into the future,* and saw that *Levi* would be born as Abraham's great-grandson someday. Before conception he was already part of the *seed* of Abraham's *loins!* Through Abraham's

168

faith and obedience, generations later *Jesus* became the fruit of *Abraham's loins* as well. If God saw these ancestors coming forth from Abraham, He is also seeing this for men today. Each man needs to consider *what future descendants* might be inside of his own loins waiting to be conceived and birthed into their destiny in God.

If Abraham had been sterilized, then the entire nation of Israel would not have come through his bloodline, including Jesus! History would have been missing out on a whole army of mighty arrows coming to this quiver all because of one man's decision. Few people realize that after Isaac was grown up Sarah died and Abraham fathered six more sons (Genesis 25:2*)*. This gave Abraham a total of eight sons to leave on earth to carry on.

How about the Hebrew slaves of Goshen? If it were not for their obedience in family planning, there never would have been a nation of Israel (Exodus 1:12, 17, 20; Jeremiah 29:4-6).

What about other men in Scripture such as Isaac or Jacob? If Jacob had been sterilized, he would not have been able to father the twelve tribes of Israel. This does not mean that there would not have been twelve tribes of Israel; it just means that because of Jacob's free will he could have disqualified himself from being used in this powerful way. This would have been sad for the family of Abraham and Isaac and their bloodline. *One man's decision* could have a devastating effect on the family's future.

God promised David that from *his seed* He would produce an eternal King. "David died and was buried but he was a prophet and knew that God had promised him on oath, that he would place one of his descendants on this throne" (Acts 2:29, 30). *That heir of King David's seed was JESUS: a very powerful arrow to add to his quiver!* Jesus says, "I am the root and *offspring* of David" (Revelation 22:16).

This is one of the reasons why Satan is working so hard at convincing Christian men to limit their own seed through birth control and sterilization by convincing them that once their loins produce a couple pieces of fruit (one or two children), they need to be shut down. When they make this choice, then Satan can steal their future inheritance.

Can you imagine the sorrow that David would have felt if he had received a vasectomy and he learned in Heaven that it caused him to miss out on the privilege of having the Son of God as his offspring? If we look at the examples of the men from Scriptures, a vasectomy for any of them would have been historically and spiritually devastating.

Some of you may be saying to yourselves that Scriptural times were a long time ago and agreeing that those men would have missed out, but times have changed since then, and things on earth are different now. Perhaps, but if you think that this is true, then what would have happened *if one hundred years ago your own great-grandfather had received a vasectomy?*

What if your grandfather was never born because your great-grandfather had a vasectomy? Today you would not be here! Neither would any of your children or your grandchildren! *It is amazing how one person's decision can affect multiple generations of people.* This is why we need to be very careful about how we choose to operate our free will concerning our families; today's circumstances are no different from those in past generations. God's people are still walking through the pages of time, and God *is still* doing something miraculous among us. Times have not changed; in fact the closer that God's people get to His return the more critical their decisions will be to the outcome of the final events of history.

Because many of God's dear people in the twentieth century chose to use birth control and sterilization, they may be missing thousands of people whom God intended to have been conceived and brought to earth. Researchers during the last forty years projected that the U.S. population would soar to 331,000,000 by the year 2000. Instead, because of widespread birth control use and abortion, the United States Census Bureau reported that the population in 2000 was 281,421,706—roughly 49,000,000 fewer people than the projected figures![12] I believe that God would have allowed these people to be here. These people could have been born and grown up to serve in many capacities: doctors, lawyers, truck drivers, school teachers, parents, artists, writers, historians, musicians, pastors, missionaries, etc. God would have blessed us with these additional lives, but man's free will chose not to receive these additional blessings.

Many believers are not even open to the possibility that God may desire to send them additional children.

If God's people understood why He desires to send them additional blessings, they would want to trust Him to plan their futures. Future warriors are still waiting in their loins to be conceived. Few people realize the value of their ability to create life, so they casually allow that gift to be taken from them.

Remember the story of the Wizard of Oz? Dorothy had the ruby slippers with her the whole time, but she did not realize their value. The wicked witch of the East constantly tried to steal those slippers. The slippers had the power to give Dorothy everything that she was looking for but Dorothy was ignorant of their value. Had Dorothy surrendered them, she would have been at the mercy of the wicked witch of the East. In Christianity the same thing is happening. God has given His people the precious ability to create new lives, but many of God's people do not realize this power. *It must be very great, or else Satan would not care about taking it away from us.*

When couples get married they do not know *who* is destined to come through their bloodline or *when* they are supposed to be born. If God planned to give them four children and they stopped at three, then they would miss the blessing of that fourth child. The fourth child would also have had a great destiny, like their other children. The fourth could have also been used to defeat the enemy and further the plans and purposes of God. Suppose child number four was to become a great leader of some kind? By their own choice, they would have blocked God from giving this special gift to them.

Most people do not realize that many *famous people of history* were *not* the first- or second-born children in their families. Many were born fourth, fifth, or sixth. Some were born tenth or seventeenth!

Six of our American presidents were *fifth*-born, two were *sixth*-born, three were *seventh*- born, and one was *eighth*-born. At least thirty-one American presidents were from families with at least *five* children or more. Both George Washington and Thomas Jefferson were from families with *ten* children. What if all of these presidents' parents had stopped birthing children after their second children were born as so many do in our country today? We might have missed out on many wonderful presidents and leaders in our society. A decision not to receive these wonderful people could have been historically devastating.

In the same way in which a person receives salvation, a person must receive a child from the Lord. Every good and perfect gift comes down from the Father (James 1:17). We have to receive His gifts. He does not *force* them upon us. God will not force a couple to have another child. He will give them signs and pull on their heartstrings, but if they are trying to prevent children from blessing their lives by using various forms of birth control, God may allow them to make the final choice. They may never know what God could do and may regret their decisions when they meet Him at the end of their lives.

The theme of history has been people creating their families. Even in America, this has been the main theme until the last forty years or so as we have witnessed the breakdown of the family. We still see families today but they do not look like the families of the past; many are void of mom or dad, void of many children, void of nearby grandparents. What we have today is a lopsided picture of what the family was intended to be. God's people have dramatically hurt the cause of Christ in the twentieth century by changing the look of the family and by choosing to curtail their numbers. *I think we have forgotten that there is great power in numbers!*

In 1931, when Protestant denominations first began to accept birth control use, their generations began to be curtailed and their numbers went down as a result. *This greatly diminished the effect that Protestants could have had upon the future.* By 1971, less than forty years after this ruling and two years before abortion became legalized in America, white Anglo-Saxon Protestants and Jewish Americans were already reproducing at or below zero population growth.[13]

Protestants today have fewer children than they would have had, and therefore their effectiveness as a group has decreased as well.

They lost their majority and therefore have lost politically, socially, and economically. I know that more people are becoming believers now than ever before but we still do not know how many more Protestant believers there would have been if Protestants had not used birth control, abortion, or sterilization. And since the sixties, even Roman Catholics have greatly curtailed the number of children that they have had, causing the numbers of people who believe in Christ to decrease. Since Protestant and Catholic parents did not birth and train as many offspring, they failed to reproduce a greater number of believers in Christ. Overall, belief in Christianity has suffered. *The enemy has been very successful here.* Globally, there is a deeper threat arising as other religions which do not believe in Christ are beginning to take hold in record numbers. These are not all new converts either. Some of these religious groups do not believe in birth control use, so they are reproducing offspring in greater numbers!

Throughout Scripture, *God told people* to "Be fruitful and increase in numbers" (Genesis 35:11).

"He will love you and bless you and *increase your numbers.* He will bless the fruit of the womb-none of your men and woman will be childless" (Deuteronomy 7:13).

"I will favor you and bless your seed and make you fruitful to *increase in numbers* and I will keep my covenant with you" (Leviticus 26:9).

"I will *multiply the numbers* of your people" (Exodus 36:10).

God has NEVER instructed His people to practice birth control or to become sterilized or to decrease their numbers of offspring.

Throughout time God has always seen an *increase in numbers* as being a tremendous blessing. In Jeremiah 29:6 God told His people to increase and ***do not decrease***! This verse specifically tells people to not do anything to *limit their numbers.* Birth control use is about limiting the number of children that come into a family and using it would definitely go against God's instructions in this verse. In today's Christian world, couples have expressed through their actions that they believe that it is acceptable to limit the size of their families even though they do not have any scripture to back this up. It is time for God's people to change this misconception.

IS SATAN TRYING TO "ROMANCE THE STONE" OUT FROM UNDER YOU?

The enemy knows all about the heritage in a man's loins. He has invested much time in trying to halt God's army. He especially despises those coming to earth to take a stand for God during the end times. He knows what the earth would be like if it were filled with the offspring of Godly people all marching together in unity in God's army against him. Satan surely does not want that!

This scenario is kind of like the movie *Romancing the Stone*. The main character (Kathleen Turner) had a treasure map which she followed to find a valuable jewel. Everyone wanted to take the stone away from her. She joined a male companion (Michael Douglas) who was really falling in love with her but who was accused by the bad guy of trying to use *romance* to steal the prized stone away before she realized its value.

Satan seems to be doing the same thing with the vasectomy operation. He is trying to "romance the seed" right out from under the men before they realize the power that they have. He wants to steal family inheritances by romancing the gift of life away. Something few have ever stopped to realize about Satan is that he does not possess the gift to procreate. One-third of the angels fell from Heaven with him, but he has no power to procreate additional demons. He wants to keep God's people from being able to procreate powerful eternal believers who could defeat him.

Will he continue to be successful at preventing
God's mighty warriors from being created?

Surely God wants to see great restoration and additional children being created and born into families, but His people must first recognize their error, repent, and turn back to His ways. When God's people do this, God says that, "He will turn the hearts of the fathers to their children" (Malachi 4:6). Fathers will once again feel compassion toward their own children by allowing them to be created and by being open to receive children into their lives.

God is giving today's generation an opportunity to repent for their own sins and the sins of their parents' generation in family planning. This repentance will allow the Lord to restore family inheritances!

God wants to restore and bless the fathers. One of the beautiful things that children do is that *they leave a man's physical mark on this world!* A man's material wealth will fade before the next generation is grown, but children are a man's eternal ammunition to fight spiritual darkness. The thief comes to steal a man's ability to create (John 10:10). Let us stop the thief in his tracks today!

God is giving men in this generation an incredible spiritual opportunity. Because of your love for Jesus Christ you will not want to miss the *intended purpose of your sperm. Recognize that this is war!* Ask God to allow you to receive God's arrows to defeat the lies of the enemy. This way, both here and in eternity, your life will be full of the *blessings of the destiny of your SEED!*

"Blessed is the man who fears the Lord, who finds great delight in His commands. His children will be mighty in the land; the generation of the upright will be blessed. Wealth and riches are in his house and his righteousness endures forever" (Psalm 112:1-3).

PRAYER for the Husband: Lord Jesus, I had no idea that my seed had such value to you. I repent of taking my seed for granted. I also repent for other men in my family bloodline who did not value our family seed. Please forgive them and remove any curse that might be on our seed. I desire for more mighty warriors to come through our bloodline if this is what you desire. Please give me the heritage that you have for me so that in Heaven and on earth I will not have any regrets. Please give me wisdom in all things, and help me hear your voice as I lead my wife in following you in this important area.

PRAYER for the Wife: Lord Jesus, thank you that I can take part in creating our family heritage. Help me to be a willing participant in your plan. As the one who houses the fertilized ovum, please help me to stay open to my purpose of bringing mighty warriors through our family bloodline. I submit to your will and not my own. I repent for myself and for anyone in my family bloodline who took this for granted. I desire to receive all of the children that you want to send to me. Please, dear God, help me to be physically capable of bearing children. Please bless my husband and put your hand upon him. Please help him to use wisdom in all of our decisions as we seek to be open to your plan.

CHAPTER 7

The Barren Womb is Never Satisfied

Most people who love the Lord would say that they did not make the choice to cease from having children because they "do not like children" or because they were "willfully choosing to be disobedient." Many would say that they chose to be sterilized because they had what they considered to be very valid reasons at the time. I believe that our churches and our society are so filled with the mindset of choice that many seemingly innocent people just do not realize what they are doing by choosing to become barren.

Because I am a mother of seven children, I get the opportunity to meet a lot of people who tell me that they wish that they had been able to have more children. Often they want to hold my baby and then share with me how they wanted another child and their spouse did not, or they could not have one for some reason. Every time I hear their stories, I can feel their sorrow. They almost always seem to have a sort of emptiness that I can feel in my own heart, and I can usually tell that also they feel that there is something missing. They do not seem completely fulfilled somehow, and it always leaves me feeling sorry for them.

I think that most people in our society want to have a family at some point in their lives, though they may not know why. Most people feel that it is the thing to do. *Unfortunately, our society does not view parenthood as being very valuable.* Feminists argue that women can do much more than be "baby factories" and that they should fulfill their career goals.

Scripture shows us that there is nothing wrong with a woman desiring to do different types of work (Proverbs 31:13, 16, 18, 22, 24), especially since some women have a natural need to accomplish goals through working both inside and outside of the home. I have this need myself. I believe that women can do many things and should try to fulfill all of their goals—as long as God gives them the grace to fulfill their goals and their children do not feel neglected. The problem that I see with the feminist message is that it claims to be liberating, but in reality it is very limiting. Feminists push the idea of having a career as the all-important life goal, and they downplay motherhood as something a woman should "fit in" if she so chooses when she has the time. They push on young women the importance of having a career, but they forget to tell them that biologically, they only get *one season in their lives for childbearing*. Often this is the same season into which women are encouraged to cram a full-time career. If they miss their opportunity, they may never have children.

Women who choose to have children and mix motherhood with their career also find this to be a difficult task. The mother is torn between the needs of her job and the needs of her children and husband. She must burn her candle at both ends and even the woman who is super-organized eventually finds herself losing out somewhere. Eventually everyone suffers because to be successful at both motherhood and a career at the same time is almost impossible.

God has outlined a perfect plan for women. If women choose to operate within His biological time frame, then they should choose to reserve those *special fertile years* to concentrate on bringing their families to earth and spend less time on their careers. It is very important for the emotional and physical health of a woman to be able to fulfill her *innate* need to nurture a child. The female body does not give a woman an indefinite amount of time to meet this need. During these special fertile years, unless there is a financial emergency, it is much easier for herself and her family when the woman places her full concentration on being a mommy instead of dealing with a full-time career. If she can be home, even part-time, during these years of her life, it is much easier and happier for her children and usually her husband as well.

Sometimes the transition from career mom to stay-at-home mom is a bit difficult. Some women find that they miss the recognition they received in their career; they find that the day-to-day routines of motherhood offer little praise. But once they get used to being at home, many times they find a creative way to express their needs for recognition and settle into a nice routine. Many times they are surprised when they realize that they find great joy in being around their children.

When women spend their time pursuing material things instead of pouring themselves into the lives of their families, they never seem to be completely happy. Even in the midst of success, there seems to be a void somewhere. This void may be a woman's heart expressing the emptiness that can only be filled as she nurtures a child. When she does not get to carry out her feminine role completely, a woman can feel a loss deep inside. Many Hollywood stars and other celebrities have proven this point to be true. They make movies, pose in magazines, attend exciting events, and spend thousands of dollars to have beautiful bodies and travel to exotic places and yet when Barbara Walters interviews them they say, "I wish I had a child," or "My children are the thing that is most important to me" or "I never thought that a child could make me feel so complete." If these people, who the world sees as *having it all* admit this then children must be a key to fulfillment in life.

By understanding this need when I run into women or couples who seem to be *longing for something,* I usually encourage them to consider having another child. I believe that this *longing* is a heart cry for another child. *I believe that God places this desire in their hearts.* They may not realize how much a child will meet their need and satisfy that *deep longing* that God put there to be fulfilled through a child. Many adults do not realize how much a child will help to inspire them. Children are a fountain, a wellspring of laughter and joy that never runs dry. Their enthusiasm for life, their innocence, their zeal, and their precious spirits can revive many a weary adult and bring back the joy of life that has been lost. Children are emotionally and spiritually healing. We can never fill the void that children fill.

Many times new grandparents will express how *they don't know how they lived without their grandbaby.* They realize how this one child has literally revived them and re-birthed something that had been lost and it excites them just to think of the child. Children re-birth adults in a beautiful, God-inspired way. We can't seem to live without them, and when we try to move on and do other things, God may send a child into our lives to help us remember what is important.

Throughout my life, I have been able to successfully encourage some couples to have another baby. When they do, they always thank me and they always seem happier. Praise God! Many times, however, people act like they are trying to convince me why they don't need another child with their rationalizations and excuses, but I am not the one who needs convincing. Whether they have another child or not is not up to me.

I have noticed that once people make up their mind not to have any more children, a *strong delusion* seems to overtake them. *Once they shut their heart* to the possibility of desiring another child, it is almost impossible to say things that will break through to them. They have made up their mind that they *do not want* another child and sealed the decision in their heart, and only the power of the Holy Spirit softening their hearts *towards loving another child* would be the only way for them to ever break free again. The Lord must open people's eyes, soften their hearts, and penetrate their minds.

Without the help of the Lord there seems to be *resentment towards having to sacrifice and care for another child* that causes people (even God's people) *to despise the idea* of having even one more! I can not tell you how many times I have run into people who get downright angry when I kindly *suggest*, "Why don't you have another child?" They answer my suggestion with a huge "No!!!" or they say "That is the *last* thing that I want to do!" People want to clearly express why they do not need any more children. I am always amazed at the *anger and resentment* that some people express towards raising their children. Obviously their experience has not been like mine, for mine has been quite fulfilling, as the Scriptures say that it should be. The anger being expressed may come from another problem in their lives that the children are unrelated to but are getting blamed for.

WHAT IS BARREN?

In the twenty-first century, the politically correct word for barrenness is *infertility*. *Barrenness* is God's word for this condition, which has existed since the first generations.

Barren means: To not produce offspring; to be sterile, unfruitful and unproductive; dull; not inventive; empty.

Sterile means: Incapable of producing others of its kind; producing little or nothing; deprived of its usual power or function; ineffective.

According to Scripture, one of the greatest curses that a person ever had to endure was to be cursed with barrenness!

God even used infertility as a punishment on the Israelites for their disobedience. The reason that this was so devastating was that people in Bible times knew what a loss this curse produced and how it prevented their generations from coming forth through them. They understood the loss of the blessings that were supposed to come to them.

Barrenness (infertility) meant that their seed would not be left on earth. Therefore to be barren (infertile, sterile) was *never ever* something that people *would choose* for themselves!

Do you understand this point? *To be barren was a curse* back then, and it is still a curse today! Since the first generations it has always been something that no one wanted to be. Throughout history, to be barren has been perceived as being a horrible curse.

"If you obey all of these commandments, *none will miscarry or be barren in the land* [promised land]; I will give you a full lifespan" (Exodus 23:26).

"You will be *cursed* for disobedience; *the fruit of your womb will be cursed*" (Deuteronomy 28:18).

"I will never again *deprive you of children*" (Exodus 36:13).

"Has Israel no sons, *hath she no heirs*?" (Jeremiah 49:1). [It was considered a curse not to have heirs.]

If you are disobedient I will cause you to eat your children (Deuteronomy 28:53-57).

In one day *you will be barren* and widowed for your sin (Isaiah 47:9).

No birth, no pregnancy, no conception (Hosea 9:11).

"Give them miscarrying wombs and dry breasts" (Hosea 9:14).

"Even if they bear children, I will slay their cherished offspring" (Hosea 9:16).

Throughout the ages, the cry of the barren (infertile) woman has always been: "Give me children or else I die!" (Genesis 30:1).

According to this verse, a barren woman would *prefer death* rather than to be without a baby to love. In Biblical times, there were quite a few women who had trouble conceiving children. The Bible says that they were all very unhappy because they could not have children and were in deep sorrow of spirit, travail, and remorse over this longing in their hearts. They longed to hold just one of God's precious blessings in their arms. *These woman cried, prayed, fasted, gave special offerings, and made vows; one even gave up her first-born* in order that God might remove the curse of barrenness and open her womb. These women were *desperate.* They had nowhere else to turn except God. When they turned to Him, His blessing was always to give the woman her wish: *a child!* God was merciful and made each woman a happy mother of children. This was how God showed His love for the woman and her husband. Great is our Lord and greatly to be praised! These are some of the examples:

Sarah was barren; then she gave birth to Isaac (Genesis 11:30).

Rebekah was barren; then she gave birth to Esau and Jacob (Genesis 25:21).

Rachel was barren; then she gave birth to Joseph and Benjamin (Genesis 29:31).

Manoah's wife was barren; then she gave birth to Samson (Judges 13:2).
Hannah was barren; then she gave birth to Samuel and three more sons and two daughters! (I Samuel 1:6).

Elizabeth was barren and she was disgraced; she later gave birth to John the Baptist, who was first to recognize Jesus while still in his mother's womb (Luke 1:7, 25).

David's wife Michal was fertile; then she was cursed with barrenness as a punishment because she made fun of David dancing in praise before the Lord. The Lord never opened her womb again (II Samuel 6:23).

The nation of Israel was barren. God also punished the Israelites with *nationwide infertility* more than one time for their disobedience.
When people read these verses about infertile women, they do

not really understand what the Scripture is trying to stress because they look at Biblical times as being different from today. But they are not! Infertile people throughout the ages have always been unhappy because they could not reproduce children. Today through fertility drugs and operations, our society goes to great lengths to try to help the infertile couple conceive just one child. Ironically, our society also makes available to everyone a *quick and easy sterilization operation* that can turn a person from being *fertile* to *infertile.* Do you see the confusion that arises from the enemy here?

Just as in Biblical times, there are men and women walking around among us today who would *rather die* than live without children. They are grieving just like the women of the Biblical times, longing to hold just one of God's blessings in their arms. When someone wants a child and cannot have one, it consumes every area of their lives. They constantly question why they can not have what they see everyone around them having. They ask themselves, "What is wrong with me? Why can't I be happy? Why am I denied this privilege? Am I cursed?" They will spend $5,000, $10,000, sometimes $20,000-50,000 just to conceive one child through in vitro fertilization!

Not long ago I visited a neighborhood moms' group and was shocked to find out that of the eleven women who were sitting at my table, six were infertile. The majority had either had a series of miscarriages or could not conceive. Four of the couples had tried in vitro fertilization, and this was how they did conceive the one child that they already had. Several had spent more than $20,000 trying to conceive. As our friendships grew, I also learned that several marriages were greatly strained due to this problem.

If and when the barren finally do conceive, they are so happy! They finally get to have the one thing that their hearts and souls had longed for. Even those who do not know the Lord will usually be thankful to Him because they recognize that life comes from a higher power. It is beautiful to see the barren no longer infertile!! "He settles the barren woman in her home and makes her a happy mother of children" (Psalm 113:9). God usually does this through supernatural healing and the removal of the curse; sometimes He opens the door for adoption as a means of breaking the curse of childlessness. Sometimes people adopt, and then God also blesses them with a biological child. Either way, when the barren woman becomes a mother, she is so happy!

I have a wonderful friend who for years could not get pregnant. She was able to adopt a child, and she has never been happier. She says that now she knows the joys of motherhood through experiencing the life of her child. She also told me that before her daughter was born, she felt like she was somehow left out of society. By having a daughter, she now fits in. She feels that she is now serving society by raising a wonderful, secure daughter who will grow up to be an asset to our world.

Why do God's people not recognize that barrenness is a curse? Today there are increasing numbers of infertile couples who would give anything to have just one child. Yet since the early 1900's, choosing to make oneself infertile by the sterilization operation has become quite popular and is *something that even God's people have actually chosen.* According to Scripture, *to no longer be fruitful* (capable of bearing children) is not a blessing, but a huge curse that leads to dissatisfaction and emptiness (Proverbs 30:16).

Even though Scripture calls it a curse and Biblical families would never have chosen to become barren, I have met many church people who see nothing wrong with sterilization. In fact, they seem to *flaunt the fact* that they no longer have the burden of bearing children. Unfortunately, they are blinded by society's trends and do not realize that they have done anything to harm themselves. Sometimes when I encounter these individuals, I wonder how much research they really put into their decision to become sterile. I believe that many people would never consider this operation if they were better informed of the potential physical side effects, emotional regrets, or spiritual consequences.

BOREDOM, BOREDOM, BOREDOM

Proverbs 30:15-16 describes the spiritual consequence associated with barrenness: The barren womb is never satisfied and never says enough! This description is not outlining a blessing, but describing a curse of a lifetime of dissatisfaction. This means that infertile people—especially those who willfully choose to be infertile—will always be searching for and longing for something to fill their void. They are actually cursed with emptiness, and the need to be fulfilled. When two married people cheat themselves out of the possible joy of creating another child through the choice of sterilization, this Scripture indicates they will be left *empty, unsatisfied, and bored!*

This proverb has a very important application for today's society, because we live in the most materialistic and selfish society of all time. We have every convenience known to man, yet people remain empty, dissatisfied, and unfulfilled. I believe that it is partly because our society has traded gaining family members for gaining material possessions. They have made birthing children a choice instead of a blessing and have made having sex the goal in a relationship while viewing children as the unfortunate consequence. By using birth control and sterilization, *the act of sex* becomes more important than *the blessing of sex*. Once the burden of conceiving children has gone away, the couple is supposed to be much happier. But are they? The lives of those who choose sterilization reflect pain, sorrow, and emptiness. Without the burden of a possible pregnancy, sex is supposed to be much better. But is it? Some say their desire for sex diminishes. When there is the possibility of creating a new life, this can make a woman's desire increase; but when that possibility is gone forever, her desire for sex sometimes goes with it.

With all of this pain in people's lives so evident, we would hope that people would make other choices, but just the opposite seems to be happening. Statistics show that *25 percent of the adult population in America, including God's people, can no longer have children!* Also two out of every three married women between the ages of thirty-five and forty-five can no longer have children because of the sterilization operation. This means that after the age of thirty-five, only one out of three women has the ability to conceive another child. If other factors cause her not to be able to conceive, then basically *after the age of thirty-five, a woman's fruitful years are over!*

Since childbearing is a God-given need that affects a woman's hormonal, emotional, and physical needs, when it is not fulfilled *to her satisfaction,* she may feel like her life has lost purpose and meaning. A woman may not be in touch with this pain and may wonder why she is so unhappy. Her husband may try to comfort her, but this is her own personal emptiness, and it needs to be filled *to her satisfaction*, not her husband's. *A man cannot tell a woman that she is fulfilled until she knows that she is fulfilled.* She may begin to look at other areas to gain stimulation and to feel satisfied within herself, and it becomes very important that she fill this void. Women instinctively know that they need something or someone to love. It is innate. This was why God chose to give a woman the gift of children. He created her with this need, and children fulfill it (Proverbs 31:28, Psalm 113:9, Genesis 18:12). When a woman allows herself to willfully choose to let go of her body's ability to create new life it causes her to have the need to look for other ways to feel satisfied within herself.

This emptiness is not good. As a fertile person blessed to still be conceiving past the age of forty, I feel sad to see this. It seems that everywhere I go, I observe people, especially women, filling their lives with activities to take up their time since they no longer have little children to care for. *Some activities are the necessary things that people must do as they finish raising their families, but some feel that they must keep busy and never stop being busy so they do not have time to reflect on their hidden sadness.* Their internal emptiness could be the need for a Savior, and when many find God, He satisfies their wounded hearts. However, many times *I see God's people* with this insatiable need to be filled, and I wonder why God is not filling them. Then at some point they casually tell me that they are not having any more children because they or their spouse is sterilized, and then I understand better why they spend their lives pursuing the things that they do. They seem to be wrapped up in busyness, longing for something more, and do not realize what that something is. Everywhere they look to find fulfillment leaves them dissatisfied and looking for something else. It is so sad, but this is one of the sorrows that our culture has been left with. We convince men and women to voluntarily become barren by vasectomies and tubal ligations. *Afterwards they spend the rest of their lives trying to fill the void that these operations created.*

People of God, do you see what God is trying to say to you? The generation that sterilizes itself may not be completely satisfied because they are not choosing to follow God's plan for happiness. What is sad for sterilized people is that because they chose infertility, they will have to live with the consequences that come from this choice. *There are so many people out there who are living with these regrets! They are either trying to hide them or are living in denial, but the regrets dictate their life's choices.*

Several women who have had their tubes tied have told me that being around my baby makes them begin to wish for just one more child. They have also told me that they are reminded of their decision every time that they see a little baby. When they see a pregnant woman, they are reminded that they can never be a new mommy again. They try to look away or try not to think about it, but it is painful, and it is their reality, and they are living with their choices. This is horribly sad for them because these ladies are wonderful people and made these decisions without knowing what they were really doing. Thank God that He can restore His people and their generations!

OUT OF THE MOUTH OF THE INFERTILE

While I have been on my *mommy journey* these past twenty-one years, I have heard a lot and seen a lot. But as our family rapidly expanded these last several years (as we ceased to use birth control) I have had to listen to mountains of comments by seemingly everybody about why we are choosing to have a bigger family.

I would like to share a few situations when my husband and I have met someone who told us that they chose sterilization. I feel that these are all sad stories because by their own choices these people are more than likely living with less than the best for their lives.

Recently my husband and I were serving in our church nursery, and we encountered a sterilized mother. I was holding my newborn while my husband was tending to the toddlers in the room, and she commented, "Oh, you have a new baby. That's so nice." As we exchanged a few pleasantries she told me that her youngest child was ten years old and that she missed having a baby. (She was probably forty.) So I said, "Why don't you have another?" She answered, "Oh no! I had my tubes tied and we are so busy, and I work, and our daughter is in private school, and we couldn't afford it." Her attitude and the tone of her voice changed from sweet to defensive. I just listened. I had not said anything rude—just "Why don't you have another?" She was the one who started defending herself as to why she chose to become barren. As she left the room, my heart sank because I believe that she may have occasionally wished for another child, but her choice to get sterilized kept that dream from becoming a reality. When those feelings arose she just stuffed them back down trying to forget her sorrow and quietly resenting herself for feeling this way. This is so sad. God probably would have blessed her with another child had she not chosen to get her tubes tied.

Some people would say, "Well God could still intervene." Yes, I believe that God could supernaturally allow her to conceive another child. This is possible, and I believe that God can do miracles. But until people have the faith to seek this kind of miracle, the reality is that they will have to live with their choice and even if they did seek a miracle, the final decision is still in the Lord's hands. I believe that because we all have our pride, people do not want to admit to themselves or others that they might have messed up. So they tell themselves that they *could not* have more children, *should not* have more children, *do not want* more children, that they *have better things to be doing with their lives*, and on and on. Every once in a while, the truth slips out, if only for a moment, and then they quickly remind themselves that their choice to prevent more children truly was correct.

In another family that I knew, their second child was born extremely premature. Infants born this early usually do not live; if they do live, they are usually left with a lifetime of problems. God in His mercy miraculously healed this baby, and their child grew to be completely normal and healthy. We talked at length several times about the consequences of choosing sterilization, yet to my amazement the husband chose to get a vasectomy. They told me that the reason why they chose to do this was because they did not want to go through a premature birth again. This is understandable, but they did not go through a premature birth when they had their first child and the doctor told her that the cause of this child's pre-maturity was a one-time occurrence and would more than likely not be repeated. Knowing all of this they still were not empowered to trust God and stay open to the possibility of one more child. Instead I think the pre-maturity may have scared them. After their ordeal, they were very concerned about the stability of their future. The husband was worried about having enough money and they wanted to put both children through private school. The mother wanted to pursue some of her hobbies and church activities, and I guess that somehow they felt that they could not do these things if they had more children. To feel better about their future, the husband chose sterilization.

Another family, who were believers and lived near me, had only one child. The wife had six miscarriages during a six-year time period. After a lot of prayer, she conceived again and they were finally able to have a second child. At that child's birth, she got her tubes tied. Getting her tubes tied made no sense to me, but she told me that they just could not go through another miscarriage. I can understand this because miscarriages are awful! But they would not necessarily have had another miscarriage.

Some people might read the above examples and say, "Well these people knew what they could handle." This may seem true, but *do people in their limited human wisdom really have any idea of what they are capable of handling?*

Only God knows what we are truly capable of handling through His strength and power. I Corinthians 10:13 says that God will not allow us to be tempted with more than we can handle. I have found that people use this verse to justify choices that they make when life gets to be a little more than they can control. Only God's infinite wisdom knows what is best. As I have walked with the Lord, I have learned that many times I Corinthians 10:13 really means that God will never give me more than He knows that I can handle and not what I think that I can handle. There is a *big difference* in His perspective and mine. This one thing is the challenge of what walking in faith is about. In each of these cases, had the couples not been sterilized, there is a possibility that their lives could have turned out differently and they could have handled the future situations and joys that God might have brought them.

In my example of the couple who miscarried six times, what if after the new baby the pattern of miscarriage had been broken and God's plan was to then send several more living children whom they really would have loved and enjoyed? *They will never know until eternity what God could have done.*

In the case of the couple with the premature infant, they could have enjoyed more children and possibly with God's grace been able to do all of their other activities; *but they will never know until eternity what God had planned.*

What about the couple who wanted to get their kids through private school and the mom who wanted to work? Again, if they had stayed open to trusting God and He did allow the joy of another child, their finances might have increased due to God's Scriptural promises concerning provision. She might have then been able to work by choice instead of having to work because of finances, *but they will never know.* Only in Heaven will each couple see how God could have changed their circumstances and how their lives might have turned out richer and full of greater joy.

When a couple chooses to be sterilized because they have very good *human reasons* it will always makes sense to them at the time, but do people also apply the same reasoning to other areas of their lives? People usually do not tell God, "Since we do not want any more children, Lord, do not give us any more money or a bigger house or greater material comforts as well." Many couples do not want more children simply because they want to utilize their money for other purposes than the cost of raising their children. They are hoping for more money, more time, and increased possessions.

When we rationalize our decisions, it may make sense to choose the money and the other possibilities over the children; but why do we want the things that satisfy our earthly needs and dismiss the things that fulfill both our earthly needs and our heavenly needs? Why don't we want both? Finances, material comforts, and children require our time, our management, and our responsibility; but our reasoning causes us to look at the situation from a human standpoint and dismiss the eternal perspective.

From the eternal perspective, one thing that children do is bring us joy. *In sterilization the couple is choosing to limit their joy.* Most couples who choose sterilization are so positive that they are making the correct decision. But what I always want to ask them is:

WHAT IF YOUR CIRCUMSTANCES CHANGE IN THE FUTURE?

What makes a couple so positive that nothing could ever happen to their children? Scripture tells us in many places that only God owns the future and that we should *never* make presumptions about our future.

All throughout the Bible we are told *not to go to fortunetellers* and *not to seek knowledge of the future.* Those who walk with God learn quickly that His style is to let us know things on a *need-to-know* basis. It is not always pleasant, but He does this for our protection. He *does not* reveal future events very often. This is to help prevent us from worrying about events that we cannot change and to prevent us from falling into fear.

When people choose sterilization they are choosing to restrict all future possibilities of children. We may not realize it, but when *we try to take control* of our future, it is like saying: *"Scoot over, God. I am calling the shots on this one. I am positive that I do not want to birth any more children. I think this is what will be best for my life and my future. Sterilization will give me the security that I need."*

Are we telling God that He does not know what is best and we do? Are we hoping that an operation will give us security?

What makes a couple positive that *in the future* their life will not change? There is *no way* that any human beings can really know *their future.*

Yet as couples begin to analyze their reasons for wanting a vasectomy or tubal ligation, they will say, "I do not think that either one of us wants another child in our *future.* Since we are positive, it should be O.K. to get sterilized." Or they say, "We just cannot afford any more children, and we know that *in the future* we will not have enough money to provide the things that we want for them."

When choosing sterilization, people are making a lot of assumptions about how they will feel in the future. This creates a *false sense of security* about their future. They may not realize how quickly their circumstances could change, yet so many couples make these choices because they are positive that they will never change their mind.

Remember the story of Job? *In one day he lost his ten children!* The day before it happened, Job had no idea that he was about to lose his entire family.

Before a sterilization operation many couples never stop to think through even the simplest possible change in their future scenario.

What if tomorrow, all of their children were killed in a car accident? What if our country had a national health crisis and all of the children died of an epidemic?
What if a terrorist act killed their children?
What if there was a war and their children were taken from them or killed?
What if there was an accident such as a drowning?
What if someone murdered one of their children?
What if their spouse died, and they got remarried and wanted another child?
What if their children ask them for another brother or sister and they also would like another child as well?
What if their spouse was healed and they were able to have another child?

Feelings and circumstances do change! Yet people still support sterilization. Sometimes parents will say, "If we ever want another child, we will just adopt." They could adopt, but a sterilization operation is not about the issue of birthing versus adopting. The truth of the choice to get a vasectomy or tubal ligation is that the couple really does not want children in their future and would rather be spending their time doing other things. Going through adoption is not as easy as most people think it is. Most couples do not want to go through a long, tedious, bothersome process unless they are deeply serious about wanting a child. Sometimes people choose to adopt after sterilization, but the majority just live with their regrets.

How can anyone know what they might want in the future? Scripture says that God holds the future in His hands. God's Word says that we are not promised tomorrow, yet couples who choose sterilizations are taking a chance and hoping that things will stay as they are. But God's Word warns us against this kind of thinking.

"Do not *boast about tomorrow* for you do not know what a day might bring forth" (Proverbs 27:1).

"Man *is like a breath,* his days like a fleeting shadow" (Psalm 144:4).

"Listen, you who say, today or tomorrow we will go and do this or that in a city, spend a year there, carry on business and make money. *Why you do not even know what will happen tomorrow.* For what is your life? You are *a vapor* that appears a little while and then vanishes. Instead you ought to say, *If it is the Lord's will,* we will live and do this or that. As it is, you boast and brag. All such boasting is evil" (James 4:13-16).

God's Word calls this kind of thinking and boasting about the future evil. When people think that they *are positive* that in the future they will *never want another child,* they are making a very large assumption about their future life circumstances.

God's people have to be very, very careful here. Sterilization takes us very close to the realms of witchcraft, divination, idolatry, and fortune-telling. There are many similarities. The reasoning involved to justify the sterilization decision mimics the process that psychics use to get their information. Both must speculate upon a future that *God says is His.* Leviticus warns us about the evils of this behavior.

"Do not practice divination or sorcery" (Leviticus 19:26).

"Do not turn to mediums or seek out spiritists, for you will be defiled by them. I am the Lord your God (Leviticus 19:31).

"Let no one be found among you who practices divination or sorcery, interprets omens, engages in witchcraft, or casts spells or who is a medium or spiritist or who consults the dead. Anyone who does these things is detestable to the Lord and because of these detestable practices the Lord your God will drive out those nations before you. You must be blameless before the Lord your God" (Deuteronomy 18:10-12).

God says to stay away from this realm!

The Bible also says that *"rebellion* is as the sin of *witchcraft,"* therefore rebellion is witchcraft (1 Samuel 15:23). God tells His people not to walk in rebellion or opposition to His ways but to line up in obedience. If we knowingly walk in opposition, then we may be committing acts of *rebellion* against God's principles, which Scripture compares to witchcraft. A person's body was created to produce offspring. Sterilization is *rebellion* against God's plan to reproduce continually.

In the area of family planning, many people have made decisions to be sterilized and had no idea that the decision could bring disastrous spiritual consequences. I do not wish to pass judgment on anyone who has made this unfortunate decision. But I am writing this because it concerns me that so many Godly couples think nothing of this operation and do not realize that it takes them into a dark spiritual realm instead of a blessed realm. Sterilization, unlike buying a house or a career move, physically alters God's original creation in a way that does not bring forth blessing. And it is based solely upon our own ability *to know or predict our future events.*

God's word calls predicting the future witchcraft and *divination.* This is serious sin! God warns people not to play with their futures. Sterilization is an evil decision that brings disastrous results in the spiritual realm, and it is time that believers see sterilization for what it is: a huge trap that the enemy has set for them.

"The acts of the sinful nature are obvious; sexual immorality, impurity, *idolatry and witchcraft*, hatred, discord, jealousy, fits of rage, selfish ambition, dissensions, factions, envy, drunkenness and orgies. I warn you that those who live like this will not inherit the kingdom of God" (Galatians 5:19).

Because of the future-predicting nature of sterilization, it is akin to divination and witchcraft.

FEAR IS A FACTOR

One of the other major reasons behind why couples choose vasectomies and tubal ligations is that people are afraid of the future and they are afraid of trusting God with it. They fear that God may give them more than they can handle. They ask themselves, "What would we do if we had too many children?" Twenty-first century Christians have run away in droves from having large families because they perceive them as a potential hardship.

I believe that people cannot stand for their lives to be any more than they *can control*. They want to prevent any surprises. But if they avoid having more children, God will use some other means to produce needed changes in their lives. I believe they will still encounter things that they cannot control. That is how life is. The only difference will be that a couple who stays open to receiving God's blessing of children will find life's hardships a little sweeter if God chooses to bless them with additional children. Children seem to make everything better.

I can understand and sympathize with the fears about bearing too many children or thinking that it will be difficult to raise another child. I personally could barely handle my first child. I was young and did not know what I was doing and was not prepared to enjoy motherhood. *I still had things I wanted to do for myself*. If it had been up to me and *my reasons* I would have quit then, and I would have told you that God was telling me to quit. I did not have any feelings of ever wanting to have another child. Even after God changed my heart and gave me another child, I still did not want any more children. Two was more than enough for me. Once again if it had been up to me I would have quit then. God knew that I was quite capable of handling much more, so He managed to arrange my life so that I could receive much more. In what I could see of my future I did not want or need any more children. I could easily have severed my childbearing ability in my early twenties because I did not know my own capabilities or how much the future could change me! Only God knew this. By the time that I became older I understood life a little better and I was able to handle much more than I first realized and found great joy in being a mother—more joy than I thought that I would find. I thank God for His mercy towards me. God wants to extend this same mercy toward you as well!

SATAN REALLY WANTS GOD'S PEOPLE TO STOP CREATING THEIR CHILDREN

There are thousands upon thousands of believers in this generation who love Jesus Christ but just do not realize what they are doing by choosing to surrender their fertility and cease bearing children. If the enemy can not keep them from having children, he certainly is happy when they quit having them! He wants *fewer of God's people on this earth*. This reason is important to Satan but there is a greater reason why Satan wants people and especially God's people to stop creating children.

> *The sterilization surgery was not possible one hundred years ago, but it is now one of Satan's greatest weapons against the family ever created.*

It has the ability to *lower man*! In the Garden of Eden Satan *lowered mankind* by causing Adam and Eve to sin. Through trickery he stole their purity, which represented their rulership (Genesis 2:28). He used reasoning with Eve and convinced her that God had kept something good from her. He led her to believe that the fruit would open her eyes and make her be *like God* and that it would be a good thing. This trickery caused Adam and Eve to sin, which lowered them to the enemy's level because they no longer had the purity that God had originally given them. They were created to rule earth and afterward they suffered a loss.

> *Satan must steal what men and woman have or shut it down in order to defeat them. This way he can try to prevent the purposes of God from coming forth while also trying to stop mankind's dominion over him all at the same time.*

The sad thing is that many people do not even realize what they have done by having this operation. I believe that the Lord and all of Heaven actually shed tears for each parent's potential loss. "I would weep day and night for the slain of my people" (Jeremiah 9:1). "Streams of tears flow from my eyes because my people are destroyed" (Lamentations 3:48). *Sterilization robs a man of being creative and lowers him to Satan's non-creative zone. He becomes mute because he loses a life purpose.* Those who go along with sterilization whether by choice or by ignorance actually come into a *type of agreement* with the plan of the enemy. Thankfully, God can forgive this choice and restore lives.

Because of these things, I am so grieved when I hear sterilization stories that it hurts my heart. Many of these stories are coming from *good people* who love God but who have been deceived by the enemy into letting go of their precious gift. This choice may cause them to miss blessings and yoke their lives to the consequences of barrenness. "Be not deceived God is not mocked. Whatever a man sows that shall he also reap" (Galatians 6:9).

I believe that part of the curse of willfully choosing to make oneself barren brings consequences that will affect each gender differently. Both the man and the woman will suffer *in relation* to their gender roles. Men and women naturally care about things differently, and this kind of loss hurts them in a way that will affect how they relate to each other. I believe that this sorrow is why some people grow apart and eventually divorce after one of the spouses becomes sterile. When sterility causes those deep emotional wounds of the heart, longings to hold a baby, regrets that they can never have another of their own, and the feeling of personal rejection, they may not even understand why they have this sorrow, but they know that it is there and they want it to stop! Often they will look for reasons to *blame their spouse* or try to make the other person *pay* just to stop their own pain.

Please let me remind you that God is so rich in His desire to heal the brokenhearted that repentance will bring healing for the man, the woman, and the marriage. First we need to look at the consequences of choosing to be infertile so that we can better understand the individual sufferings that need the Lord's forgiveness.

WHAT ARE THE CONSEQUENCES FOR THE MAN?

My husband and I had a very interesting discussion one night about the difference between how men and women view infertility and barrenness. My husband and I decided that when a woman is infertile, it feels the same as when a man is impotent. Both problems make the individuals involved feel somewhat incomplete in their gender roles. A man's ability to relate sexually makes him feel fulfilled. When a woman bears a child, she feels like she has fulfilled one of her life's goals. If either one cannot perform these roles, society makes them feel inadequate. When individuals suffer this way, usually their spouses will be very understanding, but all of the love and support in the world does not seem to take away the emptiness that people feel when they cannot fulfill their gender roles.

So, dear husbands and husbands–to–be, please understand that when a woman is infertile, she is suffering because she no longer feels complete as a woman in the same way that a man would suffer if he could not perform sexually. It really hurts! Please be sensitive to the fact that barrenness steals from a woman something that is very special from her role and that this pain can be transferred to a relationship in such a way that it can also deeply affect a man as well.

Men may think that the verse "the barren womb is never satisfied" (Proverbs 30:16) does not apply to them because they do not have a womb. But when the womb of a man's wife is empty and no longer fruitful, he may also experience grief which he may not realize is connected to this loss. God gave men the need to conquer, to produce, to be protectors and providers. They are motivated by a deep need to *imprint themselves upon another*. This is why they build buildings, ships, aircraft, cities. They compete in business, fight in wars, and love sports. They are trying to leave their mark on this world, and they want to make a difference by building a legacy to be remembered by!

Even in male animals we can see the need to stake out and claim territory. The male will leave his scent so that another male does not come close to his territory or his female. If another male comes by, there is usually a fight to the death.

When a man cuts off his seed through sterilization, he halts the process of *further staking out his territory* because he has finished producing offspring of his kind. When a man has two or three children before he becomes sterilized, he easily convinces himself that he has had enough children. Most men then concentrate on trying to be a *good dad to the children that they already have.*

God gave men the innate desire to achieve greatness! They are created in his image (Genesis 1:27). When a man makes the choice to dictate how many children he should have instead of leaving that decision up to God, he may not realize that *he is disappointed with his choice.* By limiting God, *he has actually limited himself;* eventually as his children grow up, he no longer feels needed the way that he once was. Once disappointed he may then turn his attention toward other outlets to imprint his legacy. As the Lord blesses men's efforts of hard work and provision, many times we see them pouring their lives into things that fill their idle time, such as watching sports, golfing, fishing, taking vacations, purchasing expensive toys or the latest electronic gadgets. Some men because of their boredom turn to affairs with other women, internet porn, gambling, or alcohol—anything to *fill the void* that they feel now that their fathering role appears to be disappearing.

Many men in our society would deny that this is what men are doing when they seek excitement, but I believe that this is at least part of the reason. Why do men seek excitement? Because they no longer feel valuable but still desire an outlet for their need to conquer, protect, and provide. Many times they end up conquering their golf game, conquering another woman, conquering through ownership of expensive things. *They want to leave their imprint somewhere. Sadly they leave it in the wrong places.*

Occasionally, we may see a man become so bored with his life that he discards his first wife. He is no longer attracted to her once she has her tubes tied and has gained a little weight. The excitement is gone! He then moves on to a younger woman who is exciting to him and can bear him more children, even though he may never admit that this was the reason for leaving his first wife. The man feels young after *starting over* with a newer wife and a second family with little ones *who need him* the same way that his first family did.

My family has known several different couples to whom this has happened. These men expressed a *newfound happiness and excitement* by becoming dads again, but it certainly does not justify their behavior.

Men of God, you have a need to succeed! Please see that God has given you a need to leave your *personal imprint* on this world. Please see that God desires that you leave it through your children. Do not let Satan convince you that what you have should be limited. Ask God to help you *be open to see if He may have bigger plans for you.* He may desire to *enlarge your territory* far greater than what you had ever imagined possible!

WHAT ARE THE CONSEQUENCES FOR THE WOMAN?

Can you imagine never again holding a sweet-smelling infant, never again seeing his angelic smile or staring at his blessed sleep and wondering what he is thinking? Far too many women are longing for this blessing just one more time. . . .

A woman has the God-given need to cuddle, love, and nurture another human being, and we find great pleasure in being the caretakers of society. Nurturing is part of most women's nature, which can be seen when watching little girls at play. They hug their dolls and pretend to be the mommy. They collect trinkets and share and give love. They enjoy hugging and drawing pretty cards and just stopping their play to come tell you how much they love you! They express loving and nurturing right from the start.

"The barren womb is never satisfied" (Proverbs 30:16). When a husband convinces his wife that she should have her tubes tied or that he should have a vasectomy, she may agree in theory with her husband's reasons for sterilization, but she can never *turn off* the emotional side of her nurturing heart that desires to mother. *Women cannot deny what their hearts are telling them.* Nurturing is a God-given desire. When a woman realizes what she has done through sterilization or what her husband has convinced her to do, there is a deep, deep grief in her spirit. Many women will resent their husbands because *they no longer feel equal to the fertile women around them.*

When their arms are empty and another woman's arms are holding an infant that they too could have had, deep sorrow can set in. This sadness leads to feelings of inadequacy, inferiority, and jealousy. She may not even realize that this loss is the reason that she is having these feelings, but many women experience *degrees of depression* after they or their spouses have become sterile. When this sorrow occurs, usually it also affects intimacy in the marriage because of the grieving that the woman feels deep inside. This unmet need of her heart can even affect her hormone balance, which could lead to depression.

When women no longer feel that they have any use, they become very unhappy. It is common knowledge in the obstetrical/gyneco-logical profession today that the state of women's health in our world is at a critical point. Women are falling apart emotionally and physically. They are depressed, cancerous, infertile, and obese. The medical profession cannot seem to stay ahead of the hormonal problems. More women are prescribed antidepressants than ever before, and the infertility rate is going up faster than the doctors can offer solutions to the problem.

Often women need antidepressants once they have had tubal ligations. They cannot emotionally deny what their hearts are telling them. They feel as if their childbearing years were not complete, so *they become depressed.* Ending the part of their lives involved with creating a family may seem correct at first, but later it turns to sorrow because it is so final. After tubal ligations, some women have dreams where they are holding their baby and some-one comes and rips the child out of their arms, or they themselves even have thoughts of stealing another woman's child. The depres-sion that sets in is very haunting for some women.

Most women do not really know what to do or even why they are having these feelings of sorrow, so they look to *filling this void of womb* with other things, always looking for the love and acceptance that comes from nurturing children. They pour their time into careers, crafts, hobbies, decorating their homes, vacationing, shopping, or pets. Sometimes we see them pouring themselves into church work, motivated by the desire to feel fulfilled and needed.

Often after a tubal ligation a woman may develop into a complainer, constantly whining to her husband about all the things that he has not provided for her. She now wants a bigger house, a housekeeper, or more money to spend. She does this because *she resents him* for not stopping her from having the operation or because she is upset that he cannot fix her pain. She makes him *pay* by having to *put up with her unhappiness.*

Our world needs an answer from God, and I believe that coming back to Him in this area is the answer. Some may find it a little hard to believe that so many unfulfilled women are out there, but it is evident everywhere that many women in today's world are sad. Their words reveal what their hearts are feeling. They are mourning their loss because they were cut off by a husband who would rather be pursuing his own interests rather than raising another son or daughter. These are the ones who never seem to be at peace and have hidden their pain deep inside.

Have you ever been to a baby shower and listened to the comments of the older women there? The women who are forty, fifty, sixty years old? Often they will comment about how much they wish they could have another child or how much they enjoyed raising the children that they have already had. The younger ones talk about how much they wish their husband wanted more children and how much they are wishing for grandchildren soon. They become teary-eyed when the gifts are opened, as if each present reminded them of a season in their life that has passed—*a season that they loved, a season that they enjoyed, and one that they would love to enjoy just one more time.* When Sarah was eight-nine years old and found out that she was going to have a baby, she laughed and said, "Will I now have this *pleasure*?" (Genesis 18:12). *She called having a baby a pleasure.* Baby showers remind women of the pleasure of having a baby and the feelings that come with being a *new mommy* again. At these showers you can hear the cry of the ladies' hearts. You can also hear those who are unfulfilled, for they are grieving their loss and hoping that the grandchildren will fill that void. Some of these may not see grandchildren at all due to the rising infertility rate.

God does have a road to happiness in this area, and if we look to God to find answers we realize that deep inside the heart of every woman is a need that children are intended to fill. Each woman has a personal desire to nurture, and it varies in degree for each woman. When a woman lets God bring the children needed to fulfill her personal nurturing desires, she will be truly blessed with *contentment.* Then she will not need to run to the mall to buy something to make her feel better and she will not be whining to her husband to give her things that she does not need. Her void will be filled to overflowing, and *she will be a happy mother of children.* She will find Biblical contentment in fulfilling her gender role.

Once content, as she matures and her body begins to show signs of menopause, she will welcome the change instead of fight it. She will know that she has used her body for what was intended, and therefore the whole transition to menopause will be more peaceful. Her need to nurture will have been fulfilled, and this will help her to settle into a peace within herself and with God.

We must remember that God is not the author of sorrow but of joy! A baby at any stage of life produces joy! When a woman's longing arms hold a dear precious little one, the beauty and glory of love that comes from our Heavenly Father is felt.

Woman of God, I beg you not to be added to the list of millions of women who regret either their own decision or their husband's decision to be sterilized. Do not allow Satan to rob you of the privilege of giving life!

WHAT ARE THE CONSEQUENCES FOR THE MARRIAGE?

Have you ever read any articles or books talking about the consequences of sterilization on a marriage? I have not. Every marriage course that I have ever taken and every marriage book and article that I have ever read *acts like the subject of sterilization does not exist.* However, *the problems that sterilization creates in a marriage are quite real.*

The movement for *zero population growth* in our world filters so much information concerning the consequences of sterilization that this may be why we do not have much knowledge of them. Also, since many ministers are now either sterilized themselves or have spent their lives using birth control, they too could be experiencing marriage problems as the result and may not know why. When a couple chooses to become barren through a sterilization operation or spends their marriage using birth control, it can cause emotional strain. The *freedom* that so many couples seek turns out not to be as enjoyable because sterilizations bring new problems that *no one ever talks about.*

Once a couple moves away from the most important purpose for marriage, which is to create new life together, they will begin to lose something special. The emotional losses start out small but can grow bigger as time goes by because the sterilization operation creates an emotional wound as well as a physical one. If the couple never addresses these wounds, then the two become more and more separate. (Most couples do not address these issues because they do not realize that their emotional separation is related to this.) Divorce, affairs, and marriages that have grown cold are the fruit of these wounds. The sad thing is that this is clearly *not* what God intended for marriage.

God created marriage to be a wonderful partnership, where the man and woman became as *one flesh.*

"Has not the Lord made them one? In flesh and spirit they are His. And why one? because He was seeking Godly offspring. So guard yourself in the spirit and do not break faith with the wife of

your youth" (Malachi 2:15).

According to Malachi 2:15, when the couple enters into a birth control arrangement they will *no longer be in agreement* with what God intended. Complete unity is what God intended for marriage partners to experience and the *expression of that unity* is the fruit of a child produced from the act of *one-flesh agreement.* Modern believers have failed to completely grasp how beautiful this fruit is. It is a beautiful thing in the eyes of God and a glorious picture of the true unity of their marriage. It is not supposed to be a fruit of their random choices and occasional desires. Children are an expression of who God is. When a couple goes further and chooses sterilization, they permanently stop God's goal of producing Godly offspring through marriage.

> *For many couples, using birth control starts an emotional separation that later grows into the decision to become permanently separated.*

When a couple uses birth control, the subtle message that they send is "I love you but I do not love *the part of you* that makes us *one flesh*, (in reality I do not want *you!*) I *reject* your contribution which is part of your flesh (your egg or sperm) because I do not want to make children *with you* at this time"

> *Using birth control is a subtle yet very real form of rejection and reflects a continued lack of acceptance in the marriage.*

Most people have never looked at birth control as being a form of rejection, but this is what it is! By using birth control each partner is rejecting the baby-making capacities of the other. They want the excitement but they reject its *fruit,* which is the possibility of a child. This rejection keeps them from experiencing complete unity and is not God's best for their marriage.

What God offers people is something pure and beautiful and loving. He desires complete unity when each partner completely accepts every part of the other partner and then comes into a complete agreement with that acceptance. This is what it means *to be naked*—naked in mind, body, and spirit just like Adam and Eve were in the garden—naked and unashamed. When people are naked, they want to be completely loved for who they are. Husbands and wives who experience this total acceptance find that their marriages grow extremely strong because everything is out on the table, so to speak, and their partner still loves them, still wants them, and still wants to make babies with them. This may be why couples who follow God's plan for marriages in this area hardly ever divorce! This complete acceptance eliminates fears from the marriage as well as personal fears that arise as people age: "Does she still want me?" "Does he still find me attractive?" "Do I still have value?"

When a couple is still willing to produce offspring together years after they are first married, they will feel a deeper level of emotional connection because they are still willing to be physically connected. As they age and still desire to create offspring, they still feel valued because their spouse still needs them and still needs *their sperm* or *their eggs*. This may sound silly, but this unspoken need is what makes a marriage exciting when people have been together for a long time. The idea that "I am still wanted" makes a person feel special.

After the couple chooses sterilization, why should a wife get excited about her man anymore? After all, he does not want to make a baby with her. He is basically through with that part of her, so why should she *make love to him* when she does not feel like it? Why should she desire him anymore? Why should he be thrilled about her anymore? What is she to him now that they do not want any more children together?

BIRTH CONTROL USE SEPARATES

Couples may spend their entire marriage not realizing that their spouses were feeling rejected just because they used birth control. What is interesting to note is that for many couples, feelings of rejection subside during their pregnancies. When they are creating a baby together they both feel elated and excited. There is an anticipation of their own contribution that is filled with both mystery and excitement. This keeps couples interested in each other and their marriage. Sex during pregnancy without the use of the birth control often becomes better and feels closer as neither partner feels rejected by the other.

However, when the couple goes back to using their birth control after the birth of a child, the feelings of rejection return, and the sorrow begins all over again. Could this be a reason for postpartum blues? Could this be why many women don't rush back to sexual relations after the birth of their child? Could they be fearing the rejection?

The whole concept of birth control is to protect the partners from each other. This is the opposite of oneness.

If the couple chooses to permanently cease childbearing after the birth of the new child, at first a husband may feel relieved that he no longer has to fear additional children. But over time the joy begins to leave the bedroom because the thrill is gone. Part of the act of lovemaking is the thrill, the chase, the conquering, the satisfaction. The woman may retreat into a hole of rejection that she never comes out of simply because she feels her husband no longer needs her or wants her. A woman has a need for her Prince Charming to fight for her, to conquer her, and to take her away. When a woman is talked into getting her tubes tied and ceasing her ability to give life, she will not feel protected by her man, and she will hold this against him. Even though she may be happy that she can no longer become pregnant, she may find that sex becomes more mechanical and lacking in intimacy because she no longer is conquerable. In her mind, where was her prince when she needed him to protect her? Why didn't he stand up and protect her rights, her heart, her emotional needs? In her mind she may feel that he already conquered her, used her and threw her away. So again, why bother with him?

If a couple uses birth control and experiences the subtle rejection, it becomes easier to take the next and final step which severs their partnership—sterilization. Once sterilization takes place, the rejection caused by birth control then has concrete roots. *When this happens, there is now a date and a time* when one spouse made a permanent severance from their childbearing capabilities and therefore ultimately rejected the other spouse! This unspoken vow of rejection looks like this:

On this day at this time _____*, we choose to no longer be yoked to each other in order to create new life.*

It is as if one spouse says to the other: "I reject your ability to create new lives with me.

I am permanently rejecting *you*, and I feel good about this decision."

Wow! When this form of rejection occurs, the partners are now permanently separated. *They are no longer partners in this area.* They can no longer produce life together and one of them is no longer physically whole. The sterilized spouse paid the ultimate price of rejection. They are now *physically mutilated as well.*

This form of severance kills marital intimacy!

The husband and wife no longer have the same relationship they had on their wedding day. The partnership has now changed from its original goals and God's perfect plan of intimacy through creating offspring. After sterilization, they can never be the same again. It is impossible.

Can they still have a good marriage? Perhaps. They would have to work hard at their communication, but it is possible. There is more to a marriage than creating children, but this decision to reject will always be the filter for love to flow through from that point on unless there is repentance and emotional restoration. When a spouse severs the partnership, rejects the partner's seed or eggs, and then mutilates their own body, the consequence will be a *wall of rejection* that will be part of their marriage forever!

To feel unwanted is one of the most horrible feelings that a person can experience. This opens a person's heart up to fear and temptation. The woman will fear that her husband no longer needs her. If he no longer needs her to create offspring which represent the fruit of their union, over time she may break away and feel he no longer needs her for other things. Although they may never talk about it, that feeling of rejecting her will be there. As she ages and her youth begins to fade, just knowing that she is no longer needed in the same way that she once was makes her sad. If she has been blessed with children, then as long as they need her, she may be able to cope, but once they grow and go, she may feel very out of sorts and very separated from the intimacy that her marriage once involved. Even if she has a career and enjoys stable relationships, she will know that deep inside something is missing.

Only repentance and seeking the Lord's forgiveness together will allow restoration. As the Lord forgives and begins to heal the emotional wounds in the marriage, then the couple can see some degree of restoration. Without this healing, many couples just *grow apart* over the years, some have affairs, and some even divorce. But many just live in a cold marriage filled with emotional separations. They stay together because it is too inconvenient to divorce. This is clearly not what God intended for these couples.

People of God, I plead with you: here are more reasons to seek God's heart on the family planning issue! The Bible supports the fact that using birth control and sterilization cause unnecessary pain and suffering. Those who choose this road find unhappiness in many, many areas. Please do not allow "the enemy who stalks about like a roaring lion seeking whom he may devour" (1 Peter 5:8) to devour your God-given ability to be unified in your marriage!

Let us return to the Lord! His way has blessings for us to reap.

"When all these blessings and curses I have set before you come upon you and you take them to heart . . . and when you and your children return to the Lord your God and obey him with all your heart and with all your soul according to everything I command you today, then the Lord your God will restore your fortunes and have compassion on you . . . " (Deuteronomy 30:1-3).

"Come let us return to the Lord, he has torn us to pieces but he will heal us, he has injured us but he will bind up our wounds"

(Hosea 6:1).

"Even now, declares the Lord, return to me with fasting and weeping and mourning . . . return to the Lord your God, for he is gracious and compassionate, slow to anger and abounding in love" (Joel 2:12-13).

"....Return to me and..... I will return to you" (Zechariah 1:3).

"Ever since the times of your forefathers you have turned away from my decrees and have not kept them. Return to me and I will return to you, says the Lord almighty" (Malachi 3:7).

It's time to heal the brokenhearted and preach good news to the poor, to bind up the brokenhearted, to proclaim freedom for the captives and to declare the release from darkness for the prisoners . . . to comfort all who mourn (Isaiah 61:1-2).

PRAYER for the husband: Lord, I want to do it Your way! I don't want to spend my life trying to fill the void that comes from barrenness. Forgive me if I have been doing this. Please put me on the proper path. Please give me a vision for my family that will give me peace about the future. Help me to trust You with all of my concerns for provision. I repent. Call me back to You.

PRAYER for the wife: Oh, God, please save me from this sorrow! I do not want to suffer the consequences of barrenness. Help me to want children and to see that they can fill the voids in my life. Help me to be open to You. Please help me to want what You want and not to be afraid. Please calm all of my fears and take away my pain.

CHAPTER 8

The Idol's Altar

"Break down their altars, smash their sacred stones,
cut down their Asherah poles and burn their idols in the fire.
For you are a people holy unto the Lord your God. The Lord
your God has chosen you out of all of the peoples of the earth
to be his people, His treasured possession" (Deuteronomy 7:5,6).

From the beginning of time, the devil has been using the same methods to mess up mankind. He may package them differently from generation to generation, but his tricks are the same, and over and over people keep falling for them. Century after century the devil ruins lives through his deception and trickery, and the sad thing is that people who are being deceived do not realize it until it is too late! When we are walking in deception, all we will believe is that our decisions are correct. Later we see that what we thought would be best really was not.

This very thing is what happened to Eve in the Garden of Eden. I do not believe that on the day that she committed the first sin she planned to disobey God. Her day started out like any other day in the garden, but as she happened to pass by the one forbidden tree, suddenly something drew her in and she found herself desiring something that *she knew she should not want.* Then she heard the devil speaking through the serpent, and he twisted her mind in such a way that she may have thought that by eating the fruit that she was *actually doing a good thing* by choosing to become like God. The devil was cleverly misleading her by getting her to *reason out the situation* and the variables until she fell into sin. After she ate the fruit and hid from God, she realized that her choice was wrong, but there was *nothing* that she could do to change it. She was left to suffer with the consequences of her action.

This is how deception works, and it is evil. When people are deceived, they do not realize that they are allowing *reasoning* to twist their decisions. For example, doctors who perform abortions *reason* that they are helping women. They dismiss the fact that they are also murdering innocent babies because they justify that helping women is a good cause. When scientists desire to use the body parts of aborted babies to create new medicines and vaccines, they dismiss the fact that these body parts came from innocent babies and focus on wanting to help those alive today. When people decide to steal something, they *reason* that they need the item more than the person who owns it and they dismiss the fact that it is stealing the other person's property or that stealing can hurt the other person.

When we are being deceived by the lies and trickery of the devil, he *always* leads us to a justifiable conclusion that makes sense in our situation. This is the art of deception, and Satan is a master at it. *He knows how to fool us in such a way that we do not realize it until it is too late.* (1Timothy 3:46). This is also how he operates in the area of family planning. His deception is affecting people's decisions everywhere in society, including our churches. This deception has caused us to justify our choices on the basis of reasoning and dismiss what God might have wanted for our lives.

When we disobey God's commands, Scripture calls us *idolaters* because we have come into agreement with a belief system or an idea that may go against the plans and purposes of God for our lives. After this happens we can become easily entangled in a web of *our* *own personal opinions, thoughts, beliefs, and interpretations for our future lives, based on how **we feel** about the situation and not on the Word of God.* Once we move away from God's perspective, it is hard to step back and realize that we may be involved with an idol.

God's perfect plan for our lives is then compromised and can become lost in a cloud of our own justifications and personal reasons. When this happens, we settle for living our lives by *our plan* instead of by God's design.

WHAT IS AN IDOL?

Considering that we may have given ourselves over to an idol is hard for some of us to accept. Most of us do not want to believe that *we* could ever become deceived in this way because we love God and want to please Him. But Scripture says that believers do get trapped in idolatry. To understand how we could ever become involved in any way with an idol, we must first understand what exactly an idol is and how the enemy uses deception to trap us.

An idol can be anything that robs and steals our hearts' attention from God. This is why *an idol is an affront to the Gospel and to loving God with all of our hearts, souls, and minds.* Some idols cause us to become attached to them, and in exchange they make us feel safe and secure. This security is temporary and false, but we do not realize it because we are deceived by our allegiance to the idol. Some idols steal our time and demand our attention, and we give it to the idol because we do not realize that we have transferred our time and attention to an idol and taken it away from God because we are deceived. Scripture says to turn from idols and not to defile ourselves with them (Ezekiel 14:6, 20:18, Acts 15:20, 1 John 5:21, 2 Corinthians 6:16). In other words, idols get in the way of the Lord having complete control in a particular area of our lives.

Why should we want to give Him control? Because when the Lord takes control of an area, we will *always* reap incredible blessings as well as be protected from the enemy trying to bring us harm. When we offer ourselves as servants, it also shows the Lord how much we are willing to trust Him with our lives, our hearts, and our bodies. To be truly blessed, our desire should be to give Him complete control over *every area* of our lives.

Recognizing the areas where we have displaced our love for the Lord with idols and then removing those idols will allow us to begin to receive the abundant blessings that God intends for us. He says, "I will bless a thousand generations of those who love me," those who are not idol worshippers" (Exodus 20:5). Notice that the Lord says that the blessing comes on those who love Him. Idol worship is an indication to the Lord that we do not love Him and are not willing to do things His way. This brings sorrow to the heart of God.

Scripture says, "You shall not make for yourself an idol in the form of anything in Heaven above or on the earth beneath or in the waters below. You shall not *bow down* to them or *worship* them" (Exodus 20:4).

What God was clearly communicating to His people was, "Do not make any kind of idol." He also said, "Do not worship anything but Me!" (Exodus 20:3). In other words, if you want to be happy, *"Do not give your heart away to anything or anyone but Me."*

We must remember that our God says that *He a jealous God* (Exodus 20:5). He wants our hearts' affection. He does not want us to *waste our love* on something that will not bring us true happiness. He wants what is best for us all of the time. He told us to stay away from idol worship because idols *take* our time, *consume* our lives, and *never* give anything of value back in return.

Scripture is clear that not only is idol worship a sin, but it also brings a *generational curse* upon those who are idol worshippers.

"Visiting the iniquity of the fathers upon the children unto the third and fourth generation of those who hate me" (Exodus 20:5).

"The arrogance of man will be brought low and the pride of men humbled; the Lord alone will be exalted in that day, and the idols will totally disappear" (Isaiah 2:17).

Even *ideas and beliefs* that are readily accepted by our culture can be idols. In fact, these can be our biggest idols because they blind us to the truth. It is easy to become confused because even believers have come to accept many of these ideas and beliefs without questioning whether they line up with the written Word of God. This is why many of God's dear people are involved with idols without realizing it. "He reveals the deep things and brings deep shadows into the light" (Job 12:22). Scripture is clear that anything that takes our hearts' affection away from God can be an idol. Therefore *our beliefs, our reasoning, our justifications for our actions* can actually be something that we turn into an idol in our hearts, and many of these may remain hidden until God reveals them to us.

When we try to dissect an issue like family planning, it is difficult to discern the truth from deception because *the enemy hides in the shadows of our own doubts and fears and also the preconceived ideas we have formed from the world around us.* We must ask God for discernment if we are going to disconnect our thoughts from the enemy's lies.

HOW DO PEOPLE BECOME CONNECTED TO IDOLS?

To understand how people become involved with idols, we must first think about Eve and realize that the devil's number-one trick of deception is to lead us by twisting our minds. We also need to understand a little history about God's people and idol worship. This will help us put the whole area into perspective. Idol worship is not something that people necessarily plan to do. But they are led into it *little by little* until it eventually consumes them without them realizing their deception or their involvement.

When the enemy desires to deceive us, his goal is to get us involved with something that *looks good* or *sounds good* to our human spirit but in the end, as the Bible says, *"leads to the ways of death"* (Proverbs 16:25).

Such deception worked on Eve that fateful day in the Garden. Once the devil *confused her* about the true issue, she then became *unsure* if her previous thinking had been correct. He asked her, "Did God *really* say that you must not eat from any tree in the garden?" (Genesis 3:1).

Once the devil saw that she was *wavering,* he then used reasoning to lead her into sin. "You will not die, for God knows that when you eat the fruit your eyes will be opened and you will be like God" (Genesis 3:4-5). Once she saw that the fruit was good, she then *felt good* about her choice, and she was trapped! *This is the plan of the devil. It worked on Eve. In the area of family planning, it's working on thousands of couples today as well.*

First, the devil confused church leadership about the issues so that our pastors stopped preaching and following what the Scriptures said about birth control and sterilization. At the same time the respected medical community offered us new alternatives. Because God's people no longer had a Scriptural viewpoint as their guide, they started looking to see what other couples were doing. "All we like sheep have gone astray . . ." (Isaiah 53:6), and we then lead each other astray. Couples begin by talking about family planning with each other and their friends; they even ask their parents or church leadership what they think; but both groups followed what was popular in their generations. It is hard for parents and clergy to offer sound Scriptural advice because they have not been taught it! Instead, most of them offer their *personal opinions*, which are based on their own experiences or the humanistic ideas portrayed in the media or taught in public classrooms. As time has gone by, Godly couples have existed in a state of confusion over this issue and have been told that family planning is an issue that *God does not care about anymore.*

Once a couple is confused about the issues, Satan can bring *reasoning* to the situation and whisper in many a couple's ear, "*Did God really say,* 'Be fruitful and multiply?' Maybe He meant that for ancient people, but surely not for modern civilizations." He also adds, "You know God sees *your situation,* and He certainly would not want you to be foolish by choosing to have more children than you can care for."

The devil will gently speak what sounds like truthful reasons to couples, and they will become slowly deceived into thinking that *God really does not mean what He said in His Word.* They begin to believe that somehow it just does not apply to today's situations because modern times are different than Biblical times. The decision about how many children to have is not important anymore, even though the Bible did not say "Be fruitful and multiply until the population of the earth reaches six billion" or "Be fruitful and multiply until you feel you've had enough children for your comfort level" or "Be fruitful and multiply only as long as you have the money to give your children the things that you think that they need."

Most couples just assume that God no longer cares about this area of their marriages; when told that He *does still care* about their family planning, most are in a state of shock and disbelief. With modern reasoning in mind they believe that *they must decide what to do* based on their own particular set of circumstances of money, time, career, health, mission in life and personal desires. And since they have been taught that, "God helps those who help themselves" (a quote by Ben Franklin that is not in the Scriptures), they become confused into believing that *God wants them to make this decision* for themselves.

Such reasoning makes a lot of sense from a human standpoint, but it is *deception* because this is not what Scripture says! It is the devil's ultimate *trickery* at work. A couple who fails to stand firm on the words spoken by God in the Scriptures will leave the truth behind. Just like Eve they will be tempted away into the pain and sorrow of sin. As the enemy confuses them and tricks them with valid human reasons, they will stray further and further from the Word of God.

Because of the devil's trickery, most couples will not consult the Lord or seek His heart for the size that their family should be, but instead they will use logic to conclude that they do not want a large family. They will remark, "We feel good about our decision to limit our family size. We have two children, and we are very happy having only two!"

Whether a couple ends up with two children or twenty children is not the most important issue. *The issue is not the size of a family.* A couple can be very blessed with one or two children and be in the center of God's perfect will for their lives. *What is important is whether a couple is willing to be open to the possibilities of God sending another child into their lives.*

There are definitely couples who are only supposed to have one or two children. God's plan for them is to raise one or two children and it is a good plan for their lives. Scripture has many examples of couples who were blessed by God with just one or two children: Abraham and Sarah, Samson's parents, and Zechariah and Elizabeth, just to name a few. But the difference between these Biblical couples and today's couples is that the couples of the Bible *allowed God to make this decision for them!* They did not make the decision for themselves. Scripture does not give us any indication that Biblical saints did anything to prevent God from blessing them with children. These couples *stood firm on what God said in His Word* and trusted this area of their marriages to God while receiving the number of children that God ordained.

When a couple says, "God told us to only have two children" or "God has not called us to have any more children" and then they use *the pill* for the rest of their lives or get a sterilization operation to make sure that God does not bless them again, they have seriously missed the point. They don't want to admit that they are afraid that God might send them another child someday even when the God of the universe is quite capable of shutting the woman's womb. God's ability to open and shut a mother's womb was proven in Scripture long before sterilization procedures ever entered the mind of man.

IDOLS LEAD US AWAY . . . INTO HUMAN REASONING

God's people have had a history of being *led away into idolatry*. Over and over idols led to their downfall and punishment. When the people of God lived in cultures where they could not freely worship the one true God, some form of paganism involving various forms of idol worship usually surrounded them. The devil used paganism and idolatry to separate them from loving God and led them into his lies by *confusing them* about whose people they were and about what God told them to do. They slowly began to separate themselves from how God told them to live and connected themselves with the culture of the pagans through participation in customs, ceremonies, and holiday festivities. Pretty soon, there was no clear distinction between God's people and the pagan culture around them. This sin pattern repeated itself over and over in the Old Testament and still can be seen today, especially in America.

Every time, the devil took his time leading God's people away. He waited, just like he did with Eve, to *slowly lead God's people away* from His principles through human reasoning and trickery. The people were eventually led away from Scripture into deception and didn't have a clue that they had been deceived or misled.

The Scriptures said that this was *whoredom* (Jeremiah 3:1-3, Ezekiel 16:20, Ezekiel 43:9, Hosea 4:12, Hosea 5:3), but God's people were attracted to this deception because at the time it made sense to their way of thinking. But it was evil and God's people eventually left God's way for a new lifestyle that led them further and further away from God's best. They were *sleeping with the enemy . . .* and they *liked* it!

"Was your prostitution not enough? You slaughtered *my children* and sacrificed them to the idols" (Ezekiel 15:20b-21).

When the children of Israel were living in the cultures who sacrificed to Molech, they followed the example of the pagans around them and *sacrificed their own children* on the altars of this pagan god (Leviticus 18:21, Psalm 106:37-38). God had already told them in Exodus 20:5, "I am a jealous God. Do not have any other gods before Me!" but they allowed themselves to be corrupted and persuaded into the pagan thought process, and eventually this led to sin and rebellion against God.

As far back as ancient Mesopotamia, Assyria, and Babylon there were pagan forms of worship that focused on a system of false gods and false beliefs. Since these ancient people did not know the living God nor have the written Word of God, they developed a religion that focused on the reasons *why* things happened in their world.

For instance, when it rained, they believed that the *rain god* sent rain. When there was a storm, they believed that the *gods in the sky* were doing battle. When the crops were harvested, they thanked *the mother of the earth.* They worshipped the *sun,* the *moon,* and the *stars.* Pagan gods were all given a star, and the people observed individual stars to discern whether the gods were happy. They formed elaborate stories about the gods which today we would call mythology.

In every new culture that followed, these gods were given different names, but the pagan beliefs remained very similar. One of the most popular beliefs, found in some form in every pagan culture, concerns *the fertility cycle. Reproduction was desired.* Birthing children and producing crops were both considered good things. When ancient peoples were productive in these two areas, they believed it was a sign that the gods were pleased. The people performed rituals that they hoped would appease the gods. The sins of the heathens were so great that at times God even required His people to conquer cities and kill everything because the evil practices were so ingrained in these pagans that even their animals were filled with evil spirits!

Child sacrifice (Leviticus 20:3) was one of many rituals that God called defilement. (Ezekiel 23:37, 37:23). God was especially displeased when His chosen people took part and blended with the culture of the pagans. Throughout Scripture He commands His people to *Come out and be separate* (2 Corinthians 6:7).

When the people of God sacrificed their children to Molech, Ashtoreth, and other pagan deities, this was an extreme act of wickedness before God. The Hebrews knew that this was wrong, yet they still did it because they had listened so long to the people living around them. They blended with society because *they had forgotten whose people they were.* God kept telling them that they were a chosen people who were supposed to be pure and set apart.

After blending with pagan cultures, God's people believed that sacrificing their children to their pagan deities would bring them greater crop productivity. They put their faith in their fertility idols instead of the living God to grant them blessings. This was a very serious act of wickedness and clearly an indication that they did not have faith in the true God. It reflected their lack of value for the *life* that He had given them. Since God is the author of Life, He blessed them with children whom he called His children: "You sacrificed *my children*" (Ezekiel 15:21, 23:37). When they slaughtered these dear little children that were God's to appease their earthly idols God's heart was deeply saddened. This is why the Lord kept commanding His people to *Come out and be separate!* He was trying to spare them from the pain that idols brought with them.

Idols have appetites that will <u>never</u> be satisfied. Those who wrap themselves up in idol worship get in deeper and deeper until they are consumed with pleasing the idol to which they have dedicated their lives. They will begin to believe that it is acceptable and even blessed of God in some cases to go against what God has said. Soon they will be unable to separate truth from deception because they fall into *reasoning,* and *reasoning* leads them into a comfort level that justifies their decisions. This is where the majority of couples are today in regard to their family planning.

THE DECEPTION OF CHILD SACRIFICE

When we hear of such things as *child sacrifice* we can't imagine the horrors of committing such an act, and we find it hard to imagine what kind of person could do such a thing. To fully understand how deeply people can be deceived, we must consider what child sacrifice might have been like so that we can understand just how evil this wickedness was in the eyes of God.

After carefully researching this subject I want to describe the situations that happened when God's people turned their backs on His commands and practiced child sacrifice.

"They forsook all of the commands of the Lord their God and made for themselves two idols in the shape of calves; they worshipped Baal. They sacrificed their sons and daughters. They practiced divination and sorcery and sold themselves to do evil in the eyes of the Lord" (2 Kings 17:16-17).

Parents took their precious sleeping infants out of their little baskets and carried them to the temple of their pagan god. More than likely it was the parent who stripped the child naked while the temple priest assisted. As the baby was wakened, I'm sure it squirmed a bit and cried as infants often do. Once the baby was ready, the pagan priests laid the baby on the *altar* to perform a ceremony of sacrifice to a pagan god. These types of sacrifices involved sacrificing children in the fire or running a knife through the child's heart. As the baby's blood spewed out all over the parent we can only imagine the reaction of the parent, but for the priest, this was commonplace causing no reaction. The baby's blood was then drained from its little body to be drunk by those participating in the ceremony or used in one of other the temple rituals.

In other rituals, the parents would take their darling little three- or four-year-old children to the pagan temple to offer them as a burnt offering to Baal, Molech, and their other idols (2 Chronicles 28:3, Leviticus 18:21, Leviticus 20:3, 2 Kings 17:17, 2

Kings 21:6, 2 Chronicles 33:6). What a horror to even imagine. What would a parent be telling a child at such a time? Maybe a parent would tell the child that they needed them to do something special for them. "Yes, Mommy; Yes, Daddy," replied the child, anxious to please his parents. When they got to the temple maybe the child would be told to climb up on a table and wait. Then the pagan priest (with the assistance of the parent) would tie the child to the table. Maybe the child would yell, "Mommy, Daddy, what are you doing to me? You are hurting me!" and as the child began to cry, the priest would pour a flammable oil over the little boy or little girl and then light the fire. As the child screamed out in shrill horror, "Daddy save me, Mommy save me!" we have no idea how the parents were reacting. But maybe they just stood there and watched as if hypnotized while their child was burned alive—sacrificed in a ceremony to appease their pagan god.

Isn't this horrifying? These were the kinds of things that happened many times throughout the history of God's people, and this behavior deeply grieved God's heart.

"Do not give any of your children to be sacrifice to Molech, for you must not profane the name of the Lord. I am the Lord" (Leviticus 18:21).

"Any Israelite or alien living in Israel who gives any of his children to Molech must be put to death. The people of the community are to stone him" (Leviticus 20:2).

"I will set my face against that man and I will cut him off from his people for giving his children to Molech, he has defiled my sanctuary and profaned my name" (Leviticus 20:3).

"They sacrificed their sons and daughters in the fire. They practiced divination and sorcery and sold themselves to do evil in the eyes of the Lord provoking him to anger" (2 Kings 17:17).

We ask ourselves what kind of parent could be able to participate in this and stand there and witness such a horror? We can only imagine. We believe that people in modern times would *never* allow themselves to commit such horrors by sacrificing their children to pagan deities. We ask ourselves how could someone have such a cold heart? Yet if we look at the practices of the abortion industry, we can see parallels to these scenes. At abortion clinics all over our country, babies are poisoned with saline solutions, burned alive with chemicals inserted in the womb, and sacrificed daily upon the altars of excuses like "I've got better things to do with my life"; "A baby would ruin my career"; "I do not have enough money to raise this child"; "I am too young to have a baby now"; "My parents would kill me if they found out that I was pregnant"; "I cannot give up my college education"; "We don't need a third child—we already have a boy and a girl"; "I am too old for another child. Since this child could have health problems, it is easier just to abort."

Men and women sacrifice their children every day.

"They parade their sin like Sodom; they do not hide it. Woe to them! They have brought disaster upon themselves" (Isaiah 3:9).

By the grace of God, those who have had abortions can be forgiven and healed and renewed. Also by the grace of God, many believers have avoided the horrors of abortion, but is it possible under the circumstances that we may still be guilty of sin here? When we take family planning into our own hands, we may decide that sterilization is best, or we may decide to use birth control so that we can prevent more children from coming into our families. In both instances, are we *then guilty of sacrificing our future blessings* without realizing it? Even though we may consider ourselves to be good people, we must ask God to help us recognize if the enemy is deceiving us here by causing us to exchange the truth of God for a lie in this area (Romans 1:25-27).

When we choose to end our abilities to produce more children by a sterilization operation, we are in a sense sacrificing *our future blessings* to what we think is a good reason.

Think about it: we sacrifice our God-given ability to reproduce a child on the surgeon's table (the altar), and we say to the surgeon "Burn it!" and with one swoop of the laser our vas deferens or our fallopian tubes are burned up. Our ability to ever create more children is destroyed. We sacrifice ourselves to *the idol of our very good human reasons,* and *this idol consumes our physical body parts as the sacrifice.*

This is what bowing down to an idol really means. God's Word says that people who do this "Cling to worthless idols and forfeit the grace that could be theirs" (Jonah 2:8). The grace forfeited may have been the grace to produce and raise more Godly heirs for the kingdom of God and the joy of being given that privilege!

In the midst of family planning decisions, most people simply do not realize the trap that the devil has set for them. They take God's wonderful plan out of the picture and allow the devil to steal the blessings of additional children. The devil convinces them that *God would want them to take charge of their own destiny.* God's Word says that when people act on ungodly impulses, God will allow this deception to happen because they were participating within their own belief system, which is not based on what is written in Scripture. Their decision to plan their family then becomes comfortable, and they rely on that feeling as if it has been confirmed by God.

God will allow deception when any child of God "sets up idols in his heart and puts wicked stumbling blocks before his face and then goes to a prophet [seeks counsel or prays about it], I the LORD will answer him myself in keeping with his great idolatry. I will do this to recapture the hearts of the people of Israel who have all deserted me for their idols" (Ezekiel 14:4-5).

The Lord says that *He will answer you in keeping with your deception* when you turn your face toward idols! That's powerful and scary! "Woe to the wicked! Disaster is upon them. They will be paid back for what their hands have done" (Isaiah 3:11).

Cry out for mercy! Do you see how you have been tricked by the enemy? Had someone pointed this trickery out to Eve on that fateful day, she might have chosen to obey God, but no one rescued her from the deception. Because of God's mercy and because of all of the suffering that has already come upon the past several generations, God is allowing this deception to be exposed to save couples from additional heartache. Please wake up and see the plan of the enemy!

Once we see how we have been deceived by these ideas that are associated with idols, then we can more clearly see what we need to let go of in order to run back to the arms of our loving Heavenly Father. Scripture says that He is waiting to cleanse us from all unrighteousness (1 John 1:9) and fill us with peace. Just knowing this is comforting, but for some of us, *the devil has so cleverly clouded the issues* that it is necessary to name these idols and expose the lies so that we can more easily understand where Satan has confused us.

SACRIFICING OUSELVES AT THE DEVIL'S ALTAR

It would be impossible for me to name all of the areas where God's people have become involved with idols, so I am going to list just a few that I believe the enemy is using to keep people from stay-ing open to the possibility of birthing another child.

Each idol has an altar upon which many of God's people are making daily decisions. They live their lives in agreement with ungodly thoughts, beliefs, and lifestyles. Many of these areas in themselves are not evil but when related to family planning, they cause us to make compromises that lead us away from God's goals for our families. Once this happens, the agreement *exalts itself against the knowledge of God!*

"There will be terrible times in the last days. People will be lovers of themselves, lovers of money, boastful, proud, abusive, disobedient to their parents, ungrateful, unholy, without love, unfor-giving, slanderous, without self-control, brutal, not lovers of the good, treacherous, rash, conceited, lovers of pleasure more than lovers of God, having a form of Godliness but denying its power" (2 Timothy 3:1-5a).

As you read this list, I pray that the Holy Spirit will bring His supernatural discernment upon you and convict you of any area where you may be compromising your thoughts or beliefs with one or more of these idols. These idols take our focus off of the Lord and His principles and wrap us up in believing that we have the proper wisdom to correctly choose what is best for our own lives.

1. The Altar Dedicated to the Idol of Human Reasoning

On this altar, *we worship and justify our reasons* for why we view our situation the way that we do.

Although we do not realize how limited our perspective is, we make lifelong family planning decisions based on what we can see from our own human standpoint and not on what God has told us to do. Think of all of the human reasons for why people should end their ability to create new life. With the exception of the mother's health, almost every reason is circumstantial. These circumstances could very well improve as a couple heads down the path of life. Scripture says that we should throw off the sin that entangles us and fix our eyes on Christ (Hebrews 12:1-2).

When you rely on your own reasoning, it becomes your idol, and you need to repent.

2. The Altar Dedicated to the Idol of Convenience

On this altar *we worship convenience* and strive for comforts.

Thousands of couples approach the decision of whether they should have additional children from the standpoint of convenience. They are deeply concerned about how much additional *work* more children may cause. They are also deeply concerned about how much of their *time* they might have to dedicate to raising additional children. Husband and wives do not always want to make this kind of investment. They feel they have other *more important* things to do with their time, money, and efforts.

People choose vasectomies and tubal ligations because using *birth control is inconvenient*. The wife has to remember to take the birth control pill, which is *inconvenient*. It may also cause her not to feel like herself at times and this is *inconvenient*. Most men see using a condom as highly inconvenient; they do not want to bother with having to stop during lovemaking and put it on, even though it only takes about thirty seconds! In addition, it is much more enjoyable not wearing one.

People make these choices because they do not want to be bothered or made to feel *uncomfortable*. To most couples, accidentally having a child that they were not planning for and do not want would be the height of *inconvenience!* Usually those who worship convenience also are very concerned with personal comforts.

Desiring comforts and conveniences and not wanting to be bothered are all *forms of selfishness,* but people do not see things this way. They can justify why they want things to be comfortable and convenient. *People believe they deserve these things* because they work for them and have choices.

Some people do not want another child because the woman complains that it is *not comfortable* being pregnant and the man complains that it is *not comfortable* sharing the wife's body with the baby. It is *not comfortable* being awake at 2 a.m. It is *not comfortable* for a woman to nurse her baby and then leak milk all over her clothes or to leak milk while trying to make love. It is *not comfortable* living on one salary instead of two. Some are *not comfortable* giving up additional money to raise another child. It also is not comfortable having to start over again with another child. It is easier to quit after two children and get sterilized.

If you are approaching the subject of family planning from the standpoint of convenience and comforts, this has become your idol and you need to repent.

3. The Altar Dedicated to the Idol of Materialism: A Desire for a Comfortable Financial Life

On this altar *we worship materialism.*

Our society bows down to the ownership of possessions. People's self-worth is wrapped up in their zip code. In fact we even have a TV show named after a zip code: *Beverly Hills 90210.* People feel that they cannot start their families until they have a house, they have two new cars, the wife can afford not to work, they pay off their student loans, they have traveled, or they have saved a certain amount for retirement. Material comforts rule the choice of how large a family that a couple desires. Too many children might mean *less for me or less for us.* On this altar they worship the dream of a life of new appliances, high-priced vehicles, traveling, retiring by age fifty-five! *They dream of a life full of the possessions of their choosing.* They feel that these are blessings from God, and they are but they have these blessings in the wrong place. They have become idols. Instead of utilizing materialism to accomplish great things for God, they use their material possessions to bring themselves a life of comfort and enjoyment.

"But the worries of this world, the deceitfulness of wealth, and the desires for other things come in and choke the word, making it unfruitful" (Mark 4:19).

Do not forget God in your prosperity (Deuteronomy 8).

If your view of the purpose of material possessions is that you can live a comfortable lifestyle, then maybe you do not understand the trap that possessions are. If you desire to gain possessions for comfort's sake this is your idol and you need to repent.

4. The Altar Dedicated to the Idol of Money

On this altar *we worship money.*

In American society, many Christians make family planning decisions based on the fear that children might cost too much money to raise. Many times they use the excuse that they cannot have too many children because they are being *good stewards* of their money. They are afraid that God would not provide enough money for their families if they were to have more children than the socially acceptable number. People do not take into account God's supernatural provision for large families who love the Lord; they have never trusted God to see what He might bring them. They mask their *love of money* and their lack of ability to trust God for future money behind human reasoning and Bible verses about stewardship, but they are being deceived by their *love of money.*

"People who want to get rich fall into temptation and a trap and into many foolish and harmful desires that plunge men into ruin and destruction. For the *love of money* is the root of all kinds of evil" (I Timothy 6:9-10a).

If you will not allow God to plan your family because you think that He will not provide enough money for your children or because you think that it is up to you to decide your financial future, then you have been deceived by the enemy and you need to repent of your love for money.

5. The Altar Dedicated to the Idol of Medicine

On this altar *we worship medicine, medical advances, and the advice of doctors.*

Our society comes into strong agreement with this idol. The majority of people have been taught that if their doctor advises them to do something, it must be correct. I believe that God wants us to be thankful for what doctors and modern medicine can offer us because medical advances promote greater health for all. However, just because something is medically possible, it is not necessarily right for God's people. We have already mentioned that since the medical community made abortion, birth control, and sterilization easily accessible and somewhat safe, that the majority of God's people have interpreted this as meaning that it is correct to use them and that God endorses them!

The medical community as a whole is *not religious*, and its goals are not the same as those of the Lord. If your doctor does not know the Lord, his family planning advice may go against God's principles. A believer needs to be careful and weigh all advice to see if it lines up with *the ways of the Lord.* Using birth control and getting sterilized are medically possible, but *they are not rights* that God gave us. They are *choices* that the medical community offers us. When it comes to the medical community in general, let me reiterate that needing to go to the doctor or listening to his diagnosis does not mean that you are deceived or are worshipping the god of medicine. It is where you have put your faith and trust that indicates where your heart is.

The sin comes when you are entrusting the medical community with the responsibility to discern right from wrong in areas of health. Instead the Word of God and its moral code should be your guide. If you have done this then you have been deceived by this idol and you need to repent!

6. The Altar Dedicated to the Idol of Career and Personal Success

On this altar *we worship our career advancement* and the pursuit of *personal achievements.*

Family planning decisions may be based on how children might mess up parents' career advancement or personal goals for their lives. "Their land is full of idols; they bow down to the works of their hands" (Isaiah 2:8). If your personal life's plans are more important than being open to raising God's mighty warriors, then you need to ask God if you are in agreement with this idol. Almost anything that you need to do with your life, including full-time church work, can be done while raising the greatest blessing of your life—your children.

Proverbs 31 tells us of the ideal woman who is to be one of our examples. She is very productive, a business woman, a nurturer, a counselor, a gifted homemaker, and loved by all. God's Word promotes productive people who are willing to be all that God has called them to be. A woman can have a full time career in one season of her life and in another season be an excellent mother if she wants to be.

When your whole life is wrapped up personal success and what you must accomplish for yourself and this choice becomes greater than your desire to raise your children then you have been deceived by this idol and you need to repent.

7. The Altar Dedicated to the Idol of Age

On this altar *we worship age.*

Here, our age is used as an excuse in the area of family planning. There are two groups who may use age as a factor: the old and the young. One group feels that they are *too young* to parent children and have their whole lives, career, and plans to serve God in some form of church work ahead of them, while the other group feels they are *too old* to parent children and desires not to bear the responsibilities of parenting anywhere close to their senior years. What is interesting is that both groups *could* parent a child if they had to, but since they can use birth control or sterilization, they will not have to, and they have created very *logical reasoning* as to why they should avoid parenting children in these seasons of their lives. (*Reasoning* was the devil's trickery on Eve.)

In other decisions for their lives, these same people will not let age affect their plans. They will still seek to do the things that they want to do. But when it comes to being *too old* or *too young* to have children, all of a sudden seemingly virile, healthy people suddenly become *too immature* or *too ancient* to raise children. They cannot bear the thought of spending their time doing this.

Young people may postpone having children until they believe they are ready, but some may wait too late, when their biological clocks have already advanced too far. Maturing people may cease having children because they feel they are *too old* (and to some thirty-five is too old), but they are not planning to go spend their lives living in a retirement home anytime soon. With the energy they have left, many have *big plans* for themselves that do not involve the burden of childrearing. In reality, age is just another mask for making family planning decisions to satisfy ourselves.

The Bible does not seem to consider a person's age as a factor at all especially when it comes to the area of family planning. In fact God has made it so that a person's physical body is capable of producing children from as young as eleven years old to at least sixty years old for a female, and from twelve years old to over eighty years old for a male. God does not seem to let age be a factor here. Instead the devil is using age to convince people to keep from fulfilling God's family call on their lives.

If you think that your age is the reason why you should delay or curtail family planning decisions, then you are worshipping the Idol of Age, and you need to repent.

8. The Altar Dedicated to the Idol of Human Counsel

On this altar, *we worship the counsel of those who we think are more intellectual than we are.*

We may be sincere. But in our sincerity, when we rely on how a professional with a little more knowledge than we have sees our family planning situation, we may be walking in "the counsel of the ungodly" (Psalm 1:1), especially when the counselor does not have a Scriptural viewpoint on family planning. Pastors, doctors, or counselors may be giving us unscriptural counseling if they use reasoning and human wisdom. We need to be careful and heed God's warning if they are telling us to make a family planning decision that goes against what God has clearly spoken in His Word. Unbalanced counsel can become our idol especially when we want to find a counselor who agrees with our reasoning not to obey God.

If you have relied on and listened to counsel that was not based specifically on what Scripture clearly says, then you have been deceived and need to repent.

Of course this list could go on. These are just a few areas where I see millions of people sacrificing *their present children, their future children, or their heart's focus on the altar of the idols* that govern their lives.

"The way of the fool seems right in his eyes but the end leads to death" (Proverbs 16:25). Some people never even realize that their lives are wrapped up in serving a mindset! They sacrifice one of God's greatest gifts to them to satisfy a reason. It sounds foolish but shamefully sad. This was why God warned His people: "Do not love the world or anything in the world. If anyone loves the world, the love of the Father is not in him. For everything in the world— the cravings of the sinful man, the lust of his eyes and the boasting of what he has and does—comes not from the Father but from the world" (1 John 2:15-16).

I know some of you are saying to yourselves that this whole thing is far-fetched. You are saying to yourself, "There is not an altar; we are not really sacrificing."

Oh really? What we do in the physical realm and the spiritual realm is connected. This is why God has always directed his people to be careful with symbols and procedures and cautioned them to be careful with their actions and words. The two realms are definitely connected and interwoven whether we properly understand it or not.

Scripture does not support reasons why we should not have children; instead it gives many reasons why we should be open to having all of the children that God intends for us to have.

As God's people we must remember, whenever "Everybody's doing it," we must be very careful! Today, most people in our churches, in our neighborhoods, at our jobs, and around us are either on *the pill*, sterilized, or planning to be sterilized, and everybody is justifying their decisions. And everybody is either presently hurting in some way or may suffer in the future from the consequences of those decisions.

"There is a way that seems right to a man but the end leads to death" (Proverbs 16:25).

"Wide is the road that leads to destruction" (Matthew 7:13).

God is clearly speaking to us here, and we have a decision to make. Let us cautioned by the response of those in the past.

This is what the LORD says: "Stand at the crossroads and look; ask for the ancient paths, ask where the good way is and walk in it, and you will find rest for your souls. But you said, 'We will not walk in it.' I appointed watchmen over you and said, 'Listen to the sound of the trumpet!' But you said, 'We will not listen!' Therefore hear, O nations; observe, O witnesses, what will happen to them. Hear, O earth: I am bringing disaster on this people, the fruit of their schemes, because they have not listened to my words and have rejected my law" (Jeremiah 6:16-19).

TODAY, GOD SAYS to HIS PEOPLE: REPENT!

Destroy all agreements with wrong thoughts, ideas, and reasons!

"Today, if you hear His voice, do not harden your hearts . . ." (Psalm 95:8).

How to repent and proceed with undoing the devil's Plan in the Area of Idolatry

If God has convicted you about being in agreement with an action, thought or idea that goes against His plan, then now is the time to repent and receive life once again.

Go back through this chapter and make a list of each aspect of idolatry that God convicted you of.

(Do not pray any of these prayers alone; you need a prayer partner to be in agreement with your prayer.)

Pray this prayer to break agreement with idolatry:

Thank you, God, that you grant us your forgiveness and compassion. "He who conceals his sins does not prosper, but whoever confesses and renounces them finds mercy" (Proverbs 28:13).

Help me not to conceal my sin but to confess it to you this day. Holy Spirit, thank You for your convicting power. You were kind to allow me to see the deception that I have unknowingly participated in, and I thank You for allowing me to see my sin without feeling condemned. Thank You for Your love. I repent of being an idolater. I did not feel like I am a person who is yoked to idols, but after reading this chapter, it has become clear to me that I have submitted my life to idols that govern my society. I repent. I ask that You forgive me for coming into agreement with the thoughts and attitudes that the idol of: (name the idol)_____led me to. I ask that You forgive me for allowing myself to give part of my heart's attention to these beliefs. Please forgive me for [name the behavior associated with this idol].

I command the spirit of death that this idol brought into my life to go right now by the power of the blood of

Jesus Christ of Nazareth, and I ask that *I never again* become entangled in the yoke of deception that this idol brought into my life. I repent of any and all attitudes associated with this idol and ask for a clear heart and mind so that I can think straight in this area.

[If there is more than one idol, then you need to name each idol and repent for each and every behavior associated with each idol.]

"We demolish arguments and take captive every thought that sets it self up against the knowledge of God" (2 Corinthians 10:5).

I now choose to destroy and tear down, right now in the presence of the Holy Spirit and with His help, every attitude, human reason, and agreement that I had with these false beliefs. *I renounce the pride* that I felt when being associated with these beliefs. *I renounce the false sense of security* that I have felt when going along with these beliefs and reasons and *the confidence* that I felt as I was in agreement with the ideas of those around me instead of with You.

I now claim this blood shed by Jesus for me on the cross over my life, over all of my sins in these area committed in the past, present, and in the future. *I claim Your blood* as my covering so that *death* will pass over me in each and every area confessed and repented for and will not be allowed to steal from me ever again. *I receive Your cleansing power.* Please remove all residue of *death* hanging over my life as the result of my choices, and fill these areas with Your *life* and make it as new again. I want to be in agreement with You. *Please help me desire what You have for me.* I receive Your *spirit of life* to help me desire Your way over mine.

After you pray, now give praise to the Lord:

"Lord, who is a God like you? Who pardons my sin and forgives the transgression of the remnant of His inheritance? You do not stay angry forever but delight to show mercy. You will again have compassion on us; You will tread our sins underfoot and hurl all our iniquities into the depths of the sea" (Micah 7:18-19).

Thank You, God, because You "do not treat us as our sins deserve or repay us according to our iniquities. For as high as the Heavens are above the earth, so great is His love for those who fear Him; as far as the east is from the west, so far has He removed our transgressions from us. As a father has compassion on his children, so the Lord has compassion on those who fear Him; for He knows how we are formed and remembers that we are dust" (Psalm 103:10-14).

CHAPTER 9

The Devil's Plan

Unlocking the Mystery of Miscarriage

"I will give them miscarrying wombs and dry breasts"
(Hosea 9:14).

WHY ARE SO MANY PEOPLE MISCARRYING?

During the last twenty-one years, during which I have been giving birth to my children, I have noticed a *tremendous increase* in miscarriages. Everywhere I go I meet couples who have experienced the pain and sorrow of losing a child. It seems like it has become almost commonplace for a couple to have had at least one miscarriage, and many couples have had multiple miscarriages.

Sometimes there are identifiable causes of miscarriage. A pregnant woman may unknowingly do something that causes her child to die, such as when the doctor prescribes a drug before he realizes that she is pregnant and the drug poisons the baby. Sometimes a woman has poor nutrition or a severe medical condition that will not allow her body to complete a pregnancy, or she has an accident which causes her to miscarry. These causes of miscarriage are unrelated to the type of miscarriages that I will address in this chapter. The *mysterious miscarriages* that happen for no apparent reason are what I want to consider.

"Praise be to the God and Father of our Lord Jesus Christ and the Father of compassion and the God of all comfort who comforts us in all of our troubles, so that we can comfort those in any trouble with the comfort we ourselves have received from God" (2 Corinthians 1:3-4).

Several years ago I attended a ladies' prayer group that focused on needs in our marriages. At this prayer meeting at least a third of the ladies expressed that they wanted prayer either because they had experienced miscarriages or they were having trouble conceiving. I began to wonder what had gone so drastically wrong for this many women to be suffering such losses. Was it possible that all of these people were doing something that could be causing this? If this was true, then whatever was happening, both believers and those who do not know the Lord must be doing the same things, because both groups in today's world are losing their children through miscarriage.

Women who miscarry are generally told to *accept their miscarriages* as something *normal* that just happens. The assumption is that miscarriage is part of the *course of nature* or that it is *God's will,* and there is no further explanation. This *acceptance* leaves women living in a deep void without any answers. They are often left grieving, and the assumption is made that this grief will be dealt with and eventually go away. There is no true source of help. Often I have cried out to the Lord in prayer and asked Him, "Why is this happening to all of these women?"

For many years I did not gain any more understanding about the cause of miscarriage. I watched women come into my life and experienced their great anticipation of a baby and then the intense sorrow of their loss. Sometimes I was allowed the privilege by God and the mother of praying over her womb, asking God that she not miscarry. This did seem to help because most of these women did eventually deliver, but still in some of these ladies who had patterns of previous miscarriage, this was not enough.

When this happened, I asked the Lord, "Did we not pray often enough?" "Did we not pray long enough?" I kept petitioning Heaven for answers.

Miscarriage had always been a *mystery to me,* but as I continued to pray, I felt the Lord pointing me to find what was written in Scripture. Since I had never heard any teaching on miscarriage, it had not occurred to me that God's Word might have anything to say on the subject. In fact, I found the opposite to be true. I found what I believe to be some answers to a large piece of the *mystery of miscarriage* and a clearer understanding as to *why* this could be happening to so many wonderful ladies. In every Scriptural reference, the Bible referred to *miscarrying wombs* as a punishment for sin. It also stated that miscarriage results from disobedience to God's commands.

This shocked me; my first thought was that many of the people that I knew who miscarry are really nice people and are not what I would refer to as *disobedient sinners.* But over the years as I have walked with God, I have come to realize that it is possible for believers to have an area in their lives where they are sinning but do not realize it because they do not understand what the Scriptures say about their choices. God does mercifully shed His grace upon people for their ignorance, but sometimes they still suffer consequences due to the law of sowing and reaping. They leave themselves open and vulnerable to Satan without realizing it. God's Word says, "My people are destroyed from lack of knowledge" (Hosea 4:6).

"Who is wise? He will realize these things. Who is discerning? He will understand them. The ways of the Lord are right; the righteous walk in them but the rebellious stumble in them" (Hosea 14:9).

We may not realize that our sin in a particular area keeps us from being protected.

"If I had cherished sin in my heart the Lord would not have listened" (Psalm 66:18).

241

We may not know that there is sin somewhere in our lives.

The wonderful thing about the Lord is that He will forgive us when we repent, He will heal and restore our broken lives, and because He is so merciful He will give us *endless* chances to get things right! "If we confess our sins He is faithful and just to forgive us of those sins and to cleanse us of all unrighteousness" (1 John 1:9).

WHAT IS HAPPENING IN MISCARRIAGE

The miracle of birth is an experience of God's love and *physical proof* that God exists. *His love becomes physical* through the creation of a child and allows humans to *supernaturally touch God.* The enemy knows that *if he can block this wonderful experience*, he can discourage us and bring defeat.

The greatest goal of the enemy in miscarriage is to distance a woman from the love of the Father that she feels when she connects to Jesus through her womb.

After miscarriages, women usually feel distant from the love of God and turn from Jesus toward fear and sorrow. They tend to *blame God* for what just occurred in the womb because they do not understand why it happened. Scripture says that God opens and shuts the womb (Genesis 30:2, 1 Samuel 1:5, Isaiah 66:9). In miscarriage, God is opening the womb, but the newly conceived child is not staying in the womb. The enemy is being allowed to steal the life of that baby from the mother.

Why? Scripture says that the thief comes to *steal and destroy* (John 10:10a). The womb is in a sense like a vineyard with ripe fruit in it. The thief (Satan) comes into that vineyard, *robs* from the mother, *steals* the life of the baby, *destroys* both the mother and her child's future, and plants the seed of fear regarding any future conceptions.

After the miscarriage, a woman's vineyard can still produce future fruit, but that *present fruit* is gone! *The loss of **this fruit** is what produces the greatest sorrow!* The realization that she will *never get to hold* the baby that is lost! She grieves this loss and cannot be comforted. She is like "Rachel weeping for her children and refusing to be comforted , because they are no more" (Jeremiah 31:15, Matthew 2:18).

The enemy causes further pain when multiple miscarriages occur. The woman feels cursed; she *blames God* and believes that *He does not love her!* When she believes this, the enemy wins a battle against her because now she is mad, sad, hurt, upset, and feeling distant from God. This is one of the enemy's *favorite weapons of deception* to manipulate her away from the love of the Father. In miscarriage he does this through the womb!

Why is the enemy allowed to do this to wonderful sweet ladies? Why is death allowed to attach itself to a woman's womb?

Scripture repeats the theme over and over again that when we love the Lord and follow His commands that *we will be blessed,* and if we disobey His commandments then we will *fall under judgment.* The choices of God's people determine whether they receive *life* or *death,* blessings or curses, in specific areas. Throughout life things will happen for no apparent reason. This principle of blessings and curses is repeated throughout the Bible to help us unravel the *mystery of hidden sin* and its consequences. This verse could easily be applied to miscarriage; "You will sow much seed in the field but you will harvest little because the locusts will devour it" (Deuteronomy 28:38). This verse talks about healthy plant crops, but it can also be applied to *creating life* as well. Sin allows the enemy to devour life, bringing forth *death.*

"I have set before you life or death, blessing or curse; *now choose life* so that you and your children *may live*" (Deuteronomy 30:19). When Moses told the children of Israel "now choose life," he was telling them that in order to be blessed of God, *this would be a choice that they would have to specifically make.* They would have to actually *choose life instead of choosing death* if they wanted to be blessed.

When people choose life, they choose God; and when they choose death, they choose to agree with the ways of the devil.

God wants us to *choose life*—not only for the lives of our unborn children on earth but also so that we can be blessed with rewards in eternity. He wants us *to avoid choosing death at all costs* because death always leads us further away from Him and allows the enemy to take from us. The devil uses our disobedience toward God and his clever deception to lead people *away from God* and therefore bring them into *his territory.* He convinces people to come closer and closer toward his realm of deception, where they can become his victims. When they are in his camp he can poison their hearts and minds and blind them to the truth. Then he reigns supreme over their situation. This is what is happening in miscarriage.

Why do we accept miscarriages? We have been taught to accept miscarriages by both the medical community and by our churches. The medical community gives us physical reasons for the miscarriage, and our churches tell us not to question God's sovereign will. God's people seem to *accept miscarriage* as something that *just happens* and never question whether there could be a spiritual reason for their miscarriage.

As women share their losses with those around them, often someone tells them that they can have other children and that "All things will work together for good" (Romans 8:28) in the end. But even when they know that God will somehow work the miscarriage out for their good, it does not change the fact that they will never get to hold *that baby* in their arms. This is the saddest reality of miscarriage.

I do not know why for years clergy have been training God's people not to question miscarriage, especially since Scripture does offer answers. One reason may be that most clergy consider miscarriage to be a *female health issue* and not a spiritual issue. The fact that it relates to women and most of the church leaders are men may be another reason.

Since believers are not educated that miscarriage could indicate a possible spiritual problem, they just grieve like everyone else and do not look for answers. I have never heard a sermon by a pastor telling his congregation, "Miscarriages should not be happening!" Instead, churches set up support groups to listen to and pray with those who cannot conceive or who miscarry, but they do not conduct Bible studies to help them find out what areas of sin may be taking this opportunity away from them. I do not believe that this is what the Lord wants! He came to give us the abundant *life* and to set us free from *death* and its curse. We know that God is gracious and uses these experiences to strengthen us and to teach us, but it seems that *if God's people are taught to accept miscarriage, then the enemy can keep getting away with doing this to God's precious people and their children, and they will keep being his victims.*

The deception that the devil loves to blind God's people with is the idea that *God is doing this to them instead of the devil.* If they believe this, they will blame God. When God's people are blinded in this way their anger at God separates them from His love. They turn from God's love and begin to experience doubt, fear, anger, frustration, confusion, and pain, not allowing themselves to receive anything from Him because they feel that He has stolen something precious from them. Unless they forgive God, they could stay angry at Him indefinitely.

How do we stop the curse of miscarriage? Death does not originate with God but is the result of sin. We know that Jesus conquered *death* on the cross. Miscarriages are caused because the enemy is stealing the fruit of the womb because he has *legal spiritual authority* or *permission* to do so. These unexplained miscarriages *can be stopped* once the area or areas where *death* has attached itself to the person's life are revealed. (Once again I am talking about miscarriages that have *no apparent reason* for occurring, not miscarriages that are caused by a health problem or an accident.) When God's people recognize that miscarriages *are what God allows* as the result of not walking in agreement with His plans, then they can repent and be made whole. When they have an area of deception that they are not aware of, they will do as *they see fit according to themselves,* and this opens them up to possible loss in this area.

"You are not to do as we do here today, *everyone as he sees fit* since you have not reached the resting place and the *inheritance* that the Lord your God is giving you" (Deuteronomy 12:8).

The Bible says that "the wages of sin is *death*" (Romans 3:23). When our choices violate God's principles, then we will have the reasons for why we may be suffering these losses. Religion has tried to label certain sins as being far worse than others. To God, all sin is equal because it is rebellion against God and separates us from the love of God.

As God's people, our desire should be to live lives that are pure and blameless. Miscarriage may be caused by an area of sin that is related to our choices in family planning. God desires to remove this sin so that we can be completely whole. Before people can repent, however, they must realize where they may have been choosing death in family planning instead of choosing life.

The Bible says that the devil is the *accuser of the brethren* (Revelation 12:10) and that he watches believers for areas of their lives where he can point blame and make accusations (Job 1:7). Satan desires to harm God's people. Scripture says the Lord is *our defender* and high priest who defends us and *prays* on our behalf (Hebrews 7:24-25). When the accuser tries to gain permission to bring destruction, the Lord can put *a hedge of protection* (Job 1:10) around the person so that that *particular area of his life stays protected and blessed* (Job 1:12). But someone who has not made wise choices and has left himself vulnerable could be open to the devil stealing from him because he is no longer hidden under the shadow of God's wings (Psalms 17:8, 36:7, 57:1, 63:7, 91:1). This does not mean that a blameless person will never ever suffer ill, but it will allow for victory in the end (Proverbs 10:24, 10: 28-32, 11:8, 11:21, 11:23,11:31).

> The Lord tells His people to "return to the Lord your God;
> your sins have been your downfall" (Hosea 14:1).

The following verses indicate that *God's protection is lost* because of people's incorrect choices. When this happens, God's people open themselves up to the devil's plan and *camp out in the devil's territory.* Their lives then become entangled in his yoke, and they suffer loss.

"The cords of death entangled me; the torrents of destruction overwhelmed me" (Psalm 18:4).

"In my distress I called to the Lord; I cried to my God for help"

(Psalm 18:6).

Is it possible to sever the curse of miscarriage? Yes we can find the areas where we have sinned and repent and ask the Lord for restoration. The following is a list of areas where the devil has cleverly led God's people into *choosing death,* which led to leaving God's ways in the family planning area. Once you pinpoint the sin area or multiple sin areas where you may have unknowingly been involved, then you can repent and plead for *mercy* before our loving and holy Heavenly Father and ask for His forgiveness. He can then restore your life and tell the devil that he does not have *permission* to harm you or your generations ever again! At the end there will be prayers of repentance to pray. If you feel convicted that you have made incorrect choices, then pray the applicable prayer.

> "When 70 years are completed for Babylon, *I will come to you* and fulfill my gracious promise to *bring you back* to this place. For I know the plans I have for you," declares the Lord, *" plans to prosper you and not to harm you, plans to give you hope and a future.* Then you will *call upon Me and come and pray to Me, and I will listen to you. You will seek Me and find Me when you seek Me with all of your heart. I will be found by you,"* declares the Lord, "and will *bring you back* from captivity" (Jeremiah 29:10-11).

Barrenness, too, may be caused by a spiritual blockage. Praying prayers of repentance in these same areas, where applicable, may allow God to open the womb if sin was the reason for the lack of conception.

WHAT ARE THE CAUSES OF MISCARRIAGE?

1. Could leaving God's ways and adapting to the ways of society cause a miscarriage?

Yes. According to Scripture, there have been times when women miscarried more than at other times. Miscarriages were more prevalent at times when God's people had turned from God and embraced the customs and cultural practices of the nations around them.

The vast majority of believers today do not allow God to plan their families and have instead embraced the family planning practices of modern society. God's people use the same pills, see the same doctors, and have the same operations as their non-believing counterparts. Because of these choices, God's people are experiencing the loss of many blessings. They are also suffering the sorrow of miscarriage and the loss of the lives of their unborn children. God is again allowing this to happen as judgment for sin as He has allowed it at other times in history.

Miscarrying wombs are identified in Hosea and Deuteronomy as the result of God's judgment.

"I will give them miscarrying wombs and dry breasts" (Hosea 9:14). [following the devil and choosing his ways over God's]

"I will prevent conception" (Hosea 9:11). [infertility/barrenness]

"They will bring their children to the slayer" (Hosea 9:13). [The devil is the slayer; one way he slays is through miscarriage.]

"If you do not obey, the fruit of your womb will be cursed" (Deuteronomy 28:4, 18). [Miscarriage is one indication of the fruit of your womb being cursed.]

Scripture further indicates that each time that God allowed these miscarriages, they were the result of the *sins of God's people and were meant as a punishment and as a warning* for them to repent and come back to His ways. The patterns of miscarriage that we are seeing today are at epidemic proportions, and many people are suffering because *they did what they thought was right in their own eyes* instead of obeying God. God's people seem to be at another historical point when the Spirit of God is saying, *Return to my ways!* When God's people live in ignorance of His ways or resist coming back, they are *left vulnerable.*

"But if you do not listen and carry out these commands... I will bring upon you sudden terror [fear and all kinds of phobias], wasting diseases [cancer, AIDS, etc.], and fever that will destroy your sight [blindness] and drain away your life [sexually transmitted diseases]. You will plant seed in vain because your enemies (devil) will eat it [miscarriage]" (Leviticus 26:14).

God's Word so clearly indicates that God allows this to happen but does not want to curse people or bring them death and destruction. He is trying to bless people with the abundant life, but we must follow Him to find it and walk in His ways to get it!

" *I am setting before you today a blessing and a curse. Blessing if you obey.... curse if you disobey" (Deuteronomy 11:26)* [a choice between God's ways or the devil's].

"See I set before you today life and prosperity, death and destruction" (Deuteronomy 30:15) [*the choice between God's way of doing things and our choice to do it the devil's way*].

"For I command you today to love the Lord your God and walk in His ways, to keep his commands, decrees and laws, then you will *live in increase* and the Lord will bless you in the land" (Deuteronomy 30:16). [*You will reproduce and be prosperous, with children, with money, with possessions, with lifelong success!*]

"I have come to bring you *life* and life more abundant" (John 10:10) [*We are rewarded on earth with blessings and in Heaven with spiritual rewards.*]

When God's people *choose life* and *follow His ways,* then He can keep them in a *safe* and *secret place* and *shelter them* so they can reap the rewards that are their inheritance through His love.

"He who dwells in the secret place will abide in the shadow of the Almighty" (Psalm 91:2).

"The Lord will grant you abundant prosperity—in the fruit of your womb . . ." (Deuteronomy 28:11).

". . . that you may love the Lord your God, listen to His voice and He will give you *many years* in the land" (Deuteronomy 30:20a).

2. *Could choosing death over life instead of choosing life over death cause a miscarriage?*

Absolutely! When Moses told the Children of Israel "Now choose life," he was telling them that in order to be blessed of God, that this would be a *choice*. They would have to actually *choose life* over death if they wanted to be blessed. Moses emphasized the principle that when you choose life, you choose God, and when you choose death, you choose the ways of the devil.

"I have set before you life or death, blessing or curse, now *choose life* so that you and your children may live" (Deuteronomy 30:19).

God wants us to choose life not only for our own lives on earth but also for the lives of our unborn children. He wants us *to avoid choosing death* at all costs because death always leads to destruction and takes our lives further away from Him.

"Who is wise? He will realize these things. Who is discerning? He will understand them. They ways of the Lord are right, the righteous walk in them but the rebellious stumble in them" (Hosea 14:9).

Many couples today act like they believe that their reproductive systems were created to act like faucets: they want their fertility to switch *off and on whenever it is convenient for them.* This gross misunderstanding about what their bodies were designed to do and their approach to regulate reproduction may be what is causing many to have miscarriages. When couples do not want babies because they are newlyweds or need to finish school or think that they can not afford to have children, etc. they use some form of birth control to *turn off the baby-making switch*. In reality while choosing the birth control they are *rejecting their bodies' ability to create life*.

Then, one day a baby seems like a good idea. Suddenly they want to *receive life,* and they go off *the pill* or cease their other contraceptive choices. They want to *turn on the baby-making switch*. If they are fortunate and God blesses them, then they have a baby. Sometimes, however, this is where the first miscarriage occurs or infertility shows up, and the couple does not understand. For some, the cause may be their history of *choosing to reject life*. Truly repenting for rejecting life and rejecting their bodies' abilities could restore this situation and cease additional miscarriages.

Miscarriages do not happen to all couples who treat their bodies this way. The enemy sets many traps in this area; people's thoughts, feelings, emotions, and actions all play a vital role in falling into the trap. Some are more vulnerable than others due to various factors that we will cover.

If the couple is blessed with a baby, they usually do not want another child any time soon, so they attempt to *turn the baby-making switch off again* by going back to their birth control choice. Once again they reject their bodies' ability to create life. Then several years later, when it seems convenient for their schedules, they attempt to have another child, and the process starts all over again. Sometimes this is where their first miscarriage occurs (again some miscarriages are due to nutrition issues). The couple cannot figure out why they cannot get pregnant again or why there is a miscarriage. Again the miscarriage may come from the emotions, thoughts, feelings, and actions that could allow the person to become trapped by the enemy.

Here's one reason why the miscarriage could have occured. Sometimes after the birth of their first child, the parents start *declaring* that they don't think that they can go through this again or that they are not sure that they can handle another child. Sometimes the wife constantly states that she is not sure if she wants another child because she is afraid that she might get fat. Statements like this, made in jest, are actually words that could be spoken against the creation of a new life. These statements are *declaring fear,* and fear is a hole through which the enemy can move into someone's life and steal from them. The combination of using birth control and rejecting their baby-making abilities while making statements that reject their parenting abilities could cause death to their abilities to keep their fruit. Repentance of fear and of rejecting life could break the enemy's ability to steal from them again.

Just the *attitude that the sexual reproductive cycle is there to serve our needs and desires* is what may be causing some to miscarry. The *off again, on again idea* about the human reproductive cycle is not in agreement with how God created our bodies to work. Trying to treat our bodies like a *water faucet* or a *light switch* is in agreement with the ideas of a modern society seeking convenience but clearly reflects a lack of understanding of the choice of receiving new life. *Choosing life* means to choose it all the time and to be open to the possibilities. The trap that the enemy sets here for the majority of people is that once people devalue their reproductive cycle and see it casually, then they will not realize how strongly they are *choosing death* by being frustrated with their bodies' ability to create life. This frustration with their body is a form of rejection and could also be another hole through which the enemy could come in to steal from the person. Repentance could bring restoration and stop these miscarriages from occurring.

The natural progression for those who *scorn their bodies' abilities to create life* will be to get a sterilization operation. After people turn their bodies *off* and *on* several times and get what they want, then they eventually desire to *turn their bodies off permanently* through sterilization. This is the hole through which the enemy may attempt to steal from their children's abilities to receive life. We will cover this in a moment.

3. *Could the birth control pill cause miscarriage?*

Yes. Both believers and nonbelievers use the birth control pill and consider it to be truly reliable. Few previous contraceptive options could compare to the ease of *the pill*. We also know that since the birth control pill came onto the market in 1960, *the number of women miscarrying has increased dramatically.*

There may be a real connection here. Today, the pill is a 3.5-billion-dollar industry. It has caused countless women sorrow and grief because of what it actually does inside of their bodies. It alters their chemical balance by falsifying the body's hormonal responses. *The pill* prevents fertilized eggs from implanting. Multiple medical reports show that the pill in general is causing more harm than good for women.

There are forty-four different types of pills using various chemical combinations, but *all behave similarly in the womb. All forms of the birth control pill prevent the egg from implanting after fertilization occurs.* If a woman were to conceive on either of the popular pill combinations, the pill would rid her body of the baby. There are some differences of opinion among doctors and scientists as to how varying combinations affect conception. Some doctors and scientists argue that the *mini-pill* (progestin only) allows for fertilization and the regular pill does not because it contains estrogen, which should prevent fertilization from occurring, but the *information is not clear* and doctors are not one hundred percent sure. There have not been any long-term studies that specifically focused on what each variety of pill is doing. Doctors are basing their information more on what they know generally about how *the pill* works in the body. *The birth control pill could definitely be seen as a controversial choice for a believer because of its potential abortive properties, especially if the woman chooses the progestin-only mini-pill.*

Women on both kinds of pills (estrogen only or estrogen-progestin) do not realize that they could be having *silent abortions.* When the egg and sperm unite, the hormones *the pill* releases prevent implantation of the newly formed zygote, resulting in the death of the baby. When this happens, *the pill* causes the woman's body to *commit murder* without the mother even realizing it. Murder is against God's fifth commandment; it is listed in Deuteronomy and Leviticus as sin and one of the reasons for a person's life to fall under judgment and curse. Unfortunately, these *silent abortions* could happen to sincere women who are on *the pill* but are ignorant about how it works in their bodies. In ancient days the prophet Hosea cried out to God for this same type of ignorance: "My people are destroyed for lack of knowledge" (Hosea 4:6).

Medical reports and the insert provided with *the pill* warn that women who take *the pill* may become depressed. Those who use it long term seem to have a higher rate of depression and may need prescription antidepressants. One theory as to why women may become depressed is that their bodies may be *silently killing their children* without them knowing it. They may wake up one morning and notice that they have an *uneasy feeling* that something is wrong, but they do not know what it is. Over time this feeling may gnaw at their hearts and minds and cause their physical and mental health to break down.

Another common problem that occurs from the birth control pill is that routinely preventing implantation may create scar tissue on the walls of the womb. Even if a woman desires to become pregnant at a later time, her baby may not be able to adhere to her uterine walls due to the scar tissue. This also happens with the use of the IUD and any other form of birth control that acts as an abortifacient.

Does this mean that using birth control could be connected to miscarriage? Since the majority of people today use one form of birth control or another, and more people are miscarrying now than ever, *my answer is yes! Birth control use may be one of the main reasons for the miscarriage epidemic.* With some forms of birth control the mother could be bringing her womb *death* every month and not even realize it; the pill or IUD or another contraceptive that acts as an abortifacient may be causing her to have *silent abortions.* This leaves a woman vulnerable to the devil coming into her life to steal from her.

It is clear that when believers adapted the ways of the world in their family planning, a very clear breakdown of blessing occurred.

If we look at birth control use in light of God's Word, we find that the use of birth control is an act that falls outside of God's protection. We know that *the Biblical saints of old did not use birth control,* and we also know that the majority of believers also did not use it until the 1930s. These facts are strong arguments against the "right" to choose our family size.

All forms of birth control represent *man's desire to control his own destiny.* This control is a form of fear that takes God's dear people away from His blessings and allows them to become subject to the devil's plan.

The specific goal of *the pill,* the IUD, and other abortifacients is *to rid the female womb of the child* conceived; we know that God's Word teaches us against such practices. Other forms of birth control also have the goal of *rejecting life,* making the entire issue one that leads God's people down a vulnerable path.

Birth control use means depending on ourselves instead of depending on God to handle our situation. This dependence on self is a form of pride because we believe that *we should be in control* of our own destiny instead of allowing God to do it.

Birth control use could also be seen as a form of *idolatry* because we put faith in the birth control instead of our faith and trust in God.

Birth control could be *rejecting what is good* (Hosea 8:3)

because children are good and we could be forgetting our Maker .

Since not all women who miscarry are practicing birth control, however, we need to look further for other possible reasons.

4. *Could a previous abortion cause miscarriage?*

Yes. "The Lord hates . . . hands that shed innocent blood" (Proverbs 6:16-17).

"And for your lifeblood, I will surely demand an accounting. I will demand an accounting from every animal. And from each man too, I will demand an accounting for the life of his fellow man" (Genesis 9:5).

"You shall not commit murder" (Exodus 20:13).

" . . . you are to take life for life, eye for eye, tooth for tooth, hand for hand, foot for foot, burn for burn, wound for wound, bruise for bruise" (Exodus 21:23-25).

"Do this so that innocent blood will not be shed in your land, which the Lord your God is giving you as your inheritance, and so that you will not be guilty of bloodshed" (Deuteronomy 19:10).

"I will give you over to bloodshed and it will pursue you" (Ezekiel 35:6).

Women who have had abortions are plagued with sorrow that many never seem to get over. Many mothers think about the day that their baby would have been born. They are haunted with the fact that they took a life that was not theirs to take, and the emotional scars cause them to suffer in silence. As a result of the abortion they can have severe hormonal swings; they may become depressed and not know why; they may even lack creativity and develop a nonchalant attitude towards life. Their wombs, tubes, and cervix may become covered with scar tissue as the result of the abortion procedure. Those who do not know the Lord tend to choose abortion more often than God's people; however, many a young girl has been taken in for an abortion so that her churchgoing parents can prevent the embarrassment that her out-of-wedlock pregnancy might bring.

When a woman kills her unborn child through abortion, the abortion procedure usually causes a *spirit of murder* to enter into her life. This spirit will plague her and cause negative things to happen.

Depression seems to be one of the most prevalent responses. This sorrow can cause *death* to her self-esteem, *death* to her joy for living, *death* to her hope, loss of excitement, nightmares, *death* to her finances, *death* to her creativity and *death* in any other area that was previously full of life. She will just feel unhappy and will not know why.

This negative spirit from the enemy may also *be allowed* to take away *new life* again because the woman may have a *death* cloud hanging over. Even if she was forced to commit murder (abortion) against her will, she may hide behind the guilt that she feels. Her hands have shed innocent blood, and the Bible says that this blood cries out from the ground begging for vindication (Genesis 4:10-11). After a woman commits this murder within her body, the blood cries out from her body, calling to appease the death.

The awesome thing here is that repentance can bring about deliverance of this *death* cloud and restore the woman to wholeness once again. Once her guilt is healed, she will feel free and will be able to conceive again and keep the fruit of her womb.

5. *Could having premarital sex cause a miscarriage?*

Yes. God wants the marriage bed to be undefiled before the marriage to protect the couple from the curse that this sin brings with it.

"Marriage should be honored by all and the marriage bed kept pure, for God will judge the adulterer and all the sexually immoral" (Hebrews 13:4).

". . . the Lord hates . . . a heart that devises wicked schemes and feet that are quick to rush to evil . . ." (Proverbs 6:16, 18).

"Do you not know that the wicked will not inherit the Kingdom of God? Do not be deceived: Neither the sexually immoral not idolators nor adulterers . . .will inherit the kingdom of God" (1 Corinthians 6:9).

"You shall not commit adultery" (Exodus 20:14).

"If a man commits adultery with another man's wife—with the wife of his neighbor—both the adulterer and the adulteress must be put to death" (Leviticus 20:10).

If you have *committed adultery* at any time in your life, it is possible for the fruit of your womb to have a *curse* due to defilement and God's judgment.

Premarital sex once was not commonplace in our society. Believers knew that is was not Scriptural, and they led society in a higher set of moral standards. Even many nonbelievers followed the moral code that the believers set as the example.

Sexual promiscuity rose sharply with the introduction of the birth control pill in 1960. Since that time, we have seen a rise in sexually transmitted diseases many of which cause infertility, barrenness, and defilement. Sleeping with multiple partners or having done so in the past opens up a door both in the physical realm and the spiritual realm. This act could cause a person to be *walking in death* in the area of reproduction. People who used birth control when they were being promiscuous did not want to create new life with their partners, so they were rejecting *life* and yet enjoying sex without the responsibilities that come from committed relationships.

If you have *slept around* there may be a curse over your womb or seed (men included) and over your abilities to give life. Every sexual partner that you have embraced has left a spiritual mark on your soul. In your involvement with them, you have embraced all that your partner had received from other people as well. *This can have very deep spiritual consequences* and requires repentance so that you can be restored.

Sexual promiscuity is so common and acceptable in today's society that the family life pastor at our church told us that more than seventy-five percent of the couples who were attending his recent class on *preparing for marriage* did not know that premarital sex was even wrong, especially if they were planning to marry their sex partner. This response was coming from young people in their early-to-mid-twenties, many of whom have been brought up going to church every week!

Premarital sex can bring *death* to intimacy, *death* to trust, *death* to the *life* of the relationship. When the couple has premarital sex and then wants to start a family, this death caused by their sin *may block* conception and or may be *the hole* through which the enemy gets in to steal the life of your unborn child through a miscarriage. If you have had premarital sex, you need to repent for allowing *death* to come over your womb and seed.

6. Could a generational curse cause miscarriage?

It is very likely. The Bible says that the Lord will bless a thousand generations of those who love Him (Exodus 20:6), but the sins of the fathers will be passed down to the children of the fourth generation of those who do not love Him (Exodus 20:5).

This is a curse. When people are unable to have children, the *death* in this area may be coming from the sin of a previous generation. The parents' sin could cause the next generation to reap bad fruit because the unrepented sin is still allowed to take from the family bloodline. God's holiness requires complete repentance to make a person whole.

Remember that the goal of the enemy is *to stop believers from producing Godly heirs* for the Kingdom of God! He is looking for every open door to go through to bring destruction so he can take from God's people. If the grandparents were sterilized because they did not want any more children, this could cause a curse on the next generation's abilities to conceive or keep the fruit of the womb. *The grandparents' curse* would actually be cursing the reproduction of the next generation. Because the previous generation cut off their own seed, it may also cut off the next generation's seed as well. *Instead of transferring blessing down the bloodline, it transfers a curse due to idolatry* (Exodus 20:5).

Many times this is easy to recognize. Two virgins get married; neither have ever had an abortion; and yet they cannot conceive or suffer a series of miscarriages even when their health is good. They could spend years in sadness, wondering why God will not give them children, when they could be operating under a curse as the sins of the fathers are visiting the children. When working with couples to find out why they cannot conceive, a prayer counselor needs to look for *every open door* that could cause someone to be suffering. Going back to see if their parents cursed their own fruit may help to identify one way that the enemy may be operating against a couple. If their parents did become sterilized, the couple may need to ask God to forgive their parents for cutting off their fruit, for trying to predict the future (divination), and for choosing their own desires over God's (idolatry).

After a curse such as this is broken, the prayer counselor and the couple must ask God to *restart the family bloodline* through the husband and wife who are trying to conceive. This curse may also be on their siblings (usually siblings in a family are having the same problem). We must also repent for fear of the future that either the *would-be grandparents* had or the couple may have. They need to tell the Lord that they put the future back into His hands. They may need to also repent for trying *to control their destiny*, which involves a spirit of *witchcraft*.

In rare cases, adults who were an *only child* or had only one other sibling when the parents were sterilized may have feelings of depression concerning their families that they do not understand. It may have come because deep down inside they feel that their parents robbed them of other siblings. If miscarriage robbed them, there could possibly be *depression* for those lost siblings that were never born. A couple may want to ask God to heal any depressed feelings that they may have that could be blocking their own abilities to conceive or causing them to miscarry.

Another reason why there may be a generational curse could be because the previous generations did evil. Psalm 109 is a righteous man's plea for God to judge his unrighteous accusers, who are deceitful and have lying tongues. *He asks God to bring a curse on the children of the unrighteous,* which would be the evil man's descendants.

1. May his children be wandering beggars and lose their homes. [Some families can never keep a house.]
2. May a creditor seize his assets. [Some families stay in constant debt.]
3. May he lose the fruits of his labors. [Some men cannot keep a job and struggle in their jobs all their lives.]
4. May no one be kind to him; may no one help him. [Some people are rarely shown mercy.]

5. *May his descendants be cut off and not remembered in the earth* [miscarriage, premature child death, early adult death].
6. *May the sins of the parents be remembered before the Lord so that God will cut off the memory of them in the earth* [curse over the entire line of people so that they will be wiped out supernaturally].

This is a powerful curse on the unrighteous and his family seed!

Understanding curses is a serious matter. Curses are real, and they affect the lives of people who love God every day! When Jesus set us "free from the curse," this is one of the things that He did (Galatians 3:13). We must act upon the problem and ask Him to specifically help us in these areas. Through the awesome power of God these curses can be broken and our lives can be changed dramatically!

"Whatever is bound on earth will be bound in Heaven; whatever is loosed on earth will be loosed in Heaven" (Matthew 16:19).

7. *Could personal fears cause a miscarriage?*

Yes. *Fear* is a huge problem in many believers' lives. Miscarriages may be the result of fear causing a woman to cast her fruit before its time (Malachi 3:11). In other words a woman could be allowing herself to emotionally dismiss and then physically let go the fruit of her womb because of her agreement with fear.

Do you have many fears related to family planning?

Fear can cause more trouble than people can imagine because people are often not in touch with their fears. Fear is a strong enemy that *steals from us* because we give in to fear. When we walk in fear we are *not* walking in the light of God (1 John 1:5).When we give ourselves to *shadows* and *innuendos* and *what-if's* we can become consumed with fears that control us and rob us of God's peace. If we are robbed of God's peace, then the enemy may rob from us in other areas, one of which is stealing the *life of our children*. Fear is the enemy and is able to steal the fruit of the womb because we are walking in close agreement with it.

Fear of the future:

"What kind of parent will I be?"
"Can I handle another baby?"
"What if my other child rejects this baby?"
"Can we afford another child?"
"What will my family/friends think?"
"Does my husband or my wife really want this baby?" In the case of either spouse not really wanting the child, emotional and/or verbal rejection of the seed could cause the female body to desire to empty itself.

Fear of finances:

"How can we afford another child?"
If the man rejects his seed because of fear of the future or fear about providing, it can also cause miscarriage.

Fear of not being able to be good parents:

"What if I am not being a good parent?"
"How will I give myself to another child?" I am already stressed as it is.
When we speak what we really fear, we reject the child inside.
Fear of timing:

"I wish this were happening next year, I am not ready for this baby."
This fear can lead to miscarriage, because we give fear permission by the thoughts we have and the words we speak without even realizing it.

Fear which causes misplaced trust:

Do you have your complete trust in God? God asks us to trust

Him with our lives, but sometimes we place our trust in what we can see. We can misplace our trust by looking to a pastor, a doctor, or a belief. Trusting in things or people instead of God is wrong. It is a form of fear.

There may also be other forms of fear affecting our parenthood and causing us to let go of our seed. They each need to be confessed and repented for. Ask God to reveal these other fears so that you can repent. He usually does this by bringing those fears into our minds as thoughts. When they are revealed, then ask God to forgive you.

8. Could the words a person speaks be the cause of a miscarriage?

Yes. The words we speak are very powerful and could be the source of where we are losing out on life. If people are speaking words of death concerning their family plans, this could be a key to miscarriage.

"The power of *life* and *death* are in the tongue" (Proverbs 18:21).

None of us realize the awesome power of our words. We have the ability to live or die based on the things that come out of our mouths. Are you speaking words of life and healing words, or are you speaking death over yourselves?

"I always miscarry."
"My husband is afraid if I get pregnant that he might lose me."
"I have trouble having children."
"I cannot seem to get pregnant."
"I do not know how we could afford another child."
"I do not think I could handle another child."

These kinds of words throw negative comments out into the spiritual atmosphere that surrounds us. The devil is just waiting for us to speak fear or negativity against ourselves; then he can harm us based on our own admissions. Negative comments along with fear or lack of faith may be all that the enemy needs to be able to steal the fruit of our womb. If all we keep saying is "I always miscarry," then this may be what we will do. There is a good chance that it will come true, because by speaking it we give the words permission. When words of *death* are spoken in greater numbers than words of *life,* we need to repent and ask God to help us speak *life.*

9. Could feelings of rejection cause a miscarriage?

Yes. We have already discussed how using birth control can bring rejection into a marriage. *Rejection* is a powerful force and in a sense could be seen as a form of *death* because it is saying to that person: "I reject you! I do not want you! I do not like you! I wish you were not here! Go away!"

Rejection brings pain and sorrow. The goal of rejection is to rob and steal emotional worth from a person. Many wounded and rejected people feel like it would be best if they had never been born. Eventually most rejected and wounded people desire to leave the person who is rejecting them, because everyone desires to be loved and to feel loved. Love brings *life.* If you have been rejected in your past, you may have *emotional death* hanging over you. You may be also rejecting others to try to get back at those who harmed you. Without realizing it, you may be sending *death* out toward others. This could harm your ability to give *life* or to receive *life.*

What we do with those feelings and emotions can be the key to *life* or *death* in our lives. Many people suffer from bitterness; it can be rooted so deep in their hearts that they do not even know that it is there! It can bring *death to relationships* and *death* to many other areas of their lives because it causes the person to view life through the wounds suffered by being wronged. We need to forgive those who have done evil against us and to let go of all bitterness. "Be merciful, just as your Father is merciful" (James 2:13). "Blessed are the merciful, for they will be shown mercy" (Matthew 5:7). "Therefore confess your sins to each other and *pray for each other so that you may be healed*" (James 5:16).

Rejection can also cause confusion about what we really want. Do you and your spouse really want this child? Saying "I am not sure if I want this baby" could cause the child to feel rejected in the womb; your physical body may also reject the baby because you believe this. *A rejecting spirit can cause you to lose your baby.* You may be miscarrying because you do not understand why you should want children.

People may want to understand their reasons for wanting a child. Could it be because this is what people do? Or because of selfishness? Or to feel loved? Or performance for Mom and Dad? Or to feel grown up? The woman may reject her ability to be a mother or have fear about her own abilities to be a mother.

If you have rejection issues, then you need to ask God to help you forgive those who have hurt you and you may need to seek further counseling to rid yourself of the hurtful thoughts and feelings that can torment you for the rest of your life if not properly dealt with through forgiveness. Ridding our lives of rejection isues and repenting for this could allow us to keep the lives of our unborn children.

10. Could dishonoring a parent cause a miscarriage?

Yes. God says to "Honor your Father and your Mother so that you may live long in the land the Lord your God is giving you" (Exodus 20:12). This is one of the ten commandments, with the promise of long life to those who honor it. Poor relationships with your parents could open you up to having problems trying to create your *own family* and may be a *hole* through which the enemy enters to steal the life of your child through miscarriage. Your parents represent your *former family* and will be your child's grandparents. If your relationship with Mom and Dad is strained, maybe you need to ask forgiveness of them and ask God to help you to be loving toward them. We need to recognize that our parents were doing the best that they could at the time and to show them mercy even in the worst of circumstances because it is a commandment. We do not get to pick our parents, yet God commands each of us to honor them no matter how awful they may seem. By doing this we can ask God to show us mercy as we try to have our own family. When God allows us to give them grandchildren it will show love and honor toward our parents by continuing with their family bloodline. Repentance can restore our abilities to keep the life of our unborn child.

11. Could making fun of the things of God cause a miscarriage?

Yes. Scripture gives us a very clear example of a person who made fun of the things of God and was struck with barrenness. This happened to David's wife, Michal, who ridiculed David for worshipping the Lord. God never allowed her to conceive again. If people routinely make fun of the things of God or criticize the preacher, traveling minister, or TV evangelist because they did something that they did not like or did not understand, this could be a hole throught which the enemy tries to come in and steal from them. If you are the kind of person who thinks nothing of being critical of people whom God has allowed to be leaders, you may be bringing death to your own life. Even leaders who mess up are still God's chosen until He removes them. David understood this. Before he was king, he greatly honored Saul's position as King of Israel, even though Saul had become evil and had strayed far from God. David still honored the position that Saul held. It is not our prerogative to comment even when we think that we are correct. Until we stand in that person's shoes we will not know what choices we might make or understand all of the circumstances affecting their decisions. We need to extend mercy toward God's leaders to release blessing upon ourselves. Michal brought death on her womb by laughing at David dancing before the Lord and by ridiculing him.

We also must be careful not to ridicule or criticize spiritual things that we think we understand but really do not. Those who do not worship like we do or who do not do things our way are not necessarily wrong. We have no right to criticize believers who are sincerely seeking to follow God whether we agree with their style of worship or not. We need to just keep quiet. Paul said, "I do not even judge myself. I will wait until the Lord judges me" (1 Corinthians 4:4-5). Someday God will make all the wrongs right. It is not up to us. If we want to release *life* over our lives in this area then we need to keep from criticizing the things that we do not know or understand. This way we will not be speaking death to ourselves through our lack of understanding.

12. *Could greed in the area of finances cause a miscarriage?*

It is likely. Malachi 3:11 talks about a curse of disobedience with finances causing *fruit to be cast before its time.* This passage is often used in relationship to giving money to God; however, casting *physical fruit* before it is time to be born is exactly what happens in miscarriage. This may be why after Abraham tithed to Melchizedek (Genesis 14:19, Hebrews 7:4-10), God sent him Isaac through his once barren wife Sarah (Genesis 21:7). Malachi 3 indicates that fruit vines will be more secure by obedience in releasing money in offering to God. This would very likely bring blessings over the fruit of the womb as well.

This list identifies possible areas where God's people may be suffering and falling under God's judgment without realizing it. The combination of adapting to the ways of society, while using their pills and speaking fear over ourselves about parenting, or feeling rejected in our relationships, or having attitudes of dishonoring our parents or clergy, or possibly greed toward our money all could be doors through which the enemy enters to steal the fruit of our wombs. When a person combines these areas with a possible past of abortion or promiscuity or both, the enemy has another door through which to enter. If the grandparents devalued their own abilities to give life, the next generaton may find it hard to conceive or to keep the baby once conceived. *Choosing death* instead of life yokes us to the consequences of sin. The beauty of the cross is that Jesus shed His blood to bring forth forgiveness and restoration for our sin. The Scripture is clear that God's ways are right; the righteous walk in them and find life, and those who choose their own ways lose out.

As you have read this chapter, I believe that the Holy Spirit may have revealed an area or areas where the enemy may have found *a hole* to come into your life in order to destroy the life of your child through miscarriage. If you realize that this is what happened then you need to ask God to forgive you. He is *always* willing to forgive His children and receive them with love.

I am going to walk you though a series of repentance prayers. Because of the nature of the prayers in this chapter, you MUST have at least one other person present with you who can pray with you or who can silently back you up as you speak these prayers aloud. These are prayers of deep repentance and cleansing. You are demanding that the enemy leave your life. *Do not pray these types of prayers alone!* Wait until you have someone, preferably your spouse, who can be your partner to support you as you pray. This is a MUST! If you cannot find someone then I advise you not to pray until you do.

1. *Prayer of repentance for adapting to the ways of the world:*

Lord, please forgive me for being worldly. I did not realize that I have become so much like the world. I want to repent of adapting their ideas about family planning. I desire to have Your ways and to allow You to help me create the family that You desire to send me. Please help me to desire what You what. Please make it seem irresistible to me and help me to not be afraid of what it might mean to follow You in this area. In the mighty name of Jesus, I ask You to forgive me, cleanse me, and remove any hindrances in my heart and mind that could keep me from obeying Your plan. Please restore a fresh vision for what You can and will do within my heart and life by repenting of worldliness in this area.

2. *Prayer of repentance for choosing death over life by rejecting life through seeking to turn your body's reproductive system off and on:*

Lord God, I did not realize that I had misunderstood the purpose of what my body was created for. I now realize that my body is not supposed to operate like an appliance with an off-and-on switch but is instead a holy vessel. My wonderful body was created to give life and to bring forth new creations. Without realizing this I took it for granted that I should be in charge of this process. The worldly ideas that I have been influenced by deceived me, and I repent of being taken in by this thinking. I realize that human reproduction is a process that cannot be turned off and on. It is a process that You alone, Father, should be in charge of. You know the rhythms of my body and my spouse's body, and You know what is best for our long-term health. In the name of Jesus Christ I place back into your hands what I have taken for granted. I repent and give this back to You. Please forgive me and restore what we have lost.

3. *Prayer of repentance for using the pill or IUD:*

Lord, I repent for using *the pill*/IUD as my birth control. I had no idea that this was such an ungodly thing to be doing. I do not want to oppose what You want to give me. I need Your forgiveness and plead with You to make my body whole once again.

If I have murdered any of my children unknowingly I ask for and receive Your forgiveness. I receive Your cleansing power. I command a spirit of murder to leave my life by the power of the blood of Jesus Christ of Nazareth. I command this enemy to never return. I break every curse off my life that the enemy brought, and I ask that You fill me completely with Your spirit of love. Please renew each area that the enemy has robbed me from physically, emotionally, spiritually and financially. I receive Your renewing power.

Father, forgive me for only wanting children when it is convenient for me and for wanting to control my future. I have been proud and arrogant. I was depending upon my own strength and not on Your power to decide for my own life. If I have made myself and my life's goals into an idol, I ask that You remove my thoughts from this position, and I ask that You now come and sit in that position in my heart. If I have committed the sin of divination by trying to control my life or my future, I am sorry. Please forgive me. I place the future back into Your hands, and I repent for desiring to ever control in this way. I do not desire to be close to the witchcraft realm. I ask that You remove any curse that could come to me because of my ignorance. Please remove any obstacles that this enemy has brought into my life and restore me to completeness. Please bring me to total restoration by Your power.

Lord, I also ask for healing and forgiveness in the area of depression. I receive a new mind and a new desire. I ask that all darkness and all thoughts of sorrow and sadness leave me. I repent for not receiving the children that You intended for me, and I ask that any thoughts related to this not be able to depress me anymore. I command the spirit of depression to leave me by the power of the blood of Jesus Christ of Nazareth. I ask for Your complete restoration in my mind and heart.

I also ask for forgiveness for using *the pill* and for the chemicals that it introduced into my body. Please cleanse and heal my system from all of the unnecessary hormones that have broken down my body. I ask for forgiveness and ask that you cleanse my body, Your temple, and restore me to complete wellness through the power of the blood of Jesus Christ of Nazareth and through Your cleansing power. I now make the active choice to choose life that I and my children may live! In the mighty name of Jesus Christ and by the power of your Holy Spirit, Amen.

4. *Prayer of repentance for abortion (Remember, you MUST pray this with a prayer partner!)*:

Lord, please forgive me for murdering my innocent baby. I am so sorry. I also choose to forgive any and all people who were part of my abortion. I choose to forgive my doctor, minister, parent, lover, spouse, friend, or other person who coerced me, encouraged me, or falsely counseled me or who had any part in my choice to abort my baby. I choose to consciously forgive each person now and ask for forgiveness through the power of the blood of Jesus Christ.

I repent of this sin of abortion and ask that You forgive me for shedding innocent blood. I ask that the enemy's spirit of murder be removed from my life. I believe that this enemy has caused many complications for me, and I ask that this enemy not be allowed to wreak havoc on my life anymore. I command the spirit of murder and death to leave me now by the cleansing power of Jesus Christ of Nazareth. I demand that you leave me! Lord, keep me from allowing myself to be with evil and keep from doing this ever again. I command each and every area that the enemy has used against me to be made righteous and cleansed by the blood of Jesus. I receive complete restoration in my life in the physical, spiritual, emotional, financial, and creative realms. *I now choose life* and ask that I and my children shall live. If I have become barren since my abortion, I ask, Dear Heavenly Father, that You have mercy on me and open my womb. I pray this in the mighty name of Jesus Christ of Nazareth. Amen.

5. *Prayer of repentance for premarital sex:*

Lord, please forgive me for taking something that is precious and holy to You and misusing it for my own pleasure. I ask forgiveness for not keeping myself pure in this area and ask that You will restore me to purity once again so that I may live in holiness before You.

I repent of allowing death to come to myself by misusing Your blessing. Please forgive me. I ask that You remove any and all spiritual repercussions over my reproductive organs. I ask that You restore me and allow me to give and receive life once again. Please cleanse me and make me whole. I also ask that You restore the love that this behavior took away from my heart and life and erase any and all hurts that this behavior brought to my emotions. I receive Your love and restoration. Help me to walk in complete love for myself and my spouse. I command a spirit of death that has attached itself to me to leave by the blood of Jesus Christ of Nazareth, and I receive a spirit of life from You. I ask for complete and total restoration so that I and my children may live.

6. *Prayer of repentance for generational curses:*

Lord, please forgive my family bloodline for not desiring Your children. I repent of the sins of my fathers and forefathers, mothers and grandmothers who were not open to receiving the wonderful gift of life that You wanted to bring our family tree. I repent of the waste that is now connected to our family and for the lost people that should have come down through our family bloodline. Please forgive the family for our sin. I command the enemy's spirit of death that has attached itself to the generations of the family tree to go! I renounce its curse over the female wombs and the family ancestral seed of the men. I command this spirit of death to unattach itself and to leave our bloodline through the power of the blood of

Jesus Christ of Nazareth. I command any and all curses to be broken by the blood that Jesus Christ shed on the Cross. *I renounce the attitude that children are not desired in this family,* and I now receive with joy a spirit of life and ask that any and all children that have been withheld from our family lineage be restored through the power of Jesus Christ. Please open the wombs of this family and allow the family seed to flow once again. Please restore all of our family's losses in this area, Lord.

I ask that financial blessings that have been withheld because we did not receive these children also be restored and that the money and wealth of our family bloodline be loosed right now through the power of the blood of Jesus Christ of Nazareth. I ask that every area of life be restored to the family.

I also repent for evil that my ancestors may have committed. I ask forgiveness for evildoers in my family and for poor business practices, for cheating and lying and falsehood. In any area where death has been allowed to attach itself to me by their sins, I ask for life now to come.

Your Word says that there can be a curse on the generations for those who put their faith in idols. I repent for idol worship. I repent for trying to control my destiny, which is a form of idol worship that has attached itself to me through a bloodline curse. I repent through the power of the blood of Jesus Christ of Nazareth, and I command a spirit of death that has attached itself to me through idolatry to go by the power of the blood of Jesus. I receive Your cleansing power and ask for the blood of Jesus to now cover my finances, my business practices, my family planning decisions, and my life so that I and my children may live.

7. *Prayer of repentance for fear:*

Lord, please forgive me for walking in fear. At times it seems like I am afraid of everything. Please help me turn my fears into trust and to pray through my deepest fears. I repent for not allowing You to have complete control of my future. It is hard for me to trust You with something that I can not see. Lord, I am scared about so many things and I feel so inadequate at times with the small things, much less the larger things of life. Please help me not to be so afraid.

I ask your forgiveness and command the enemy's spirit of fear that has attached itself to my mind to go right now through the power of the blood of Jesus Christ of Nazareth. I ask that a spirit of life come and give me new thoughts and a new mind over the events that have happened in my life. I ask for this spirit of life to bring me clarity and a sound mind and a peace that I have never had before— peace that only Your spirit can give. I receive Your peace through the power of the blood of Jesus and ask that I never walk in fear again. I ask that You show me any and all areas where I have not walked in peace so that death may never attach itself to my mind again. I receive the life that comes from Your spirit so that I and my children may live.

8. *Prayer of repentance for the words that I have spoken:*

Lord, I ask for your cleansing power over the words that I speak. I did not realize the incredible power that I have to create life and death. I have spoken repeated negative words over myself, my body, and the people around me. Please forgive me and cleanse me. I repent of speaking ill words about other people. I have used my tongue in gossip and slander and to cause others to think ill thoughts about people. I have also used my tongue to speak words that have cursed my own health and physical body. I have also lied by embellishing the truth. I ask that You forgive me for this misuse of the gift of communication. I now turn my words over to You. I ask that you forgive me and cleanse me of misusing my tongue to hurt people and to speak words of hate against myself and others. I command the enemy's spirit of lying that has been attached to my tongue to leave my body right now throught the power of the blood of Jesus Christ of Nazareth. I command my tongue to line up with the words that the Holy Spirit would desire that I speak, and I receive wholeness over my tongue.

I also command the enemy's spirit of murder to leave my tongue by the power of the cleansing blood of Jesus Christ of Nazareth. I no longer choose to ruin others' reputations through gossip or slander, and I also choose to no longer tell others that I hate them or that I hate myself. I choose life, and I ask that You fill me with Your life, Holy Spirit, and renew Your love inside of me so that I may love myself and others. Please heal me, cleanse me, and forgive me by the power of your Holy Spirit and in the mighty name of Jesus Christ of Nazareth. Amen.

9. *Prayer of repentance for feeling rejection:*

Lord God, I have felt rejected all of my life. Sometimes this causes me to dwell in the negative instead of the positive. Please help me. Please forgive me for not believing that You desire to bless me with a child simply because You love me. I am afraid to accept this completely. I repent of rejecting my own seed. I did not realize that this is what I was doing. I desire to have children and do not want to push them away. Help me not to reject my child, myself, my spouse, or others. Help me to not walk in fear that leads me to reject myself as a parent. In the name of Jesus help me to take authority over the lie of rejection in my life, and I rebuke rejection and send it back to where it came from. No longer will I receive rejection in my life. NO MORE! I desire to be made complete and whole and happy with myself. Lord, please help me to see myself as You see me and help me to receive new life.

10. *Prayer of repentance for not honoring my parents:*

Lord, please help me to honor my parents, and please help me not to judge them. I desire to obey You in this area, but I need Your supernatural help. I receive that right now. Lord, please help me because my parents do things that I do not agree with, and this bothers and upsets me because they make decisions that seem foolish. Sometimes they do not see me as a grown adult. Please help me as I struggle with understanding them. I am thankful that they have contributed to my life in good ways. Please help me to focus on this and to remember that they did the best that they could. As I honor them, please help me to have my own family. If there is any resentment in me or attitude toward them that may be blocking conception or causing a miscarriage of their grandchildren, please forgive me and help me to repent. Thank You for the parents who molded and shaped my life, and help me to hold them in high esteem.

11 . *Prayer of repentance for making fun of the Holy Spirit and the things of God:*

Lord God, please forgive me for passing judgment on your leaders. You told Job that he spoke of things that he did not understand, things too wonderful for him to know. I believe that I may have passed judgment because what I was seeing on TV or in a leader's life appeared wrong. It may have been wrong, but I put myself in a place of judgment, and I judged your leaders instead of allowing You to judge them. Please forgive me. Also forgive me for thinking that I understand every religious thing that comes across my path. Help me to realize that I do not understand all things; therefore I do not need to comment. Please restore my life. If my judgments have caused me not to be able to birth my children then in the name of Jesus please remove this curse from my life and grant life to my children once again.

12. *Prayer of repentance for not greed in the area of finances:*

Lord, I try to give my money. If I have lacked in this area, please forgive me. As I grow in my understanding, I will desire to give more money to the church. If by not giving I have caused myself to cast my fruit before its time, please forgive me and help me to hold onto my child. In the name of Jesus I break any curse over my seed, my womb, or my life in relation to money.

After you repent, it is a good idea to thank God for His great mercy extended toward you:

Prayer of thanksgiving:

"Who is a GOD like you? Who pardons my sin and forgives the transgression of the remnant of His inheritance? You do not stay angry forever but delight to show mercy. You will again have compassion on me; you will tread my sins underfoot and hurl all my iniquities into the depths of the sea" (Micah 7:18-19*)*.

Thank You, God, because You "do not treat me as my sins deserve or repay me according to my iniquities. For as high as the Heavens are above the earth, so great is Your love for those who fear You; as far as the east is from the west, so far have You removed my transgressions from me. As a father has compassion on his children, so you Lord have compassion on me when I fear You; for You know how I am formed and You remember that I am dust" (Psalm 103:10-14).

I thank You, Lord, and now claim this blood shed by Jesus for me on the cross over my life, over all of my sins in these areas committed in the past, present, and in the future. I claim Your *blood* as my covering so that *death* will pass over me in each and every area confessed and repented for and will not be allowed to steal the fruit of my womb ever again. I receive Your cleansing *power* and ask that you help me not to fall into judgment again for this sin. Please remove all residue of *death* hanging over my life as the result of my choices and fill these areas with your *life* and make it as new again! Help me not to walk in sin again in this area. Please also forgive me for any other area that I am not aware of. If I am made aware of it, I will also confess it to You.

LORD JESUS:
I want you.
I need you.
I choose you and
<u>I now CHOOSE LIFE that my children may live!</u>

I claim Exodus 36:13 and ask that You please never again deprive me of children, and I receive any and all children that you want to bring me!

CHAPTER 10

Truth Or Consequences

What Happens to Us When We Desire to Change The Intended Role of Our Physical Bodies

"Be not deceived. God is not mocked. Whatever a man sows that shall he also reap" (Galatians 6:7).

"There is a way that seems right to a man, but the end thereof are the ways of death" (Proverbs 14:12).

When I was a child, there used to be a game show on TV called *Truth or Consequences* on which the contestants had to perform silly duties to win prizes. The name of that show has stuck out in my mind for some time because the name reminds me of a Scriptural truth. One of the themes of Scripture is that if God's people will seek *truth* and follow His ways, their lives will be full of blessing. By obeying they will avoid the many *consequences* of sin. If they disregard truth and disobey God, they will eventually reap what they have sown.

I do not know many people who want to go through life purposely making poor choices so that they can see how bad things could get. We would consider someone who wants to suffer needlessly as being foolish. Yet every day, people make foolish choices that can take years to recover from; some take an entire lifetime! When Hosea the prophet mourned for the sins of God's people, he cried, "My people perish for lack of knowledge" (Hosea 4:6). What an incredibly true statement this is. This is one of the reasons why I wrote this book. Many couples are suffering sorrows from their family planning choices because they did not know what God's word says about family planning or have accurate and complete medical information to guide them.

In this book, we have talked about the *spiritual and emotional consequences* of using birth control and sterilization, but we have yet to explore the *physical consequences* that are causing harm to people's good health. Unfortunately many people have not been informed of the *physical side effects* that some forms of birth control and sterilization can bring to their bodies. People need to know this information before they make decisions that could drastically affect their health.

For reasons unknown to me, there seems to be some sort of *unspoken agreement* between doctors and the media to keep the general public from knowing the possibility of side effects related to family planning.

> In 1977, Dr. Reimert Ravenholt, the head of USAID's[14] population office, publicly inferred that the agency intended to sterilize one quarter of all women which they have successfully proceeded to do. The World Bank has explicitly indicated that population control is more important than reproductive freedom. Today it is estimated that over 140 million women have been steril-

ized to date. The tool to reach this goal was not done with soldiers but through misinformation, propaganda, and the hands of the women's health care providers and the medical community.[15]

If people were better informed they might make different choices.

When researching information for this chapter, I was amazed at how fast I came across information that the general public does not seem to know concerning birth control and sterilization choices. I have summarized much of what I researched to allow you to see that many of these choices could be and are detrimental to most people's long-term health.

The American medical community has been documenting in medical journals for years that there are physical consequences that come from birth control use. *The pill*, the IUD, birth control injections, sterilizations, and so on have been linked to such health problems as every form of reproductive cancer, heavy menstrual bleeding, emotional hysteria, weight gain, headaches, mood swings, autoimmune diseases, heart disease, blood clots, and even death. The average patient has some idea that these risks may be involved but they also do not realize that these complications *are not rare* but happen quite frequently to a wide spectrum of overall users. When a woman visits her doctor and he prescribes *the pill* or IUD or recommends a tubal ligation or hysterectomy, she is seldom informed of all of the health risks.

There is a growing movement of unhappy people who have utilized some of these choices. They are speaking out in record numbers against various methods of birth control and sterilization choices. What is interesting to me is that these movements are not coming from *religious organizations* but from *secular groups* who are saying, *We have had enough sickness, there must be another way!* They have trusted their doctor's medical wisdom and now feel that sometimes the advice that their doctor gave them let them down.

WHY HAVE I NEVER HEARD THIS BEFORE?

I do not know.

Most people are uninformed because they have never thought about researching the topic of reproductive health.

The Internet is full of web sites with medical studies, testimonies, drug information and general information from those who have made choices that harmed their health and who are trying to warn consumers that most forms of birth control, abortion and sterilization carry *long-term consequences.* People provide this information so that others will not make the same choices and find themselves living with irreversible and painful health situations that will plague them for the rest of their lives.

I can only offer a fraction of the information that is out there. Those of you who really want to know more can study this subject in greater detail and do further research. If more people had information about the physical consequences of some of the most popular choices, they might *turn* before they are *burned* by an irreversible decision.

Medical science does not deny that every 6.4 minutes, over eighty times per day, a woman in the U.S.A. is diagnosed with some form of gynecological cancer. It was projected that in 2003 over twenty-six thousand women would lose their lives to some form of gynecological cancer.[16]

GOD'S WORD IS TRYING TO WARN US!

God has given us the free will to choose to do whatever we want, but God's Word warns us what will happen if we make choices that go in the opposite direction of what God says is best. In Psalm 81:13 God says, "If my people would but listen to me. . . . " Why don't we listen?

Why would a Godly woman want to get a tubal ligation? Maybe she does not realize that she has come into agreement with society's plan for women instead of God's plan, and perhaps she has not thought about the impact that this surgery could have upon her long-term health and emotions.

The feminist movement wants women to believe that *the pill*, abortion, and sterilization are wonderful options because these things give them *freedom from unwanted childbirth.* As I have already said before, one of the goals of their movement is to set women free from God's primary purpose for their lives, which is to birth and raise children. Feminists view childbearing as a hindrance which prevents women from fulfilling a better purpose.

Before birth control options became popular, safe, and available to the masses, childbearing and childrearing were the woman's primary role. Women were not free to do other things; feminists interpret this as a form of imprisonment for women. Caring for little ones and caring for the home have been the main objectives for most women throughout history. God created motherhood and intended for that role to bring women happiness. What the feminists push is the false idea that women have always despised being mothers. Many women did enjoy motherhood, but caring for little ones and household chores took all of the women's energy so that they hardly had time left for anything else.

Luckily for today's mothers, times have changed. In today's world even a woman with many children has greater options available to help her than at any other time in history. She no longer has the same elements working against her. Because of modern appliances, chores that used to take days now take hours and chores that used to take hours now take minutes. With the addition of computers, cell phones, fully equipped vehicles, and husbands that actually help with many childrearing tasks, women today are not in the same boat as many of those in the past.

I am grateful for the road that previous women paved to give women additional choices, and I am happy that technology has made women's jobs easier. But these things seem to have created other problems. The attitude of *"Release me from the burden of bearing children"* has produced women, even Christian women, *who are no longer focused on giving their lives to nurturing and rearing their children.* Many women have become *quite selfish* as they are trying to *go for the gusto* themselves, while expecting their physical bodies to cooperate. They want their bodies' reproduction switches to *turn on* when they want and to *turn off* when they want, and they cannot figure out why their bodies will not always cooperate.

Are women happier now than in the past? We cannot go back to the past to ask the women, but what the feminists have promoted as *good* has not always turned out to be the best thing for women.

Feminist attitudes have even been adopted by churchgoing women, who appear to be no different in many of their views from their worldly counterparts. Many women from religious homes grow up desiring to be mothers someday, yet once they are married, they allow the pressures of society to shape their views on motherhood. Some join churches where it seems all of the women around them—possibly including the minister's wife—have gotten their tubes tied. *Female believers rarely research this topic in Scripture.* Unless a woman happened to be blessed with a mother who had strong convictions concerning motherhood or her female body parts, she may be vulnerable to go along with the church crowd.

I have been in churches where all of the women that I knew were getting their tubes tied or their husbands were getting vasectomies. I have also listened while the other mothers talked in the nursery about their operations. Many times they expressed how happy they were that this would be their *final baby* and now they could move on to *other things.* Some of these statements were made by women under thirty years old! Some women had been pressured by their husband, parents, or in-laws to get their tubes tied. Of course *no one wants to admit to the emotional sorrow that comes later.* I wonder if they were still happy about their decision when they turned thirty-five, forty, and forty-five years old and were surrounded by friends or church members who kept having babies. It would be sad to have to watch the new baby ceremonies knowing that you could *never again* be a participant. The emotional trauma is real and causes some women to resent their husbands, especially when they may not have been *one hundred percent sure* that this is what they wanted.

TUBAL LIGATION

Tubal ligation is a permanent form of birth control. It is the number-one choice of birth control for women over thirty years of age. Fifteen million women in America and over one hundred fifty million women worldwide have been sterilized.[17] In 1994-1996 more than two million sterilizations were performed, for an average of 11.5 sterilizations per 1,000 women.[18]

Tubal ligation been called the "Band-Aid surgery" by family planning groups such as Planned Parenthood and by doctors so that women will think that it is no big deal.

Women are *not routinely informed* of all of the health risks or how the operation will change them bodies physically, spiritually, or emotionally. If more women knew these facts, I believe fewer of them *would allow such a horrible crime to be committed against them.* The medical community and world population planners have been allowed to *downplay this operation* for years, but the complications have become so prevalent that doctors are now being forced to recognize the post-operation symptoms that have ruined the lives of millions of women. Doctors now label these consequences as *post tubal-ligation syndrome.* Dr. Vicki Huffnagel, who first described the syndrome in 1980, has written numerous reports in medical journals describing her findings. She also wrote the first papers demanding that there be a change in the *medical consent forms* given to women informing them of the risks of sterilization operations. You can visit her website for more information: www.tubal.org.

The effects of this operation have ruined such a great number of women's lives that one of the chapters of NOW (National Organization for Women) calls it the *"medical malpractice operation of the century!"* NOW desires for the medical community to immediately inform women of the possible side effects.[19]

NOW is a radical feminist organization which has done much to dismiss the role of the mother in the family and to advance the cause of feminism. I believe that for an organization such as this to be crying out for legislation and to document this crime against women is humbling. They lead these ladies into feminists ideas and now they have to rescue them from procedures caused by the consequences of these ideas. Where is the church's voice in this issue? Christians are not speaking out about this crime to women because many of God's people have also been sterilized themselves and may be suffering their own consequences without realizing the cause.

God's people are supposed to be the leaders in protecting the rights of people everywhere. We should be pointing the world to truth. Since the church is silent about this and is actually in agreement with these practices, I believe that God is using this radical feminist organization to be speaking out against this crime towards women.

Tubal ligation is the most widely used form of birth control for women over thirty. Between 750,000 and 1,000,000 women in the U.S. each year undergo this operation; of these, 143,000 per year have tubal ligations after c-sections.[20] Twenty-five percent of women (up to 140,000,000 to date) have been sterilized.[21]

During this procedure, a woman's Fallopian tubes are severed using a variety of methods. Years ago, the doctor cut the tubes in half and then tied them in a knot. Sometimes this was unsuccessful because the ends of the tubes grew back together! (Maybe God was trying to let them know that He was *not in favor* of their decision!) The couple then found themselves with a mid-life "oops" baby; some got abortions when this happened. To insure that this did not continue to happen, doctors began using laser techniques, severing the tubes and burning the ends, causing the tube to be left irreparable. After a woman has a laser tubal procedure, the chance of a successful reversal is almost impossible. A supernatural healing may be the only way that she could ever have another child again.

On the financial end, most insurance companies will pay for the sterilization but *will not pay for a reversal.* Some stipulate that they will only pay for the operation if the woman has it done right after birth. This is the worst time to make a decision such as this because a woman is very emotional due to hormones and is also tired from her pregnancy. She is hardly in the right frame of mind to make a permanent decision never to give birth again. Many women are being pressured into tubal ligations by their husbands. Doctors take advantage of women by performing this operation right on the spot without a waiting period. When a woman realizes what she has done to herself, her body, and her future, this can cause irreversible damage to her emotional psyche. Many become severely depressed because they feel robbed of their *female parts* and of their *motherhood rights.*

PHYSICAL RISKS THAT MOST WOMEN ARE NOT AWARE OF

Women are rarely informed of any of the complications of the *"Band-Aid surgery,"* even though these complications *are not rare* and happen in some form or another in almost every woman. Symptoms have been reported in at least fifty percent of the women, yet because the media will not report it, most women have no idea that other ladies are also suffering! [22]

Doctors have known for more than thirty years that tubal ligations cause adverse symptoms.

Women sign informed consent forms and are told that the surgery could cause risk of bowel injury, risk of ectopic pregnancy, slightly heavier periods. Women are routinely not informed that in addition, their tubal ligation might cause *heavier periods* due to a hormone imbalance created by the surgery or that the *ovaries could die* altogether. They are also not told about how bad the bleeding could become and that they *could develop anemia* as the result or that the tubal ligation could lead to *ovarian cysts.*

Women are told that they will have a decreased chance of developing ovarian cancer, but they are not told that this is because the surgery may lead to a hysterectomy and the removal of the ovaries. A woman with no ovaries will have no cancer in them. But the surgery increases her risk of *endometrial cancer.*[23]

The following is a synopsis of the problems that are arising in thousands of women. Details can be found at www.tubal.org.

1. *Major complications:* It depends upon which sterilization technique is used, but between 800 and 2,000 women per 100,000 can expect a major complication at the time of the operation according to the Alan Guttmacher Institute. These complications are: infection, injury to the bladder or bleeding of blood vessels or burning of the bowel. There also can be complications from anesthesia. Laparoscopy can cause perforation of the bowel and can lead to infection in the abdominal cavity, with the risk of hemorrhaging and infection. Some women have died from cardiac failure.

2. Post-tubal-ligation syndrome symptoms occur in one-quarter to one-third of all women who have this operation. Women complain of *heavy menstrual bleeding* (gushing and flooding of blood for days), *intense pain in the ovaries, menstrual disturbances requiring hormonal treatment, erosion of the cervix, tumors on the ovaries, and regrowth of the tubes* necessitating a second operation. If the couple ever decides to have the operation reversed and the woman does get pregnant, there is up to a sixty five percent chance that she may have a tubal pregnancy, which results in a failed pregnancy and is life- threatening if not treated in time.

Young women usually do not care about the long-term consequences, because they are young and also because they do not think that this will happen to them. But as they age, these factors increasingly work against them and steal their health from them at a time in their lives when they could be doing much and also while trying to enjoy their adult children and grandchildren.

3. *Hormone Replacement Therapy:* The operation can cause a *hormone imbalance* requiring the woman to go on *the pill* in order to try to balance her system. The hormone imbalance causes the blood supply in the veins, arteries, and capillaries to be cut off to the ovaries and uterus, and they begin to *atrophy* because of lack of use. This can lead to *hormone shock* and *bone loss* (possibly one of the causes of osteoporosis in so many women), *loss of sex drive, memory loss, confusion, hot flashes, uncontrollable outbursts of*

anger, and loss of balance in up to *50 percent* of the women!

4. *Risk of ovarian and endometrial cancer* increases when a woman does not have additional pregnancies. Pregnancy uses a woman's reproductive body parts and acts as an added protection for a woman's reproductive organs because each pregnancy is the completion of a cycle. The decrease in estrogen because of the pregnancy-induced lack of a menstrual cycle further protects these organs. *Risk factors for all reproductive cancers decrease with every pregnancy that a woman has.* James G. Tappan's study of 489 women after their tubal ligations found an increase in the rate of cervical cancer to be three and a half times the normal rate.[24]

5. *Tubal ligation can also lead to future hysterectomy* because the complications can't be controlled and the woman suffers to the point that removal of all reproductive organs is the only solution. *This happens in many cases. You hear of a woman getting her tubes tied and then a few years later, you hear that she needed a full hysterectomy.* One study found that hysterectomy was 17% more likely within the first fourteen years after tubal ligation, depending on the woman's symptoms before the tubal. A history of heavier periods, menstrual pain, ovarian cysts, and endometriosis increases the further possibility of future hysterectomy.[25]

6. *Increased PMS:* Symptoms intensify following a tubal ligation because progesterone is blocked from the ovaries. This can lead to *heavier bleeding* and *cramping*. Plus, when a woman is menstruating, it reminds her that she is not pregnant. This sorrow can produce *fear* and *anger*. The woman can be difficult to live with. She may feel inadequate and unproductive worsening the PMS.

Some women use progesterone cream, which can be purchased at local health food stores, to alleviate symptoms. The results vary, but women report this cream can help with mood swings and PMS type symptoms. Health researchers are not sure if this cream is healthy in the long term because it affects the endocrine system. The body actually stores the progesterone in its tissues and this may cause detrimental damage to the balance of organ systems over time. While using this cream, women should be monitored by a doctor to prevent imbalance.

7. *Weight gain* is common and *rarely avoided*!

8. *Intense heart palpitations* have been reported in many women.

9. *Depression*: Most women who have had their tubes tied need antidepressant drugs to cope. Why? The doctors do not really know; they just prescribe the antidepressants as part of the treatment because they help with the symptoms. Depression may be caused by emotional sorrow. Deep inside, some women are sad that they cannot have children anymore; since they did not wait for their bodies to cease the process naturally during menopause, they feel incomplete. Some long for another child and also for the feeling of knowing that their body could produce another child if they wanted one. This feeling of being incapable leaves some women feeling empty and depressed.

THERE IS A WHOLE LOT OF BLEEDING GOING ON

I am shocked at the number of women I have encountered recently who have shared their *feminine health horror stories* with me. Some family planning choices are ruining people's health, their sex lives, and their marriages.

For example, one friend of mine who is almost forty has fibroids on her uterus. They do not know what has caused them but she has been on *the pill* for almost twenty years. I do not know if this is in any way related to her problem. She told me that she bleeds all but three to four days each month! The rest of the month she is bleeding so heavily that she continuously wets menstrual pads. She is so weak that she has had to move to part-time hours at her job. *She cannot have regular sexual relations with her husband* because she only has three or four days a month when she is not bleeding. She is losing so much blood that the doctor wants to remove her uterus to stop her bleeding. She has also become anemic from her blood loss.

Another friend had been receiving birth control injections, and after several months she developed severe menstrual bleeding very similar to my other friend. Her doctor has not figured out how to stop the bleeding. It has been this way for more than six months! *She also cannot have regular or enjoyable sexual relations* with her husband. She is also weak from blood loss.

Another friend had a tubal ligation four years ago, and now her periods are so painful that she bleeds heavily for fourteen days and her cramps are so bad that she is in bed for seven days straight. She is a mother under forty with three small children! *She cannot have regular sexual relations with her husband* because she is either bleeding, cramping, or feeling lousy. She only feels well enough to have sex during ten days of her monthly cycle.

I know three other women who have been on the birth control pill for more than twenty years. All three are in their early to mid forties. One already has developed osteoporosis, although it does not run in her family. Another is experiencing extreme mood swings, hot flashes, and depression. The third is rapidly gaining large amounts of weight and is also experiencing intense hormonal disturbances. In each of their marriages, this is not only affecting how they feel on a daily basis but is also affecting their attitudes towards their husbands and towards *having sexual relations* in general.

I look at all of these women's lives, and my heart breaks. Their lives and health are messed up because they followed the advice of the media, a medical professional, friend, or family member. They are now suffering daily, and what does it benefit them? In every case it is causing an interruption in their sex lives, feelings of inferiority within themselves and emotional pain in their marriages. These stories are not rare. I have a friend who is an OB/GYN nurse who tells me that every day women come into their office with similar problems. All are suffering in a physical way as the result of their choices or as the result of what someone else persuaded them to do.

I know of several other women including myself who have not chosen to do as these women have and they are not suffering needlessly. In fact they are not suffering at all. They do not have any problems with their reproductive organs. *Their health reflects the blessing of wise choices.* Some people would say to me, "Well, they are just lucky." But are they lucky? Or are their lives a picture of what can happen when someone does things the way that God intended? God's way is *always the best way,* and yet people do not realize that they are not doing things God's way. Sometimes when people are informed of God's plan they will say that they know *a person* who did everything wrong and still appeared to be blessed so they would rather take their chances. (People hope that they will be like that one person). Why do they live in this deception? It is because people actually think that what they have found is a better way than God's way, so they go and make their decisions. Then they end up sick and sad and cannot figure out why.

God does have a road to blessing, and when God's people come into agreement with how God wants things done, then they will find those blessings! It seems so simple. Why can't people stay pure before they are married, enjoy their sex lives, and also enjoy the fruit of sex? This is God's plan that they reject. People want sex *without* responsibility and the fruit of children, and this leads to suffering.

> *All of this suffering is so unnecessary. If people would just do things the way that God intended they would not take their lives down this painful path.*

The irony of this whole thing is that the desire for *increased sexual relations without the risk of pregnancy* is one of the main reasons why husbands want wives to get their tubes tied. They desire to have all the sex that they want without the fear of getting her pregnant. But *when a woman is suffering with the consequences that come from pills and operations, is in constant pain, and is bleeding heavily, she is not going to want to have sex.* In fact the thought of making love will be the *last thing* on her mind if she is feeling this way. A couple's sex life virtually being shut down is another consequence of these choices. She may develop feelings of resentment because she is suffering so much and may become very difficult to live with.

> *What man wants to live with a woman who is angry at him, unhappy, feels sick, bleeds constantly, is fearful and*

complaining, and no longer cares about meeting his needs?
The marriage becomes vulnerable to an affair.

Why would people of God choose to suffer with all of these consequences? Usually they already have several children that they are trying to raise in the midst of these additional problems. Of course some people get these operations and nothing bad happens to their health right away. But as time goes by the complications do eventually surface or another situation arises that the woman has no idea is really related to the choice of the tubal and its deterioration of her body.

GOING THROUGH "THE CHANGE"

When a woman watches TV, during the course of the day she will see twenty or thirty commercials describing female health problems. There are commercials about *arthritis formulas, bladder control, drugs for depression, breast cancer, osteoporosis, feminine energy-enhancing drugs, douches*, etc., all describing poor health symptoms of those experiencing menopause. Younger woman in our country have become frightened of menopause because they are subtly being convinced that our futures involve cancer of some kind, menopausal nightmares, and dramatic declines in our health as we age. Instead of being a time or season that one looks forward to as the time when the body ceases one role but transfers itself to another, menopause has become a season to fear. More and more young women are living in *fear of menopause* and do not look forward to the problems that multitudes of women are already experiencing.

Did God intend for this season of a woman's life to be feared? I do not believe that He did. This will probably shock most of you, but menopause problems are not mentioned anywhere in the Scriptures. I believe that they are being produced by the choices that women are now making. We need to realize that menopause problems are *not* a problem of past generations, but a modern paradigm.

In the past, when women transitioned into menopause, the time was *peaceful and unnoticeable.* Many women did not even realize that this was what their bodies were doing because the change was slow and quiet. This is why for centuries it was called *the silent passage*. Women just ceased menstruating one day, and then they knew that their childbearing season was over. No hormone swings, no heavy bleeding, no cancer, no cramping, no weight gain, no emotional trauma, no mood swings, no unusual health problems. *Nothing but peace followed the ladies who did not alter God's plan and who used their bodies to fulfill the purpose that it was created for.* Over the centuries this would have been the majority of women because birth control was not available to the masses until the twentieth century.

When artificial birth control for women appeared, so did menopausal complications, as well as every other problem affecting the female reproductive organs.

What is this telling us? Birth control choices must be the cause of the majority of our menopausal problems and reproductive complications and cancers!

God made it so that each pregnancy would increase a woman's chances of having a smoother transition into menopause. Every time that she uses her reproductive organs for what they were intended for, it acts as a *shield of protection* and decreases her chances of experiencing deadly complications in her reproductive cycle. Even doctors will confirm this to be true. They tell women that if a woman has at least two children, she is less likely to contract breast cancer than if she does not have any children. If she nurses those two children, then her chances for breast cancer decrease even further.

If we research the topic in Scripture, we will not find *menopausal horror stories*. Scripture does not speak of women who had these kinds of complications. The Bible speaks of menopausal women in a peaceful way. In fact if these types of problems were occurring to the masses like they are today, wouldn't the Bible have mentioned at least one menopausal complication? I believe that female problems and reproductive problems in general were *very rare* amongst God's people. Women with these types of complications were outcasts because people did not understand them and because people were continuously reproducing. They also were not doing unnatural things to jeopardize their reproductive health. The story of the woman with the issue of blood is the only reference to a female health problem. It was considered unclean for a woman to be in public when she was bleeding (Leviticus 15:25), and this woman was out in public seeking a healing touch from the Lord. Scripture does not indicate her age; we only know that her condition lasted twelve years and that Jesus did heal her (Matthew 9:20, Mark 5:25, Luke 8:43). Since God does not mention menopause anywhere in his Word although he does mention many other diseases, this may be a strong indication that this is a modern health problem and not intended for our lives.

Scripture makes few references to older women's illnesses. Peter's mother-in-law was healed of fever. Naomi was a grandmother, but there is no mention of her ever being sick. Timothy's grandmother Lois who taught him is not mentioned as being sick in any way. Scripture tells us that Deborah the prophetess and Anna the intercessor were older women. There is no mention of Eve, Rebecca, Rachel, Leah, Ruth, Hannah, Samson's mother, etc. as having menopausal problems or complications. Both Sarah and Elizabeth were old women when they gave birth, but neither was sick or had menopausal problems. In fact Sarah was quite a post menopausal beauty! Scripture refers to the old as being wise, feeble, or slow, but not being sick with sexual dysfunctions. There are a few verses comparing certain situations to the trauma that a woman experiences giving birth, but none speaking of a woman's transition into menopause. *God does not mention it anywhere in His Word.* This is a strong indication that this *modern health problem* was not intended for our lives and is an area where we can make better choices.

HYSTERECTOMIES

Hysterectomies were invented to save women's lives. The word *hysterectomy* comes from the Greek word *hystera,* which means womb. Because women seemed to be more emotionally excitable than men, hysteria was attributed by the ancients to problems with the womb. Eighteenth-century women on whom doctors attempted female operations usually died; those who survived sometimes became hysterical, having uncontrollable emotions. This is how the name hysterectomy stuck.

The first successful hysterectomies, for various conditions, were in 1824, 1847, and 1878. From 1900 to1940 in the United States, a procedure called subtotal hysterectomy was most often performed, which included removing all of the womb and cervix. The technique was considered simpler, safer, and had a lower mortality rate with less loss of blood than total abdominal hysterectomy. During the 1940s and 1950s doctors decided that leaving the cervix intact might give a greater success rate long-term, because women later died from earlier procedures due to cervical stump cancer that developed. Removing the cervix also decreased sexual pleasure.[26]

Hysterectomy is the second most common surgical procedure performed in the U.S.A. each year!

A hysterectomy is a common operation used to solve a variety of female problems. When medically necessary, a hysterectomy can either save a woman's life or alleviate complications that could lead to very serious health problems. Forty percent of women will have a hysterectomy by the age of sixty. One in ten of these will have a serious complication of the hysterectomy surgery, some resulting in death.[27]

Most women are not told that hysterectomies carry a death rate of between one and two women per thousand. This works out to between six hundred and twelve hundred women dying annually. Between forty and fifty-five percent have complications such as infections, abnormal bleeding, blood clots, hemorrhage, bowel problems, bladder and kidney infections, and loss of nerves and sensation. Many times these conditions require additional surgeries.

As the result of women speaking out against this surgery and voicing their anger, today complete hysterectomies are being considered more and more as being too drastic. Doctors are offering other health choices for patients because the long-term effects of this operation on women's health cause new problems to develop and do not necessarily solve the old ones.[28] Doctors are currently searching for new options to avoid hysterectomy.

What are the negatives of this operation? One of the biggest complaints that I found is that this operation is not needed as often as woman are receiving it. More and more woman's groups are advocating that doctors recommend other treatments over hysterectomy. They are encouraging women to ask questions and only to agree to surgery as a last resort.

How is sex after a hysterectomy? After a hysterectomy, many women may experience sexual dysfunction because the removal of the uterus and cervix lessens the sensation of orgasm. After hysterectomy, the vagina becomes narrower and shorter, which can make sex very painful and penetration difficult. The nerves may be damaged due to the surgery, causing loss of sensation as well. Sometimes there is surgical damage to the bladder or intestine which could cause incontinence. Hysterectomies also cause hormone changes which could lead to loss of libido, vaginal dryness, and difficulty achieving orgasm.[29]

Are there any psychological effects of hysterectomy? The researchers have not come up with any concrete evidence that hysterectomies cause harm to a woman's psyche, but they admit that it could cause mild depression. One report said that there is increasing evidence that women feel depressed after hysterectomy due to hormone levels, sadness that childbearing is over, the psychological feeling of loss of femininity, or ongoing illness.

Is it true that many women end up having to get hysterectomies due to complications from their tubal ligations? Yes. This is a common occurrence. In a recent study of 374 patients who received tubal ligations, 18.7% returned for a hysterectomy. It also depended on which sterilization method was used. Those who had their tubes burned instead of tied had a higher return rate for hysterectomy. Another study conducted between 1971 and 1987 analyzed 80,007 women; approximately one half were sterilized and the other half were not. The study found that the sterilized women were more likely to return for hysterectomy and were more willing to have the procedure done due to increased complications from their sterilizations.[30]

People of God unless there is a severe medical emergency, why would you want to get sterilized and possibly suffer with all of these consequences? We have already talked about the spiritual and emotional consequences of sterilization, but why would you want to do this to your body? Our bodies are God's temples. "Do you not know that your body is the temple of God's spirit? You are not your own; you are bought with a price, therefore honor God in your body" (1 Corinthians 6:19-10).

We are to offer *our bodies* as a living sacrifice (Romans 12:1). Part of that sacrifice may mean laying down our lives to birth children. "We are to glorify God in our bodies" (1 Corinthians 1:20). "Know that the Lord is God. It is He who made us and we are His people and the sheep of His pasture" (Psalms 100:3).

THE DOCTOR SAYS THAT I SHOULD NOT HAVE ANY MORE CHILDREN

Why did your doctor tell you this? Do you have a serious medical condition? Is your problem so bad that you would die if you got pregnant again? Or is this the doctor's professional opinion based on your medical condition. If this is the case, would you still like to consider having another child?

When a woman is faced with this kind of a decision, she must be very careful to weigh the advice of the professionals against the voice of God and the truths of His Word. She needs to be very discerning. The Lord wants what will bring forth blessings in our lives, and children will bring us blessings. But if bringing those children here would kill us or seriously harm our health, I believe that God would want His people to be very careful to make decisions that would be in the best interests of their own physical wellbeing but at the same time still stay in agreement with His principles.

When making a decision as important as our future health, we need to be very careful in selecting our doctor. Unfortunately not all doctors are the same, nor practice the same techniques or principles. The selection of the doctor who will deliver our babies and advise us on reproductive health is a very important decision. It is a spiritual decision and responsibility. When making a selection, believers need to investigate and ask a doctor what their thoughts are on the following types of questions.

Does this doctor practice reproductive medicine according to what God teaches in His Word?

Does he/she have any problem with a woman's desire to have more than the standard number of two or three children? Will that desire be protected?

Does this doctor routinely perform c-sections? (You can ask the doctor for his c-section percentage and also ask what he thinks about c-sections. You may also find out information by calling the local hospital where the doctor delivers.) If a doctor has a high c-section rate, a woman is more likely to get a c-section with this doctor. She may find a doctor who might make a different decision in the same set of circumstances. Sometimes doctors will even admit that they perform c-sections to avoid malpractice lawsuits and also for convenience. If a woman wants to have multiple pregnancies, unnecessary c-sections could cause complications down the road as she tries to complete repeated pregnancies. In 2002 more than one-fourth of all children born were delivered by C-section.

> *The total c-section rate was twenty-six percent, which was the highest level ever reported in the United States.*

The number of c-sections given to mothers who had no previous c-section jumped seven percent and the rate of vaginal births after c-section (VBAC) dropped twenty-three percent in 2002. The c-section rate declined during the late 1980s to the mid 1990s but has been on the rise since 1996.[31]

Does this doctor routinely use sonograms and are they mandatory? If so how does the couple feel about this?

Speaking of sonograms, do we know what they will do to our children long term? Are they really safe, or are we going to find out later that they cause cancer or sterility or some other long term complication that no one ever thought of?

Does this doctor's practice promote a lifestyle of *easy reproductive choices* including giving abortions, placing IUDs, and putting women on the pill for birth control or for reasons other than birth control? Does the doctor routinely perform tubal ligations? Many doctors have been accused of pushing this decision on a woman as she gives birth. It is easier to perform the tubal ligation right after birth.

During labor, does the doctor allow a laboring woman who is not having complications to move around, or is she strapped to a bed and a monitor for hours? Must she deliver her baby on her back or will she be given a variety of delivery options?

Does this doctor allow the mother to *give birth naturally as God intended,* or are epidurals encouraged? Speaking of the epidural drug, where does it go in the body after birth? Can it harm a woman? Can it harm her baby? How safe is it long term?

Does this doctor allow God to choose the baby's birthday, or does the doctor control this decision by inducing the mom before her due date? (What woman 38 weeks pregnant who is tired and uncomfortable will not agree to an induction?) But is it safe for both mom and baby? Routine inductions usually start out by using the drug pitocin. Is this drug harmful to the uterus? If the woman does not progress, could she end up having a c-section and could this be avoided if she were allowed to wait a bit longer?

God's people need to be careful about their choice of a doctor because we are all individuals. We each carry our babies differently and labor differently. We deliver better in different positions based on the curves of our spines and positions of our pelvis. *If we are not given options, then we will have the type of birth that the doctor chooses for us.*

I have had seven children. During three of my births I used an epidural drug and delivered on my back with my legs in stirrups. The last four of my births were in the hospital utilizing a midwifery practice without drugs and utilizing other birthing positions. I have been treated by a variety of obstetricians and have found that each practice seems to do certain things routinely. When women get together and discuss what happened to them at these OB/GYN practices, the stories are all about the same, including my own. For some women this is OK. But for others, this may not be what they really wanted; this is why some choose midwifery. Some even opt to give birth at home, although most health professionals consider this risky and it has been outlawed in some states.

Please do not misunderstand me here. I believe in doctors and am so very blessed to be living in the twenty-first century with all of the modern medical advances. But I also believe that *we have a spiritual responsibility to take care of and guard our reproductive health.* When we choose a doctor who does not agree with what God intended for our reproductive health, then we may find our childbearing opportunities curtailed—not because God is curtailing them, but because something routine was used on us that may not have been the best thing for our individual bodies.

When choosing a doctor, please remember that there are doctors out there who are Spirit- led in this medical field. They may be a little bit hard to find, but I found a practice like this by calling the local Catholic church. You may also find a pro-life practice by calling a local pro-life group. The Catholic church I called knew of a wonderful practice where the doctors understood and accepted the idea of a woman having multiple pregnancies and where they were extremely careful to help her be able to be in the best shape to complete those pregnancies. They utilized c-sections only in emergencies; they did not routinely induce; they rarely used pitocin; and they did not *routinely* use sonograms. They encouraged patients to try natural family planning and taught patients how to do it ; they refused to prescribe the birth control pill, IUD or other abortificient. This practice was definitely pro-life and unfortunately a rare find in obstetrics. But if you will look, God can lead you to something similar or to a doctor that will work with your personal convictions.

The other option might be to try to find a good midwifery practice. Midwives are mentioned in the Scriptures (Genesis 35:17, Exodus 1:17). They tend to understand a more *natural approach* to birth, but most will allow you to choose an epidural if you want it. Many work under an agreement with a doctor in case a doctor is needed for an emergency. Many require that a mother meets with the doctor at least once during her care just so that they can become acquainted. Some midwives utilize herbs and natural, holistic treatments as well as other options. I have used a midwife for four of my seven births and have been quite comfortable; these midwives all delivered me at the hospital. Some midwives can also deliver at home in some states.

What is most important is that each woman recognize that if she is a believer, she *has a spiritual responsibility to choose a doctor or midwife* who lines up as much as possible with God's Word. Then she will rest assured that the advice that she will be given will not go against God's principles. If that doctor informs her that there is a serious problem, then she can be at peace that this doctor believes as she does and would be trying to alert her to the possible dangers. Once informed, then she and her husband can pray and seek God, and He will lead them to make the proper decisions that will be best for her long-term health.

If you are reading this and you know that your dear doctor is a doctor who may compromise God's principles in this area but you just "love his bedside manner," please realize that I am not telling you that you must leave his practice. Please understand and recognize that even though you like his style, there may come a point when his ideas could go against what God desires for your life and you may need to make a decision that may not be what your doctor would prefer. If you feel that you can do this and still be comfortable in a practice that does not adhere to all of your principles, then there is no reason to leave your favorite doctor especially if you have had a very beneficial long term relationship.

VASECTOMY

In several places, the Bible talks about men who were eunuchs— men who were castrated to hinder their sexual performance (2 Kings 9:32, Jeremiah 52:25, Acts 8:27). Scientists have been trying for centuries to allow men to still be able to forego castration yet remain sexually active while relieving their abilities to impregnate their female partner.

The vas deferens was named by Berengarius of Carpi (1470-1530). During the dissection of a cadaver, a man named John Hunter came across an occluded vas deferens. Once scientists realized there was a special chamber for sperm, they began to try to figure out if there was a way to do something with it. No one knows for sure who first attempted the vasectomy operation on humans, but around the turn of the twentieth century much experimentation was being done on criminals and social degenerates.

The vasectomy has become the most common surgical intervention to render a man infertile. It came into vogue in the 1970s when world-population planners vasectomized large groups of men in both America and overseas.[32]

Today the vasectomy has a failure rate of one-tenth of one percent, and is thus considered almost one hundred percent effective in making a man completely sterile. (The only operation that is one hundred percent effective is castration.) This is why men choose to have it done. There were an estimated 493,000 vasectomies performed in 1991, with a rate of 10.3 procedures done per 1,000 men aged 25-45. Most were performed by urologists in physicians' offices under local anesthesia.[33]

Why would a Godly man consider a vasectomy? Most men choose vasectomies because they want convenience. Even Christian husbands believe that a vasectomy will end the possibility of pregnancy and the bother of condoms so that they can enjoy sex with their wives. Most have no idea that this operation is like lighting a piece of dynamite.

COMPLICATIONS OF VASECTOMY

We already know that a vasectomy is a permanent form of birth control in which a man surrenders his ability to allow his seed to impregnate his wife. Most men do not research the operation at all. They ask a few co-workers or friends who had vasectomies about their own experiences and then make their decisions. If the men that they ask have not yet had any ill effects, then most decide that it sounds like what they should do as well. Men are routinely told by the clinic that the vasectomy operation will make him sexually sterile by cutting his vas deferens tubes. Most are told that the operation is quick and relatively painless but that there may be a bit of swelling.

Reversals are usually discussed; men are informed that this operation is very hard to reverse successfully because the vas deferens are tiny (about the size of a pin) and severing them forms scar tissue that hinders effective reversals. Because of this they are advised not to choose vasectomy unless they are positive that they do not wish to father any more children.

Men are not told of any long-term complications from vasec-tomies. Few know that sometimes vasectomies cause severe pain. The Internet is full of testimonies from men who are trying to warn others of the complications and pain that their vasectomies have caused them. One very popular website is www.dontfixit.org. The men on the website have not only had occasional pain after their vasectomies; they have had nonstop pain which has ruined their lives. Testicular pain is quite common, as documented by many studies. In one study of 172 patients four years after vasectomy, 33% reported that they were experiencing chronic testicular pain.[34] This is *one-third* of the patients!

The long-term health risks involved were harder to find because research is still being done in this area. Right now there are ongoing studies that are seeking conclusive evidence of how vasectomies affect men's long-term health. Since the 1970s, medical researchers have suspected that vasectomies may affect men's immune systems and their long-term abilities to fight off disease, yet for now doctors have declared the operation *medically safe*. This may be only for the short term, because medical researchers have become increas-ingly curious about the effects that the sperm has on the immune system when it is *being forced to be reabsorbed back into the body.*

COMMON SENSE

God designed the man's body to release this sperm. After a vasectomy, the man's body still produces sperm—about 50,000 spermatozoa each minute—but since it no longer has a way to leave the body, it must be reabsorbed, which can cause problems with the man's immune system.

Doesn't common sense tell us that this cannot be a good thing? A healthy immune system is a man's day-to-day defense against disease. When sperm can no longer go out of the body they way that God intended and instead is forced to be reabsorbed back into the body is this wisdom to allow this?

Because of the abuse to the man's system his immune system becomes weak, confused, or compromised as the man's defenses are weakened. The immune system is unsure whether the sperm is foreign or friendly. This confusion produces antigens, which cause the man's immune system to build up an immunity to his own sperm. This is sort of like an *allergic reaction* to the sperm. Because the body becomes confused, over time it becomes *auto-immune*, or allergic to itself. The antigens flood the bloodstream and cause the body to manufacture antibodies to defend against them. One study stated that within *two years* of having the surgery, *these antibodies could be found in 55-75% of men.*[35] These antibodies were found to leave the man vulnerable to other forms of disease.

In these nonconclusive studies, researchers found that these types of diseases develop in men who had enjoyed good health prior to their vasectomies. Diseases that have been mentioned as being linked to vasectomies include heart disease, hardening of the arteries, prostate and testicular cancer, possibly diabetes, rheumatoid arthritis, Addison's disease (malfunction of the adrenals), lupus, and erythromatosis. Nothing is conclusive. Men who have been sterilized for twenty or more years showed an increase in non-Hodgkin's lymphoma, multiple myeloma, and kidney stones.[36]

Prostate cancer is the second leading cause of cancer deaths among American men, claiming 300,000 lives each year. Studies conducted through the Harvard Medical School and published in 1993 were nonconclusive. This does not mean that it is one hundred percent safe; it just means that in those studies they did not find conclusive evidence across the board. Several studies found no evidence of a prostate cancer link, and two studies found an increased chance after twenty years. A long-term study in the USA which started in 1992, plans to have conclusions by 2015. There are also studies being conducted in Japan and England at this time.

Do we want to wait that long for medical science to tell us what God has already told us? Common sense tells us that vasectomies were created by man for men who no longer wish to bring forth new life. We know that God wants us to be available to create life and that this availability allows our bodies to function as created. Prostate cancer is on the rise, but no one seems to know exactly why. We know that the prostate is in the same area of the body as the vas deferens. We also know that cancer is a breakdown of the immune system, and vasectomies may break down the immune system.

 Husbands, why would you want to take all of these risks? Your reasoning may come back to haunt you if the operation takes away your health in the future. You might not be in good health or even alive to enjoy the future. Without God's mercy, which comes from repentance, you could reap what you have sown. A sterilization operation to prevent more children may ruin your sex life, bring forth great physical pain, decrease your libido or sexual pleasure, mess up your immune system, get in the way of raising your own children, and even prevent you from ever meeting or enjoying your grandchildren!

REVERSALS

 Can either the tubal ligation or the vasectomy operation be reversed? Sometimes, depending on how severe the original surgery was. Many people enjoy successful reversals. Some believe that successful reversals only occur as the result of the mercy of God.

 If God leads us to attempt a reversal of a tubal ligation or a vasectomy, what will that entail? A reversal surgery is the surgical attempt to restore an individual's ability to have more children by reconnecting the damaged tubes that have been cut or blocked by surgical procedures. These tubes are the vas deferens in men and the fallopian tubes in women. Reversal surgery is considered a major operation and usually requires a hospital stay. Success rates are judged by the conception of another child. Reports have stated that approximately 60% of women and 50% of men become fertile again. Some reports have found that after a man reverses his vasectomy, he still has the antibodies created by forcing his body to reabsorb the sperm and these antibodies still affect his immune system even after he has a successful reversal.

 Several factors rule out candidates considering reversal. A patient needs to be in good health and have a fertile partner. A female patient needs to be under forty and still ovulating monthly. A male patient needs to be under fifty. Less than ten years should have passed since their sterilization, and success can occur only if small sections of their tubes were damaged during their sterilization operation. If their tubes were clipped or tied, they have a greater chance at attempting reversal than if their tubes were electrocoagulated (burned). This procedure of burning the tubes is considered very effective and is rarely reversed because the procedure usually damaged too large an area of the tubes. Electrocoagulation has been used for years in the U.S. due to its high success rate on both men and women.

The average cost for reversal surgery is $5,000 plus hospital expenses; it is rarely covered by insurance companies, although Medicaid will cover partial expenses in some states. Choosing a doctor to perform this surgery is very important. The skill and expertise of the surgeon can greatly affect the outcome of the surgery, especially in vasectomy reversal where the tubes are so small that the operation requires microsurgery.[37]

When researching this subject on the internet I found that the *reversal industry* is actually becoming big business as more people desire to reverse their decisions to become sterilized.

Several websites may be helpful to those seeking reversals. The sites will give you basic information and a *list of doctors and testimonials* from those who have used them before. I am not endorsing these groups because I don't know anything about them, but I do wish to pass on this information because it may be a good reference point for those of you seeking this type of surgery. These sites are: Blessed Arrows and By His Mercies.

(You can find both sites on an internet search engine.)

Reversals also involve a spiritual side, and this requires repentance. When a couple recognizes that they have sinned by trying to control this area and then attempts a reversal, it is important that they go through steps of repentance. The next chapter includes prayers for sterilization reversals.

Before attempting a reversal it would be a good idea to pray those prayers together and to follow the steps listed about healing the emotional wounds that this creates. A reversal affects all areas of a person's life: spiritual, physical, and emotional. A couple needs to make sure that the choice to reverse is made with the proper guidance and counsel so that afterwards the marriage can become even stronger.

Physical complications are the result of the choices that we make. I have only scratched the surface of the information that is available. There is also information out there that can refute some of what I have said, because the world wants us to be like them and does not have the light of God to lead them. Society wants to offer us their lifestyle as forbidden fruit; the believer who partakes may pay a physical, emotional, and spiritual price just as Adam and Eve did.

As people of God we need to *use common sense* and refuse to accept today's trends, which are just demonic deception plots— trends that are being pushed by our doctors offices and the media, and the beliefs that have been adopted by those who are Godless in our society. We must remember that God created the womb to give birth and perfectly balanced the hormones; medical science offers a tempting unnatural artificial substitute. Do we decide to partake? God created a way for a man's sperm to leave his body; medical science offers an operation that does not allow sperm to go out anymore. Do we partake? Can we use our *common sense* to see that this is not what God intended for our bodies to accept?

The choice is ours.

PRAYER for the husband:

Lord, thank You for this information. I needed to be informed this way, and this has helped open my eyes. I desire to obey You in all that I do. I never realized just how serious the complications of these operations could become. Help me to make proper decisions as the leader of my home so that I can honor You in all that I do.

PRAYER for the wife:

Lord, thank You for this information. I don't want to suffer as so many women have. I desire to be a mommy who is healthy and whole. Help me to make choices that will be correct for my life and that will always bring honor to Your name. Help my husband to do the same. I love You, Lord, and desire to always give You my best.

CHAPTER 11

Should You Seek A Supernatural Healing in the Area Of Family Planning?

"By His stripes we are healed" (Isaiah 53:5).

During the last few years, I have had the wonderful privilege of witnessing the power of God healing people of diseases. Afterwards I have also had the privilege of continuing to see that these people really were healed and stayed healed! This experience has increased my faith level to such a degree that I believe that *God is capable of healing anything* in our bodies, including our reproductive organs. As I have been sharing this message of birthing God's mighty warriors with people, many times they tell me that there is *no way* that they could have another child because they have had their tubes tied or are infertile. I respond by encouraging them to seek God for healing. Most ask, *"Is it possible for God to heal this? Do you really believe that God wants to heal my womb, my tubes, or my husband's vas deferens? Is that kind of thing possible?"*

My response is always, *"Why not?"* I have seen other things healed, and as believers we should at least believe that this *could* be possible. Scripture says *ask and you shall receive* (Matthew 7:7). I know that the subject of healings is controversial for some people's theology, but Scripture is clear that we serve the God of the universe who created our physical bodies. He is quite capable of putting us back together when we are broken. He has done this down through the ages, and He can still heal us even in today's world.

People tell me that they have *never heard* of God doing miracles or healing people in modern times except maybe through a doctor. (Just because a believer has not heard of other kinds of healings does not mean that God is not doing them somewhere else in the world). In foreign countries that do not have the kind of medical care that we have here in America, believers *must ask God* to heal them because they have *no other choice*. Missionaries often report stories of miraculous healings because the people must go to God out of sheer desperation. With a little bit of research it is possible to find many documented accounts that American believers are not hearing about from their ministers. These healings are still happening somewhere in the world. If God can heal a person's broken body in a foreign country, He certainly can also heal a person's broken body in America. God can heal anything that we ask Him to heal. I have great faith that God wants to heal complications caused from birth control choices, abortions, and sterilizations.

How often do we hear a spiritual leader ask God to rebalance hormones disturbed by improper use of the birth control pill or recreate wombs that have been taken out by hysterectomy or recreate tubes cut through tubal ligation or vasectomy or even acknowledging that there is a problem with this area of people's health? I have rarely seen a minister ask God to heal people in these areas, and I do not know why.

I believe that the barren and hurting have been overlooked and seem to be forgotten by everyone except God.

I know that God wants to heal people of infertility. I have witnessed such miracles even here in America. Every Mother's Day my local church has a special time of prayer for people who want to be parents but are having trouble conceiving. Those who need prayer stand up, and then groups of believers surround them and pray for their need. Every year, nine to twelve months later, babies are born to some of those who were prayed for. These happy couples proudly bring their babies before the congregation on the following Mother's Day and share their miracle stories with the members. This is a beautiful thing to witness as each parent seems so happy and blessed. It would be wonderful if more churches across the country adopted this plan for Mother's Day. I believe that God would greatly honor these prayers. It is wonderful to witness what can happen when God's people ask!

We must remember that God loves the infertile and wants to heal them of their barrenness! God loves the barren and wants them to be able to have the children that He desires for them to have. He wants to see husbands and wives made complete again and He wants to restore what the enemy has stolen from them through sterilizations, the pill, the IUD, and miscarriages. God wants His people to be whole once again through Christ's blood that was shed on the cross. The power for healing our physical bodies has already been paid for by Christ's sufferings.. All we need to do is ask for it!

Why doesn't God heal 100% of the time? I do not know. In Scripture, I have observed that Jesus healed when the Father directed Him to heal. At times everyone was healed, and at other times He healed only one specific person. I believe that God's people should always desire to stay open to His healing power. God's people need to be asking God for healings, but it is still up to the Father whom He chooses to heal. It would be sad to get to Heaven and find out that our lives were not healed because we either did not ask or did not believe that God wanted to heal us.

What if God does not heal me? That is possible, but it is not for us to speculate. It is Scriptural for us to ask. Even though it has not been popular to pray over someone's reproductive organs or to ask God to recreate organs, this does not mean that He cannot do it.

Where does God heal people? We never know the arena in which God will choose to perform His miracles. This is why it is important to believe that anything could be possible. It is possible to be healed while reading this book! God is a God of miracles. Jesus often referred to healing by telling His disciples that healings glorified the Father and brought attention to His name. God's people may never know where He may choose to heal them but need faith to believe that it is possible. God may choose to heal His people out in the open in a church service or He may choose to heal people in a small group setting where the church leaders pray over their bodies for healing. Sometimes God chooses to heal some people when they are all by themselves as they believe and pray for healing. It is completely up to God.

What is the difference between healings and miracles? I just read a wonderful article written by an evangelist which helped me to clearly understand the difference between the two. A miracle is something that there is *immediate evidence* of with instantaneous results; for example, a blind person receives sight or a crippled person walks. Much of Jesus' ministry was in the realm of miracles. Healings can be received immediately, but they may take time to manifest themselves to be recognized. People may have to keep believing that they are healed until the healing takes hold in the physical realm. This confuses many people. They think that if they are not instantly healed, then God let them down and did not heal them. This is inaccurate. Many times God is in the process of healing them, but because they do not see it immediately, they lose hope and then tell all of their friends that God did not heal them. Once they start to speak that they are not healed, the enemy comes back and steals from them once again.

When people ask for prayer for their infertility to cease, *they could be healed instantly by God,* but it may take months to be manifested. For this healing to come about, a couple must act on their belief and go *make babies together.* After they come together God can bless them with a pregnancy. This result could easily be months from the actual prayer asking God for the miracle healing.

Since it may take months to be revealed, this may cause people to question whether God really brought forth the pregnancy through a miracle or if it *just happened.* Let me caution you, if you ask to be healed and it does happen: *to God be the glory!* Do not forget who healed you and made you whole! God is in the *business of healing and restoring lives!*

Do I have to do anything? Yes. First you must believe that is possible to be healed. Then sometimes people need to ask God to heal them, and sometimes they need to forgive someone. They may need to forgive a friend or family member against whom they have held wrong feelings, or they may need to forgive themselves. They may even need to repent of their resentment against God for allowing the events that made them sterile or infertile. Everyone has a differing set of circumstances; unforgiveness in a person's heart could be the only factor separating him from being healed. Unforgiveness causes a barrier that blocks a person from being able to receive God's love. Removing that barrier somehow opens people up to be able to receive the love of God and to be able to receive His healing touch.

I do not have all of the answers as to why God heals and how to be healed. But one thing that I do believe is that God wants your life to be whole and if healing is involved in that wholeness then God wants it to happen for you. If people will just believe that a healing is possible, then God can begin to work in their lives.

Since some people do not know how to ask God for healing, I have written down some steps toward healing for people to pray.

HEALINGS MUST BE RECEIVED

The first step in asking for healing is to ask the Lord to change any *wrong attitudes* that may have been received through teachings that discount healing in today's world. People cannot receive a healing touch from the Spirit of God if they do not believe that God wants to heal them! If deep inside of their hearts they are *not sure* that God wants them healed, their lack of understanding *will block* their healing, because when the Holy Spirit comes to heal, *they will not believe that He can or will not believe that He should!* Healing is something that *must be received by faith* just like salvation is something that must be received by faith. If people do not relax and let go of their fears, they cannot receive their healing and will unfortunately stay sick.

Many, many people of God have been sold a bill of goods through incomplete teachings on healing. For years I was told that illness, sickness, and disease were part of God's will and God's plan for my life. I was told that He brought these things into people's lives to teach them new things.

This may be true at times, but it is not always the case. I now believe that these teachings caused me *to accept years and years of lack* in many areas of my life because *I thought that God wanted me to.* Since I loved God and was trying my best to please Him, I accepted these problems as something that came as part of the Christian life.

This same thinking has caused countless believers in today's world to accept *all illness* as if it came from God and to *never ask God for healings*, not even if they have a headache. If they do have a headache they take an aspirin; if their child is sick they go to the pediatrician; and if they can't get pregnant they go to a fertility specialist; and on and on. They never even stop to consider that they are supernatural believers serving a supernatural God who still heals people today. They may hear stories about God healing people, but most believe that they are either not true or that healings are only possible with the help of the doctor or with the help of a medicine. This limited thinking is keeping God's people just where the enemy wants them to be: sick and accepting his lies.

The Word of God tells us that Jesus died for our infirmities (Isaiah 53:4) and that He desires to set us free from them. Jesus came to bring good news to the poor and to set the captives free (Isaiah 61:1). Illness, death, and poor health are some of the main things that the enemy uses to make people his captives. Too often God gets blamed for the things that the devil is responsible for. God wants people to be well; He wants them to be able to pay their bills; He wants them to be happy; He wants them to go to Heaven. He especially wants to see them enjoying the abundant life on earth

(John 10:10b).

Does this mean God's people will always be well, successful, or rich? God's Word promises abundance. It states that the children of the righteous should never have to beg for bread (Psalm 37:25), so if His word is true and if His people will be obedient, then God's people should be able to at least feel good, be able to pay their bills, and have enough left over so that they can give to others out of their abundance.

Does God want everyone well? I believe that the answer is yes! I do not believe that God created sickness or death. I believe that they originated with sin and the enemy uses illness to bring sorrow into our lives. If God wanted us sick then Isaiah would not have said that He died for our infirmities (Isaiah 53:4).

Does He allow illness? Yes, I believe that He does. He allowed Satan to attack Job, but Job did pray for healing! He did not just *sit there* and take what the enemy was giving to him. He sought the reasons why and asked to be delivered (Job 30:20). This is what I am encouraging each of you to do. We have already established that the enemy has set a trap here for God's people, but this does not mean that God wants His people to stay trapped. Many times He will bring healing when His people ask for it; this is what I am encouraging you to do.

SUGGESTIONS FOR HOW TO ASK GOD TO HEAL YOU

A common misconception about healing is that if God ever were to heal people, they would have to be at a church or in a church service. You do not necessarily have to be in a church service to ask for healing. God is GOD. He is everywhere and can do anything. He can heal people anywhere.

If you need God to heal you in the reproductive area, there are two ways to go about it. You can visit your local minister and ask him to pray for you, or you can pray for that healing yourself in a private setting, or you can do both things. If that minister believes in healing—and most do to some degree—this may be an excellent place to start, but it is not out of the realm of possibility to ask God to heal you in the privacy of your own home. Since God is everywhere, He can heal you at home in your living room the same way that He could heal you in front of a minister or while in a church service. It is the same power (1 Corinthians 1:18). We have to believe that God wants to do this for us and accept His outcome. Some healings may be instant, and these would be miracles; some may take time to manifest; and some may not come because they are being blocked somehow; and sometimes it is simply not God's timing. But in all cases it is Scriptural to ask God, and He wants us to ask Him. Pray about what God may be leading you to do.

If you would like to pray for healing yourself in the privacy of your home, then here are a few suggestions to assist you with this process. Before asking God for healing, most people find that they need to get their hearts in tune with the Lord first. This may work best when you can set aside some uninterrupted time away from children, the phone, work, or people coming to the door. One of the easiest ways to begin to focus on God is to listen to a CD of worship music. Some people find that they want to spend this time alone, while others may want to spend this time with their spouse. During this time, some people may sing to God; some may quote Scripture or prayers that they have memorized that bring them closer to God; while others may feel more comfortable keeping silent and thinking about the words of the songs. Some people may be comfortable just sitting on the floor allowing the music to relax their souls. As you begin to worship God in whatever way you feel comfortable, it is not uncommon for distracting thoughts to come into your head, so keep a pad nearby to jot these thoughts down. As you write down business information, grocery lists, what to wear, errands to run, etc., you will find that you become less stressed out and can more readily focus on God. After a few minutes a feeling of peace will come as you draw closer to the spirit of God.

Worshipping the Lord and getting quiet makes most people feel better. This in no way a formula for healing; it is just a suggestion to help establish an atmosphere of comfort that alleviates stress and outside distractions. I believe that once we feel more *in tune with the Lord,* we may feel ready to concentrate on the next step, which is to tell God how much we love Him.

During worship, begin to tell God that you *love Him,* and thank

Him for His blessings and for being faithful to you. You may want to name the things that you are thankful for. There are no rules. This is your time. You need to concentrate on God your way and enjoy this time focused on Him.

After you have spent some time feeling closer to God (each person will be different), you may feel ready to begin to pray for healing. If you have another way other than in private worship that you can connect to the Lord, then do it that way. Some people may want to go sit in a prayer chapel. There is no secret formula. Getting in tune with God is a personal thing, and everyone is different. But God's presence is the most wonderful place to be.

When you are ready, you may wish to pray this type of prayer or something similar:

"Lord Jesus, I know that You died for my healing. At Calvary, Your blood set me free from the laws of sin and death. Through that precious shed blood I can come to You today and ask for a supernatural healing. Lord, please forgive me for not believing Your Word and for not realizing that You did die for my infirmities. I lay down all of the lies and incomplete teachings that have convinced me that You wanted me to stay this way. I believe that You can and do want to heal me. Please remove any and all of the lies that I have believed in my heart and mind. Please cleanse my mind of these thought patterns. I receive the mind of Christ (Philippians 2:5) and *ask, Lord God, for the supernatural ability to believe You for this healing in my body.* Please help me to receive from You now, Lord. Thank You for forgiving me and for dying to set me free!

PRAYING TO REVERSE A STERILIZATION

Can we pray for this, or do we need a doctor to perform a reversal? This depends on what you believe about healing. If you believe that God has the *supernatural ability to heal you* without a doctor, or if you want to at least ask God to heal you before you seek the assistance of a doctor, then it is not out of the realm of possibility to ask God to heal your physical body.

If you are praying for God to reverse a sterilization, one of the most important things is that you need to confess that the sterilization operation was a sin and that it went against God's plan for your life. You need to start with repentance. If you have already prayed and repented of this at another time, then you may want to either repeat the prayer or proceed to ask God to supernaturally heal you.

Prayer of repentance for a sterilization operation:

1. Lord, I love You. I want You to hear my prayer and heal me today. Thank You that I have received a new mindset and that now I know that it is Your will to heal me and set me free from this hardship. Lord, I have made so many mistakes in my life, and sometimes I chose to disobey. Sometimes out of my ignorance to Your plan for my life I have done things that I did not even know were wrong. Lord, I allowed myself to get sterilized and this decision has hurt me, my spouse, and my family. I now realize that I was deceived by society and its worldly thinking, and I am sorry. Please forgive me, Lord, for being ignorant. Your word says that many times Your people perish for lack of knowledge. I allowed myself to have this surgery because I did not know that it was wrong. Had I known I might have made a different choice. I repent of my ignorance. Please forgive me.

2. Lord, I also choose to forgive this day (date of the prayer) *my spouse* for agreeing with this surgery or for thinking of this surgery and or for not stopping me from having it or for pressuring me into having it. I choose to forgive my spouse for not wanting any more children, and I ask You, Lord, to forgive me for not wanting any more children. I choose to forgive my spouse for being in agreement. I confess to You this day that I forgive my spouse.

3. Lord, I choose to forgive this day (date of the prayer) *the doctor* who performed my surgery. I forgive him (whether he informed me of my rights or not). I know that this doctor felt that he was doing what was best for me. Please forgive me for any resentment that I have had in my heart toward this doctor and forgive me for allowing myself to submit to this doctor's wisdom and knowledge over seeking what You say in your Holy Scriptures.

4. Lord I choose to confess and forgive this day (date of the prayer) *myself* for ever considering this surgery, for listening to society, for listening to other believers who influenced me, for being selfish and putting my own concerns and desires for life above what You may have planned for me. Please forgive me for thinking of myself and for not seeking You first, Lord, before I had this operation performed. Please help me to forgive myself in all areas. I receive Your forgiveness.

5. Lord, I choose to forgive this day (date of the prayer) *any family members friends, or clergy* who influenced me, whom I have held a grudge against or resented for not stopping me from getting this surgery. I forgive my parents, in-laws, grandparents, cousins, aunts, uncles, brothers, sisters, friends, minister, etc. who I feel did not honor me or those who were just trying to help me. I choose to forgive them.

6. Lord, I choose to *repent of my anger toward You, God,* this day _____ (date of the prayer). Lord God, I know that You love me, and yet somehow I wish that You had *supernaturally intervened* and stopped me. This operation has brought me much pain and sorrow. I *choose to let go of my anger towards You.* This is anger that I should not have but anger which I may have hidden deep inside of my heart. I have been angry at You for not stopping me or sending someone to intervene. If I have held any resentment or grudge in my heart toward You, Lord, please forgive me and cleanse my heart and mind and spirit with Your precious and holy blood. Lord, thank You that You hear my prayers and that You are willing to heal me. Today I would love to *be made whole again,* and I would love for You to heal me. A healing would mean so much to me, Lord, and would take away my sorrow. Lord, I thank You that You are the God who heals, saves, and delivers. Your Word says that by your stripes we are healed through your shed blood on the cross (Isaiah 53:5). I ask that that blood of Jesus cover me and I ask this in the name of the Lord Jesus Christ and by the power of your Holy Spirit I ask to be healed.

I ask Lord that You heal (name the body part that needs to be healed; e.g. Lord, please reconnect my tubes, or Lord, please reconnect my vas deferens). Lord, please allow my body to do what it was created for. Please allow sperm to swim through my tubes again and to fertilize my eggs OR (for the man) please allow sperm to come back through my vas deferens again. Lord, please remove any and all scar tissue that could block this healing. I speak to my body and in the name of Jesus Christ of Nazareth I command it to be made whole. I command my tubes to open and to be reconnected. I command the eggs and sperm to be youthful and fully functional, and I command my body to receive this reconnection as I receive this healing through faith in You. Thank You, Jesus. Praise Your holy name!

FEMALE REPRODUCTIVE COMPLICATIONS

Some women have hysterectomies and know that this was not God's plan for their lives. If you believe that God has shown you this, you may want to ask for a healing. It is not out of the realm of possibility for God to do something *supernatural* for you. But this is a prayer that most would consider foolish to pray because so many believers today do not believe that God can heal a person in this way. I caution you to seek your own heart before you choose to exercise your faith. If you feel that God may want you to seek Him in this way, then proceed and ask for this miracle; if you do not believe that this type of thing is possible, then ask God to lead you in whatever way you feel most comfortable.

Prayer to ask God to recreate your womb after a hysterectomy:

Lord, You have given me the faith to ask for something impossible. Just as You made Sarah a mother at ninety and Elizabeth a mother after menopause was completed, I believe that You can do something supernatural for me. Your Word says that "With God all things are possible to those who believe" (Matthew 19:26, Mark 10:27, Luke 18:27), and I am believing something that the people around me think is impossible. I am executing my faith to believe that You can do this for me.

Lord, please give me a *new womb* because my old womb caused me to have complications. I believe it may have been cursed or made sick as a result of choices that I made. Please forgive me if there was sin covering my old womb from previous lifestyle choices. I want to repent for anything that could have made it cease to function. I plead for Your mercy and forgiveness, dear Father.

Lord, also please forgive me of all of the times that I put my faith and trust in the wrong place. In the past, I trusted medical advice and the advice of others who guided me to make decisions that may not have been the best thing for me but appeared to be my only option at the time. Lord, I believe that I was deceived by worldly influences and because I was not aware of what was going on. Please forgive me.

Lord, please remove any residue and scarring from my past. I command my body to receive this healing from You, and I speak to my body and I say *"Be made whole through the shed blood of Jesus Christ of Nazareth and by the mighty power of Your Holy Spirit!"* Thank You, Jesus! I give You praise!

Please rebalance and restore my hormones to complete wellness once again and any other parts of my system that is not in full balance. Please make me whole in every area again. I command my hormones and body to line up with the power of the Holy Spirit and I receive complete wellness. I release all fear and all rejection coming at me that could in any way block this healing, and I release love and forgiveness toward others around me. I thank You, Jesus, for Your miracles. I praise You, Jesus, for You alone are great!

Prayer to balance female hormones or other female issues:

You may not have felt led to pray for a new womb, but if there is an imbalance in your system due to reproductive complications, you may wish to ask God to heal this.

Prayer: Lord, I desire for my body to be made whole once again. I ask that You balance my system and help my whole body to come back in tune with itself. I speak forgiveness over the parts of my body that I may have desired to shut down and ask that You forgive me for any time that I may have rejected using my body in

Your plan. I desire to obey You and to be made whole once again. From this point on I submit my reproductive organs to Your will and not my own interpretations. I speak to my system and command it to line up with the power of the Holy Spirit and will Your will for my life. I ask that the blood of Jesus cleanse my physical body and make it whole once again. If there are any other health factors that are blocking this healing, I ask that You heal those areas as well. I believe and thank You that I can receive Your supernatural healing power to be as You created me to be.

MALE REPRODUCTIVE COMPLICATIONS

Prayer for low sperm count or other male issues:

Lord, I desire for my body to be made whole once again because I want to submit to Your will. I believe that You can put my body back into rhythm once again and make me whole. I ask that You renew the health and balance that You intended for my system, and I declare that my sperm count be renewed and replenished within normal ranges. I speak to my body and command it to line up with the power of the Holy Spirit, and I receive Your *supernatural healing power* to renew my body. I also ask that if there are any other health factors that are blocking this healing that You also heal those areas as well. I believe and thank You that I can receive Your supernatural healing power to be as You have created me to be. In the mighty name of Jesus Christ of Nazareth I speak to my body an command it to be restored back to youthful wholeness and a state of well being. Thankyou Jesus!

BEING HEALED OF BARRENNESS

We have already covered this a bit in previous chapters. We looked at how various factors may be the reason that so many people miscarry or are infertile. If you have already prayed these prayers, there may be a few more things to look at that may explain in further detail the issue of being infertile.

Upon examining the lives of individuals in the Bible who found themselves barren, we may find that they did things that opened the door to the release of infertility. Hannah, Rachel, Sarah, Rebecca, and Elizabeth were all barren and were all healed of this problem.

The first family of the covenant, Abraham and Sarah, were barren. The Bible says that God found Abraham to be a righteous and blameless man, yet they could not seem to have children until God healed Sarah's barrenness (Genesis 21:1,2,7). Abraham did not sit around waiting. Abraham acted on his faith and moved forward in his relationship to God, and this may have aided in the release of barrenness. In today's world most people are infertile because they have sinned in the area of family planning. When someone asks for forgiveness they may be instantly released of the consequences of this sin, but sometimes other things could still be blocking a conception and keeping God from blessing the individual with a child. As you read what Abraham did, the spirit of God may quicken you and impress upon your heart that you may need to do something in addition to asking for forgiveness.

1. *Abraham believed God when things looked the opposite.* God made a promise and it took twenty-five years to fulfill that promise! God told Abraham that He would make a great nation out of him even though Abraham and Sarah were old and had never conceived.

2. He *tithed* to Melchizedek one-tenth of his money.

3. He *entertained* 3 angels.

4. He *prayed* for Sodom and Gomorrah. (He asked for deliverance and God's mercy for two anti-family cities.)

5. He *lied* to Pharaoh about Sarah, which caused Pharaoh and his household to become barren. God forgave Abraham after Abraham *prayed* and asked God to break the curse of barrenness off of Pharaoh. These prayers indicated that Abraham was a man of prayer.

6. Abraham *obeyed* and was *circumcised* at 99 years old (ouch!), along with all of his household including thirteen-year-old Ishmael.

After all of these events happened, then Sarah got pregnant—twenty-five years *after* God first spoke the covenant to Abraham.

There appears to be a correlation between *prayer, pleading with God,* and *breaking off the curse of barrenness.* Scripture says that God was gracious to Sarah, *remembered* Rachel, *remembered* Hannah, and allowed Rebecca to conceive after Isaac prayed. The word *remembered* indicates that Rachel and Hannah did something to get God's attention. The Scriptures are full of verses about how prayer gets God's attention.

Abraham prayed, tithed, was circumcised, and showed hospitality to angels; then

God was gracious to Sarah (Genesis 21:1-2).

Rebecca was given a verbal blessing on her fertility by her family and yet she was barren

Isaac prayed and broke the barrenness off her womb (Genesis 25:21).

Rachel prayed and God remembered her (Genesis 30:6).

Hannah prayed and God remembered her (1 Samuel 1:19).

If you feel like God is speaking to you and telling you that your infertility may take additional prayers, you may want to pray this prayer or something like this and *continue praying* until God releases you from the curse of infertility.

Prayer for conception and for healing barrenness or infertility:

Lord, thank You that I have received a new mindset. Now I know that it is Your will to heal me and set me free. Lord, I desire to have a baby. I want to birth and raise mighty warriors that will be part of Your end-time army. I desire to love these children and to raise them to love You. Your Word says that Your favorite way to bless me is to give me a child. I receive that child and future children that You want to bring. I claim Psalm 113 that says that *You make the barren woman a happy mother of children.* I want that for myself and my spouse. We want to be having children, and we do not want to limit You in the process.

Lord, I repent for any and all things that I may have done that could have blocked You from allowing a conception. I repent for my own sins past and present that could have blocked Your gift to me. I repent for careless statements that showed my lack of faith or disbelief. Lord, please forgive me for every word that I spoke against myself, my spouse, and my future child due to disbelief or ignorance on my part. Please forgive those words and please *remove* any and all curse that those words created. Please let every false word that was spoken against me fall to the ground (1 Samuel 3:19) and render them powerless through the power and blood of Jesus Christ of Nazareth. I repent for every statement that my tongue brought forth, and I ask, Lord, that today You take over the words of my mouth so that I will not allow any more statements to be said that would speak against my healing. Please send an angel to guard my tongue as I continue to believe that You desire to release me from this curse.

GENERATIONAL BLOCKAGES

We have also already covered how the decisions of a previous generation could be causing complications in our lives today. We have already prayed prayers of repentance for how their sins could be causing miscarriages, but we did not completely address barrenness. Generational sins could be blocking future conceptions if parents, grandparents, or other direct blood relatives were sterilized. Their choice could be blocking their descendants from being conceiving because the previous generation's sterilization made a statement that they desired to end their family's bloodline. This one fact alone, once repented for, can remove a history of conception problems in some families.

Prayer for forgiveness of ancestral sins:

Lord, please forgive the mistakes of anyone in my family's bloodline who could be blocking the conception or birthing process of my children. Your word says that you will punish the generations of those who were idol worshippers to the fourth generation (Exodus 20:5). Lord, wherever my ancestors may have walked in idol worship, fallen into witchcraft, worshipped falsely, or *chosen to control,* I ask that You forgive our family bloodline and stop this from robbing us of our blessing.

Today (date) I ask for forgiveness and healing over my family bloodline in the area of birthing and receiving children. Lord, please make the _____ (insert family name) family bloodline whole again. I declare this day (date) as the day that our family decided to follow the Lord again in this area. Whether it was out of ignorance on my ancestors' part or if they really did not desire children—no matter what their reasoning was, I speak forgiveness and wholeness in Jesus' name over their sins. Lord, I ask that You do not hold me or my future generations responsible any more. I ask that You forgive their ignorance and disbelief and cleanse our bloodline of this sin so that children *may once again be restored* as a fruit of the_____ family tree. I declare the _____ family tree to now be restored to wholeness through the power of the blood shed on the cross by Jesus Christ of Nazareth. I receive my healing and ask to be restored to complete wholeness and desire to receive all of the children that You want to give me, Lord.

REVERSAL OPERATIONS

We have already mentioned that there are doctors who will perform a reversal operation on you or your spouse. There are websites dedicated to people who have had a reversal and still cannot get pregnant, and there are support groups for those who are having trouble conceiving. These can be helpful, and wherever you may be in this decision process, you may find informative answers. I personally believe that if we spend a great deal of energy focusing on accepting what we do not have, this can prevent us from having because our focus is on the negative. This can also prohibit healing.

After you have prayed these prayers, every word that comes out of our mouths should be as positive and hopeful as possible: *I know that I'll be pregnant soon! I know that God is going to give me a blessing!* Try your best to stay away from negative and discouraging people who may not agree with your faith. They may tell you that you are crazy to believe that God can restore you.

"Return to me and I will return to you" (Malachi 3:7).

EMOTIONAL HEALING

If you prayed for a reversal or have had a reversal operation for the purpose of having more children and have not yet conceived, is there a possibility that you have not repented of the emotional scars that this operation brought into your marriage? It is possible that there may be an area of *emotional pain* that has still not been healed. Events such as barrenness or sterilization often wound people (especially women) on such deep emotional levels that they may not be in touch with their pain. This pain can be blocking them from receiving God's gift. If you have been using birth control and now realize that it was sinful to use it, then you may want to pray the repentance prayer in the miscarriage chapter. Many couples do not realize that using birth control breeds rejection. When people feel emotionally rejected, they will usually shut down and shut out the other person.

Sometimes the best remedy for a couple to heal emotional wounding is by seeking intimacy. If they will *confess* their thoughts and feelings to each other this may help. Many times a wife's pain may be so deep that she can not figure out why she feels sad. She may need her husband to gently hold her. Playing soft music, reading poetry, or saying prayers to each other all may allow the wounded spouse to feel loved and accepted. Emotional scarring and the feeling of rejection may be all that is blocking the healing of barrenness. When a husband and wife draw close emotionally and physically, they can receive what they may not have been able to receive before. As they make love they will be demonstrating their greatest physical, emotional, and spiritual unity; this is intense spiritual warfare against the power of the enemy.

What if nothing happens and these prayers do not work? If this happens, at least you tried, you asked, and you believed God. This is all that can be expected of us. Healing is still up to our Heavenly Father. It is at *His option.* Sometimes there are *reasons why* that we do not understand and sometimes there may still be unknown factors *blocking our healing.* I am positive that after you pray these prayers of forgiveness or similar ones, you will feel *a release of your pain* because all confession of sin brings forth greater intimacy with God. This is a Scriptural principle. If you were sincerely praying, you will definitely feel forgiven and cleansed. This alone is worth asking for! My prayer is that you will receive your healing and be made whole.

PRAYER of thanksgiving for both husband and wife:

Thank You, God for Your cleansing power! Help us to receive all that You are saying in this chapter. We want to be healed and made whole. Thank You that Your Word says that *Your mercies are new every morning. Great is Your faithfulness to us*! (Lamentations 3:23). We claim mercy over our lives and are grateful that You are willing and ready to bring Your healing power. Thank You, Jesus!

CHAPTER **12**

God Is Calling Us "Back To Our Future!"

*"This day I call Heaven and Earth as witnesses against you
that I have set before you life and death, blessings and curses.
Now choose LIFE, so that you and your children may live
and that you may love the Lord your God and listen to
His voice and hold fast to Him for the Lord is your life"
(Deuteronomy 30:19, 20).*

In the movie *Back to the Future*, the main character, Marty, had the opportunity to go back in time to witness the events that led up to his parents becoming a married couple. Marty quickly realized that if certain events did not take place in the exact same way and at the exact same time as they had before, that there was a chance that his parents would not ever get together. This would mean that he and his siblings would never be born! Marty also realized that if a few things changed even slightly that there could be positive changes in their family's future. At the beginning of the movie, the audience sees Marty's parents as nerdy and un-cool. After he is able to go back in their past to help make a few slight changes, in the end the audience sees Marty's parents being much cooler.

I named this chapter "God Is Calling Us Back to Our Future" because this is exactly what I believe that He is doing right now with the family planning issue. If it were possible for God's people to do what Marty had done and go back just seventy years to make a few corrections, then things would be different today. If all of God's people had continued to follow Scripture in this area, today we would not see the breakdown of the family that is so prevalent in our churches and in society. Although going back is impossible, it *is possible* for God's people today to *go forward* and to change the future by not allowing themselves to continue along the same path that they have been on. If you are a believer and the Lord has been impressing upon you that He wants you to make a few changes, then *now is the time* to decide what you need to do. The *decision* to *choose a new way of life* is yours. God can erase your past and bring a new future.

LOOKING FORWARD TO A BRIGHTER FUTURE

All throughout the Scriptures we see God desiring that His people have a mindset of *forward motion*. This is how God wants His people to be positioned when He returns. They are to be *focused forward* and awaiting Him. They are to be forgetting what was in the past and *reaching for what is ahead*. Paul said, "I reach for the mark of the prize of the High calling of God" (Philippians 3:13-14) Hebrews chapter 11, known as "The Faith Chapter," talks about a people of faith *looking forward* to a city with foundations whose architect and builder is God (Hebrews 11:10). These great men and women of faith were not living for the *now* or living as if things were over when they died. They were *looking forward* to something far greater than what they received on earth. God's people should all be positioning their lives towards future goals.

This is something that previous generations could see but did not *have the privilege to attain. "They were all commended for their faith yet **none of them** received what had been promised" (Hebrews 11:39).*

The Bible says that the greatest saints of all time *did not receive* what had been promised (Hebrews 11:39). Many had visions of things that were far off in the future. They could see these things happening in the future, but they could not yet attain them because they were not born at the time of fulfillment of those events. They prepared for the future but died without ever getting to see the events happen. Because of the beauty of God's grace, they did not die in vain. The things that they planned for did eventually happen and are still happening.

Abraham saw his offspring too numerous to count; Moses saw the Israelites happily living in Canaan; David saw a Savior sitting on his throne; the prophets saw Jesus the Messiah coming to earth; Paul saw the Gentiles receiving Christ; and John saw the events of Revelation unfolding. Many missionaries have dreamed of the gospel spreading to their country and around the world. Every one of these dreamers knew that one day God would bring a generation here who could attain what they were hoping for. They died looking forward to the times that we are finding ourselves living in!

Today, God wants us to be *looking forward to* and *planning for* our futures and beyond. When we birth God's mighty warriors in this generation, we are reaching toward our own futures. The Scriptures say that we need to *keep working until He comes* some-day (Luke 19:13). This way we will be found sober and alert and prayerfully awaiting his return. We are to be just like Abraham who received God's vision for his future. He was looking forward to what God was going to do (Hebrews 11:10). He was not caught up in his own finite existence but was looking at himself in comparison to God. He realized the awesomeness of God and His plan.

Hebrews 12:1 says that we are *surrounded by* and are *being watched* by a great cloud of witnesses. These witnesses are the faithful who have died and gone on to be with the Lord. I believe that they are watching from Heaven because they have a vested interest in seeing the *rest of their story* being played out on earth by their descendants. These Godly relatives want to *cheer on their faithful offspring on earth* in their pursuit of advancements for the kingdom of God! They want to see the continuing of their own legacies and the great things that will be accomplished for their Lord through their own family trees. Many times the spiritual gifts that people have and the things that they accomplish on earth are the direct results of the prayers of a generation that they may not have even known! God says that he is "showing love to a thousand generations of those who love me and keep my commandments" (Exodus 20:6).

If our ancestors knew God and asked Him to accomplish certain things through them, then we may be the people chosen to fulfill those prayers and complete those tasks! We can complete the things that may not have been possible to accomplish in their lifetime because the season of time was not yet ripe.

Someday in the future God's people will have a place in that perfect *Holy Jerusalem* as the *completed Bride ready for her beloved Savior* (Revelation 21:2). Until He comes back, God's people are to be *working for, planning for, and believing in His cause* as they make preparations for His return. As God's people faithfully birth new members of His army and train them up to love Him, we will be saying, *"God, we agree with your vision for the last days."* We will also leave earth knowing that we completed our part of this task faithfully. Corporately, as God's people come into agreement and reach unity in this area, we will be helping other believers in their quest to serve God because we will have helped to strengthen His anointed group on earth by leaving behind more fighters in God's army. "They will not contend with the enemies in the gate but will possess the land" (Genesis 22:17-18). Our children and grandchildren will build upon the very foundations that we leave behind! They can keep the momentum going that was started generations ago and passes from generation to generation. With each new child that is born, the wealth of promises will continue to increase as God's people live closer to the time of the Lord's return. The children being born later in our families will be even greater as everything is increasing, and intensifying and accelerating toward

the climactic events of history!
PLEASE DO NOT MISS YOUR OPPORTUNITY TO BE BLESSED!

Trust God and stay open with your family planning. Let Him choose to give you the number of children that He plans to give you. Open up your heart to receive God's favorite gift—*children*: a *heritage, a voice* into the future, an *arrow* to defeat the enemy, an *opportunity to possess the land* for generations, and an *opportunity to come back to your future!*

AS A PEOPLE READY TO AGREE WITH GOD, LET US SAY "NO MORE" TO SATAN!"

No more, Satan, will we listen to your lies about planning our children.

No more, Satan, will we follow in the footsteps of our humanistic culture.

No more, Satan, will we allow you to deceive us into thinking that additional children are not valuable.

No more, Satan, will we allow others to influence our family planning.

No more, Satan, will we refuse to receive all of God's gifts to us.

No more, Satan, will we allow you to keep us from intimacy with our Savior that comes through trusting God in family planning.

LORD, PLEASE HONOR OUR RIGHTEOUS DECLARATION

We PRAY and DECLARE that we will be a people who will

return to *Your ways*!

We PRAY and DECLARE to call back all of the financial and generational blessings that have been held back from our family bloodlines due to our disobedience with birth control, sterilization, and abortion!

We PRAY and DECLARE that we are a righteous people, holy and set apart, surrendered to Your plans and purposes!

We PRAY and DECLARE that we will **CHOOSE LIFE** so that our children, grandchildren, and great-grandchildren will **LIVE** and will possess the gates of your enemies!!

WE PRAY THIS IN THE MIGHTY NAME OF JESUS CHRIST, OUR SAVIOR AND LORD. AMEN!!

APPENDIX

Common Questions and Answers

Do you think God wants everyone to have a large family?

No, I do not. I *do not believe* that every couple is supposed to have five, eight, twelve, or fifteen children, etc. There are many couples who have trusted God with their family planning throughout their entire marriages and have smaller families of one, two or three children. Many Biblical families were not very large unless the man had more than one wife. A few examples were:

Noah had 3 sons.
Abraham had 2 sons with 1 wife and 1 concubine, then later fathered 6 more sons with another wife.
Isaac had 2 sons.
Jacob had 12 sons and 1 daughter (but he had 2 wives and 2 concubines).
Joseph had 2 sons.
Moses had 1 son.
Boaz and Ruth had 1 son.
Job had 14 sons and 6 daughters. (His was the biggest Biblical

family that I could find. He had 20 children from what appears to be one wife—10 children before his hardship and 10 children after God restored him.)

The whole issue is *not the number of children that a couple is blessed with* but whether they are trusting God to make this decision. I believe that when God's people do trust Him, He will allow them to receive the children that He knows will make them happy.

Does every couple who chooses to trust God with their fertility have child after child? I am so afraid to trust God with my womb. Pregnancy is so hard on my body and I just cannot be having baby after baby.

I can sympathize with your feelings. You are not alone. Many women feel like you and have a problem with allowing God to plan their families because of this very reason. *Be of good cheer.* I subscribe to an online digest of families who all believe that the Lord should be in charge of their family planning. Many times, the women write in and express that once they decided to allow the Lord to be *in charge of their family plan* that they were expecting to get pregnant right away, and yet they did not get pregnant for a long time. Some have waited two years, three years, even as much as five years. During that time, the Holy Spirit just grew a deeper desire for more children.

This message that I have presented here is one that a person has to be led to follow. God has to help a person see that they can trust Him with this part of their life. As people give God their fears, He will grow a deeper desire to allow Him complete control. *You may not be ready yet.* God loves you enough to allow you time to become comfortable trusting Him with your family planning. He is *not trying to force you to obey* something that you are not ready to receive for yourself. Just keep seeking Jesus and *do not allow the enemy to cause you to be afraid to trust your sweet Savior.* As you seek Him He will lead you to the faith to trust Him with your family planning, your body, and your future.

I want to trust God, but my parents get so upset with me.

They think that we are being irresponsible. How do I tell them that I am pregnant again?

This is sometimes one of the hardest things to do because we want our parents and in- laws, those who will be our children's grandparents, to be happy for us. Instead many times they make rude comments that hurt our feelings. After my fourth child (after my husband's angel dream), we knew that God was telling us that we would have more children, and I knew that this would upset my father because he was worried about the money. I called up my Father and told him, "Dad, I want you to understand that we are probably going to be having more children someday." He told me that he thought that I was crazy, but I then said, "We like children and we feel God wants to give us a few more. If you love me, just tell me that you are happy that I am giving you another grandchild. Please do not worry about where we will get the money because we believe that God will provide." And then I said, "And if you are not happy *tell someone other than me* about it, and please just tell me that you are happy for me." When I got pregnant with my fifth child he said, "I am happy for you and I think you are crazy all at the same time!" Now that we have had number six and number seven, he told me that it is OK because now he always wins the Father's Day contest at his church for having the most grandchildren!

Here is a really cute way a mother-to-be let her parents know that she was expecting again. Her parents were also quite concerned about how they would be able to afford all of the children that God was blessing them with. She wrote a poem to let them know that they were about to be grandparents again.

> I bet you never thought when your children left the nest
> They'd give you twenty-three grandkids;
> Why, that's way above the rest!
> No friend of yours could ever boast of having more than you,
> Your kids keep multiplying, it's really quite a ZOO!
> We are a loving family, who could ask for any more?
> But come this next December, there will be twenty-four!!

The Bible says a quiver full of children is a blessing. Aren't five children a full quiver? Once we had five children, I got my tubes tied, and we feel like we did the right thing.

A quiver in ancient times could come in a variety of sizes and could hold a varying number of arrows. A quiver was never limited to hold only five arrows. A warrior's quiver could hold over twenty arrows!

Since I have three children, haven't I already obeyed the commandment to be fruitful and multiply?

Yes, but maybe not as completely as God may have planned for you to obey it. Think about this: how thoroughly does God want us to obey His other commands? Jesus told His people to evangelize the earth. Most believers would agree that He did not set a limit on how many people to evangelize. What if a person shared the gospel with someone two years ago, and then again with someone else this year, and then kept silent for the rest of his life? Would he be fulfilling the Great Commission to the best of his ability? Most believers would say that God would want this person to continue to share the gospel because God wants others to come to Him.

Why is this command any different? If a couple decided to be fruitful and birthed children in 1993, 1996, and 1998 and then decided that they wanted to stop, would they be completely fulfilling the commandment to be fruitful and multiply? If God's people do not apply this same thinking to other commands, then why apply it here?

People create this kind of reasoning whenever they do not like one of God's commands and are looking for ways to get around what God has spoken. If people want to be continuously obedient here, then just as with other commands, they need to continue by *staying open* to allowing God to bless them. After all, only He truly knows what is best! I have heard of couples having two children and then never conceiving again. The rest of their marriage they concentrated on the other things that God desired for them to do. One of the greatest privileges a parent could be blessed with would be to fulfill the Great Commission by birthing children and raising them to be followers of Jesus Christ and then training those children to share their faith.

You do not understand. We have prayed about this, and we both feel called to have a certain number of children, and we are both in agreement that when these children are born, we will be through.

I think this is great! You should have *no problem* trusting God with your family plan! What you are saying is that you are in agreement that when a certain child (the next son or daughter) is born or when a certain number of children are born (such as after number three) that you will be through. If either of these scenarios is the case, then you should easily have no problem with trusting God to then stop sending children without needing a sterilization operation or using birth control.

Sometimes people get confused because they do not know the Word of God on this subject, and they think that when they have heard a specific number from the Lord, this means that once those children arrive they are *free to get sterilized with God's blessing.* Not at all! The Lord would have to go against His own mandate in Genesis and His other principles in Scripture to be in agreement with your permanent operation. Sterilization was only invented approximately ninety years ago. Why would God put something in His word that would only apply to believers born after the early 1900's? If you both correctly heard the voice of the Lord then why don't you have peace to trust Him to close the womb? Trusting the Lord always leads to rich rewards.

But we are in *agreement* not to have any more!

Agreement is a wonderful thing in marriage and is one of the principles of marital harmony. Agreement is an excellent guideline to keep a couple from missing the voice of God. However, just because *you are in agreement* does not mean that you are making a correct Scriptural decision. You can be *in agreement* and not be aware of God's commands and end up missing God's blessings.

The Word of God has many examples of this.

1. *Remember Adam and Eve*? (Genesis 3:6) They were *in agreement* to eat the forbidden fruit in the Garden of Eden and it led them to spiritual death. Their *agreement* put a curse on the entire human race!

2. Scripture commands us to give our money if we want the blessing of the Lord on our finances. A husband and wife may be *in agreement* not to give money to the church, but their agreement could lead them to miss God's blessings in the area of finances.

3. *Remember Ananias and Sapphira?* (Acts 5:1-10) They were *in agreement* to lie to the Holy Spirit. They sold property and agreed to lie about the price so that they could keep some of the money for themselves. Then they lied to Peter and the church. Their *agreement* led to their deaths. God instantly struck them dead for agreeing to lie.

4. The crowd who yelled "Crucify Jesus!" were *in agreement.* They said "Let the curse fall on us and our children" (Matthew 27:25). They were *in agreement* because they hated Jesus so much. The curse fell on them because of their *agreement* and has lasted more than 2,000 years!

If you and your spouse are *in agreement* on any subject it is definitely a step in the right direction; however, agreement does not necessarily mean that you are correct. We must seek out answers in Scripture *before* we make a decision. If couples would only seek Scripture for answers about birth control, sterilization, etc. they would easily see that God's Word is clear that children are our heritage and meant for blessing. Most couples just ask others around them what they think without God's Word to back up their decisions.

Today can sterilization be an option for Christians if there are valid reasons for it, such as health problems?

Sterilization has only been around since the early 1900's. *Before that time (almost six thousand years) it was NOT an option.* Believers had to trust God or use abstinence when the woman had health risks, diseases, or other physical maladies. A health risk to the wife is something that each couple must carefully consider in prayer. Even when there are health complications, I do not believe that sterilization is the best option, especially since there is increasing evidence that sterilization can lead to further medical complications. Would God want His people to break one of their healthy body parts to try to solve one problem while at the same time creating a much larger problem? This kind of reasoning does not agree with Scripture. Just because sterilization is medically available does not mean that it is now a healthy option for God's people.

When we look back in history we can see that sometimes there were *valid reasons* why people might not have wanted to birth children: health risks to the mother, famines, inadequate living conditions or inadequate medical care , mothers dying during childbirth, various diseases. But this did not stop people. With all of these negatives, *women still went to great lengths* to bring children into this world. Each of us, who is alive today has a woman in our past to thank for our existence.

Our ancestors had to trust God that their children would be born normal and healthy. Sometimes both the women and their babies died during the delivery as a result of unsanitary conditions and complications. We have the finest medical procedures available today; many of the complications encountered just fifty years ago would result in success today.

Even though people have the most advanced medical techniques in the world available to them, they are led to believe that it is unwise for a woman who has *any health risks* to try to bring children into this world. We will risk a woman's life by giving her an abortion or sterilizing her or risk her long-term health by putting her on *the pill*, but when she wants to trust God with birthing a child when the circumstances look risky, we call her stupid.

If a wife has cancer or another debilitating disease, then options should be considered through the advice of Godly counsel. There are many wonderful testimonies of people who have trusted God when things looked risky, and God came through in miraculous ways. This is what walking in faith is all about, but someone must be carefully led to trust God under these extreme circumstances.

Many times OB/GYN doctors may advise women with health risks *not* to have children because they are afraid of lawsuits if there are complications. I believe that the vast majority of doctors, however, have the best interest of the woman in mind and are trying to look out for her future health. They do not want to see a woman have repeated c-sections or make choices that could lead to further complications, so they tend to err on the side of caution and tell the woman not to get pregnant again.

A couple has to make wise choices in these circumstances. If they feel that God is leading them to learn more about trusting Him, then they may have peace about moving forward when the situation could be medically risky. *Is it wisdom to take such a risk?* Sometimes it is not. God's people really need to take into consideration the doctor's advice and the principles of Word of God, and carefully decide what God is showing them

A woman should never feel like she has *let the Lord down* if she must make a decision that will protect her health, as long as that decision does not go against God's principles. Women who do take such risks should have spent much time in prayer, possibly fasting (if their health allows) and waiting for God to *release the faith to make the wisest decision.* When someone feels that God is leading them to trust Him under difficult circumstances, great things can happen. *We are people of faith and it is in these kinds of situations that our faith can become a reality. Walking out our lives as God carefully leads is what it is all about.*

What about being over thirty-five years old when you have a baby?

I believe that if God did not want women to bear children over the age of thirty-five, then He would not have given their bodies the ability to do so. In God's eyes, when is a woman ever too old? He allowed Elizabeth and Sarah to give birth in later years, and we know that women over thirty-five have been successfully birthing children for six thousand years.

Why is it suddenly considered a huge risk factor for a woman to have a child after age thirty-five? I believe that during the last forty years in our country a few medical studies have been used incorrectly to scare women over thirty-five into thinking that *it would be rare* if they gave birth to a normal child. This is simply untrue! Yes, there are very real risk factors over thirty-five, but many of these same risk factors are true at any age. Pregnancy is hard on a woman's body. A woman's health and nutrition before she gets pregnant play a huge part in a successful pregnancy and delivery.

During the last forty years, when increased numbers of women chose *the pill* as their birth control method, they delayed childbearing until they were older, and we saw an increase in pregnancy problems, especially in those women over thirty-five years old. One reason may be that *the pill* tends to drain a woman's body of many nutrients and natural body reserves. If a woman does not concentrate on rebuilding her nutrition prior to pregnancy, she may suffer physically as a result. Another reason for problems with women over thirty-five years old could be the American diet. The types of foods that people eat have changed drastically over the last forty years, with more and more processed food and the depletion of minerals in our soil. People have more x-rays now and eat irradiated food more often and we also cook with microwaves. Another thing is that lots of women go on crash diets while drinking and smoking, and this also depletes them of needed nutrients. People are constantly being exposed to chemicals in their food and water. All of these things can cause health risks. Last, if the woman has been sexually promiscuous or has had an abortion or several abortions, this too could affect being able to conceive and also affect the success of her pregnancy.

By age thirty-five, some women's bodies are so depleted that their abilities to conceive and successfully deliver a healthy newborn are greatly affected. But *not every woman over thirty-five is in these risk categories.* Many factors need to be looked at before a woman over thirty-five decides that she should not have a child. A woman should see her doctor and get a complete health assessment if she feels that she may be too old.

For most people, age is just an excuse. Women who want to have children are having them later and later. Last year more women in their fifties gave birth to healthy children than in previous decades.

I recently met a woman whose husband told me that he wanted another child but she just refused to get pregnant again after their first. She is now forty-seven years old, and she tells him that she is too old. Women can use any excuse they want. If they want to have children after they are thirty-five years old and they are healthy enough, then they will, and if they do not want to, then they will look for reasons why they cannot. The reasons for not desiring children are usually deeper than their current states of health.

Since menopause in a normal woman (who has not altered her cycle through hormonal birth control) usually occurs in the early to mid-fifties, I believe that its clear that God intended for people to birth children until their early to mid-fifties when their bodies complete menopause.

Recently I was in a bookstore, and I needed help. The older-looking woman who helped me had a picture of a little girl on her name badge. I asked her who the little girl was, and she said, "That's my daughter, she's three!" "Wow!" I said. "She's cute. Are you going to have more children?" She replied, "Well, I would like to, but I am fifty-one and already have a thirty-year-old and a seventeen-year-old, so we will see. My doctor said that I am fertile, so we are trying to decide." I told her that I thought what she was doing was great, and she shared with me how few people react the way that I did. Most fifty-one-year-old women are not thinking about having any more children. But they could be. God has made it possible. Many times women are the ones who are limiting this possibility. Very few ladies are willing to be open to having a baby when they are this old.

You mentioned in the first chapter that America has already forced people in the past to be sterilized against their will. In the future do you think that our country could ever force people again to be sterilized for something like global population control?

Yes. I do think that anything is possible. In fact I believe that if the body of Christ does not wake up and unify, this is exactly what will happen. Right now, *America has voluntary sterilization and many Christians voluntarily submit to it.* If we want our children to be able to have as many children as they want, we must stand up and ask for legislation that will prevent forced sterilization in the future. If we don't do this now, we will be suffering the consequences. Just like when abortion became legal while God's people were asleep, we could see a two-child limit come upon us. Consider China's one-child policy and forced sterilizations and abortions.

What is the number-one reason for women choosing to get their tubes tied?

I personally believe that people get sterilized for two reasons: convenience and short-term exhaustion. They make decisions without considering the long-term effects and how their parental feelings might change in the future. Because increasing groups of people have not had the privilege of growing up around younger siblings, they enter parenthood without a clear understanding of the sacrificial lifestyle. Too many decisions are made to end parenthood because parents are wondering about *what they have gotten themselves into,* without realizing that after the initial adjustments they may really enjoy parenting a lot more.

If a couple was not ready for parenthood, after the birth of their first child they will immediately feel overwhelmed. Parenthood is harder than they expected. When they experience sleepless nights and doctor bills, they quickly realize that if they do not do something soon to prevent more children that they might find themselves in *an endless lifestyle way over their heads.* The only solution that they can think of is sterilization. So without considering their future parental feelings, they make the decision for one of them to get sterilized. The spouse with the most fear is usually the one who gets the operation.

I believe that they make their decision *because it makes sense at the time* and since they see others around them making the same decisions, they do not take into account the long-term effects of that decision. They do not realize how quickly time flies and how fast things change. As children grow, things become easier and the *pleasures of parenthood* begin to increase. The children are fun to be around. They say the cutest things, and they reward their parent's efforts with hugs and kisses. They draw a special picture or make a mold of their hand *just for their Mommy or Daddy!* They also make their own Mother's Day and Father's Day cards and seal them with a kiss. They tell Mommy and Daddy how much they love them and how they want to grow up and be just like them! Their love is pure, sweet and irresistible.

Suddenly, one or both parents realize how nice it would be to have more children. They never thought that they would enjoy raising children so much, and they like how their children are turning out. The only problem is that now it's too late. A reversal of the operation costs several thousand dollars, and the insurance company won't pay for a reversal like it would for the sterilization. Besides, it may not work! Unless God supernaturally intervenes and heals or provides a way, the couple has to live with the finality of their decision. They may consider adoption, but many just have to live with the regrets, the sorrow and the feeling of *what if?* Unfortunately, most couples will end up sad. I believe in a merciful God. I believe that He wants to heal couples who have made this kind of decision.

You're making such a big deal about this issue. I am Godly in other areas and I do not see how getting sterilized is going to affect me, especially since by limiting myself to just a few children I will have more time to serve God.

The Scriptures already quoted say that God would prefer that we trust Him with our family plan. He knows what we all need to be happy and He stands willing and ready to bless us if we want it. He may stop sending children so that we can do church or charity work, but if we let Him do it, we will be truly trusting God instead of trying to take control of something that is Scripturally His to begin with.

I'm actually in shock over this whole subject. I have been an avid pro-lifer for years and have vigorously fought abortion. I know you have shown us the evils of birth control and sterilization, but I still think that abortion is worse because it is actually committing murder and using birth control is simply *not* the same thing.

Today we hear so much in our churches about the evils of abortion. God's people are *very outspoken* about this issue because we believe that the life of the child is precious to God, and it is! At the same time that we see abortion as being wrong, however, we fail to see that there is a connection between birth control, abortion, and sterilization.

Both abortion and sterilization are founded on disregarding the inherent value of human life. We have deceived ourselves into thinking that the two are separate issues, but in reality they are very similar. On one hand we do not want to see babies killed, but on the other, we think nothing of getting sterilized to prevent children from coming. I believe this is a conflicting standard.

Let's look at sterilization versus abortion to see why we need to take both issues seriously.

1. Abortion *kills* the life of one child.
   Sterilization could *prevent* multiple lives from ever being created.

2. Abortion is murder and *breaks* the fifth commandment: "You shall not murder."
   Sterilization *breaks* the first command that God gave mankind: "Be fruitful and multiply."

3. Abortion *takes a life* that God has given.
   Sterilization *prevents a life* to be given by God.

4. Abortion *leaves hope for new life* to be given again.
   Sterilization *takes all hope away*

Now that we have looked at these two decisions side by side, do you see the similarities between sterilization and abortion? Sterilization prevents multiple individuals from ever being allowed to be conceived; it takes all hope away unless God supernaturally intervenes. Abortion at least leaves hope; God could send new life and continue the cycle of the generations.

When we compare birth control and abortion, we realize that abortion really is another form of birth control. With birth control, the issue is to control whether a child is conceived or not. When an "oops" baby is conceived and the parents decide that they do not want this child, the abortionist then kills the unwanted child that could have been prevented had the parents been using a more reliable form of birth control. Birth control users are far more likely to consider abortion than those who do not use birth control. Some methods actually cause *silent abortions,* where the mother does not even know that she has lost a conceived child. *The pill* and IUD are responsible for thousands of silent abortions.

God says that when a person is murdered the blood of the innocent cries out from the ground (Genesis 4:10). When a woman aborts or has silent abortions, the event happens inside of her which means that *the innocent blood cries out through her body.* This will curse her unless she repents. Many God-fearing people shout at abortionists and condemn their behaviors but *fail to see their own hypocrisy in using birth control.* If their method fails, they could find themselves in the position of the ones choosing abortion; and if they are using birth control methods that are causing silent abortions, then they are already guilty of abortion.

We feel that as good stewards, we need to be responsible with every gift that God brings. We feel it necessary to plan our future and to have an understanding of what we are trying to accomplish.

Having a plan is a great idea. Scripture reinforces the need to plan. God is a planner, so it is not wrong for a couple to have a plan. What can be wrong is when the couple decides how many children that they should have and do not consult God. They then plan what they want and leave out what God may want to send them. People believe that they know what God wants because they do not feel like they want children, so therefore they think God must not want to give them. They feel that they know what they can handle physically and emotionally, and they forget that God knows their abilities even better than they do. Most people do not take into account what the supernatural grace of God can do.

One of the reasons why I wrote this book was that as I studied this subject in Scripture, it became clearer and clearer to me that making this decision for ourselves is not a thought coming from the heart of God, but is a human desire. What the Word is clear about is the overwhelming evidence that God does know what He is doing with our lives and that He has a strong desire to bless each of our marriages with children. "Many are the plans in a man's heart, but it is the Lord's purpose that prevails" (Proverbs 19:21). The Scriptures that I have presented are clear that God wants this choice. If we decide to make it ourselves, He will allow us to do that, and we will get what we have chosen. "We will continue with our own plans; each will follow the stubbornness of his evil heart" (Jeremiah 18:12b).

We simply have no guarantees, whether we want to limit our family size for good reasons such as retirement, college education or tuition expenses, or short-term exhaustion. All seem like great reasons, but all are reasons that are human. Couples should make a plan and seek God for understanding, and then as they do in other areas, be flexible so that God can change things if He chooses.

You mentioned something about people losing out on finances because they are not open to having children. Do you believe that being open here brings money? Is there a connection between allowing God to plan your family and wealth?

We believe that trusting God with our family planning allowed God to bless our finances in a greater way. At the same time that God began to increase our finances we also took and taught the Crown Ministries course (a financial planning course based on Scripture). This helped us to further line up in obedience to God's

347

financial principles. If God considers each child to be a blessing, then it is His job to release Scriptural wealth to those He blesses. The Lord always takes care of the obedient. I believe that Scripture is clear that if couples who choose to obey in this area will also obey by giving and getting out of and staying out of debt, that there is no reason why they cannot prosper financially.

It is interesting to observe that in the Body of Christ there are some Godly couples who tithe and have little or no debt but struggle financially because the money that they make seems to always disappear. It is easy to wonder why they are struggling financially even though they look like they have done everything according to Scripture. But if either the husband or the wife has been sterilized, this could be the cause of their problem. I believe that *when people cut God off from blessing them, they allow the enemy an opportunity to steal from them.* He will do this in whatever way that he can, and with some couples this will be in the area of finances. People need finances and resources to raise children. "My God shall supply all your needs according to His riches in Christ Jesus" (Philippians 4:19). When people decide to have more children, the Lord will provide for them; and when they decide not to have any more children, this does not guarantee that they will end up with more money.

In your opinion, what should a pastor or Christian leader do if they realize that they've sinned in this area by either getting sterilized or trying to control through using birth control?

The best thing for anyone to do when convicted of sin is to confess it to the Lord and repent. If a pastor decides to make a change in this area, He may feel led to preach a sermon series on what the Scriptures say about birth control and then share from his own experiences. Honesty and humility can go a long way. Confessing before a congregation could bring great healing to many congregants and release curses of infertility/miscarriage from the people in the congregation.

What about Natural Family Planning (NFP)?

Natural Family Planning (it used to be called the rhythm method) is when a couple abstains from having sexual relations during the wife's fertile time. This is the only method of birth control that the Catholic Church agrees with, and they have only allowed for NFP since 1950. Few people realize that before 1950 the Catholic Church believed that Scripture was clear that couples should trust God completely in the area of reproduction.

The benefits of NFP are that it is an all-natural method, it costs nothing to follow, and couples who use this method (as well as those who completely trust God with their family planning) have a divorce rate of practically zero. If a couple would like further information about NFP, there is a national organization called The Couple to Couple League which helps couples with Natural Family Planning. (You can find information about this organization on the internet by using a search engine.)

I believe that practicing NFP is a good place to start, but I believe that God intended something far greater than this if His people will trust Him. My husband and I did not start out with NFP. When God moved our hearts to trust Him with this area of our marriage, we felt like we needed to trust Him all the way. God gave us peace to make love even during fertile times. Other couples who have followed God and trusted Him during fertile times will tell you that God really does open and close the womb as they have found; not all women get pregnant when their cycles indicates that they are fertile.

The problem with using NFP is that a couple *must abstain* at the one time in a month when a woman's body is most craving sexual relations. As a woman's body gets ready to drop her egg, her desire increases. Even though a couple can still be close and enjoy a special time, some couples find this not as satisfying and very difficult. Some say that NFP is wrong because a woman should not be paying attention to her body with charts and diagrams. I disagree because we know that during Biblical times women had knowledge of their cycles so that they could follow the strict Levitical laws of cleanliness after childbirth and monthly menstruation. The women had to appear in the temple and be declared *ceremonially clean* by the priest after childbirth or monthly menstruation, so they needed to know when their cycles began and ended (Leviticus 12).

In the New Testament Paul addressed the issue of sexual abstinence in marriage (1 Corinthians 7:5). He told couples that they should not abstain from sex except for a mutual season of prayer and fasting. Some say that Paul was trying to make it clear that couples should have sex often and should only abstain when seeking God while fasting. Some say that Paul was saying that sex should not be used as a weapon. Some say that Paul was allowing for NFP as a season of rest, and some say that he was addressing the issue of mutual agreement. I believe that he was addressing all of the above in some way.

We know that for the last six thousand years, sometimes couples had to mutually abstain from relations, especially during times of war when the men had to go away and fight. This was one of the reasons why King David's sin with Bathsheba was exposed; her husband Uriah refused to sleep with her while the king's army was at war (2 Samuel 11:11). People also abstained during times of purification and if the wife was ill or could not have children for a health reason. This very issue was mentioned in the movie and the book *Gone with the Wind.* When the character Melanie was too weak to be able to bear children her husband was known as being *a gentleman who abstained* and did so for most of the movie/story. In today's society, most men would not even consider abstinence. The birth control pill brought an attitude that sex should be for *any time, in any place,* and *to get all that I can get.* Sometimes in a marriage this cannot happen. After the birth of a baby is a good example. A man may need to wait until his wife heals from giving birth. This is part of what love is all about.

What about if one spouse becomes ill or travels frequently?

These types of circumstances do come up in life. When the spouse is able or when the spouse returns and things are back to normal, then the sex is seen as a celebration of being able to be together again. This has been a fact of life down through the ages.

As far as using sex as a weapon or one spouse withholding relations from the other spouse, if a husband desires sex and his wife does not, Paul says that she should have sex with him and vice versa. But if they both come into agreement that for a specific time period they will abstain, then they are still following Scripture. There may be times in a healthy marriage when couples do not need relations. The couple may even find that God allows for a season where they do not necessarily agree to abstain; it just happens due to the necessities of life. I have known people who can not seem to get together due to their schedules, children sleeping in their bed, unexpected travel, or one spouse getting sick with a cold of the flu. Sometimes *things just happen,* and life and children get in the way. During this season a couple could become very vulnerable, however, and they need to guard their hearts and begin relations again as soon as possible.

What about the issue of rest?

After a child is born, Scripture allows for a woman's body to rest through abstinence. This is where many believe the custom of the six-week checkup after birth came about. The old-time doctors were actually following the Levitical laws concerning waiting until six weeks (44 days) had passed after the birth of a boy and waiting 88 days after the birth of a girl before a couple began to have relations again. These rules of abstinence have to do with hormones in the woman's body returning to normal. If the mother nurses full time, it may be months before her reproductive cycle even begins again.

Can a couple use NFP while the wife allows her body to have a season of rest?

This is between themselves and God. This may be wisdom for some women, especially if they were ill and could not nurse for some reason. Couples may feel comfortable doing this so that the wife can regain her health before the next baby. When a woman has had multiple births, the couple may find this necessary to prevent her from harming her health.

I believe that this entire decision involves growing in our faith. When a couple is first feeling led to agree with this message, it may be a big step to just stop relying on an unnatural birth control method. Using NFP for some could be a first step toward completely trusting God with family planning. If the majority of today's believers just came to the point of using NFP and got off all of the unnatural hormones and avoided unnatural operations, then we would see the vast majority of God's people healed emotionally and restored physically in less than a generation!! God's people have to start somewhere, and many couples do try NFP. If you love Jesus and if you desire to trust Him, He will show you how to trust Him in your personal circumstances. As you rely on Him more, He desires to take you into complete trust with this area of your life. As you grow, you will see that the whole idea of allowing God to plan your family is a great and wonderful adventure with God.

Footnotes

[1] All Scripture quotations are taken from the New International Version (NIV) unless otherwise indicated

[2] Much of the information about the history of birth control came from the Marie Stopes International website: www.mariestopes.org.uk

[3] P. Scott, "The Green Revolution," *Twin Circle* (April 23, 1972).

[4] *Apology* 9:4; quoted in www.epm.org/abortohs.html.

[5] Quoted in www.epm org/abortohs.html.

[6] Rima D. Apple, *Women, Health and Medicine in America: A Historical Handbook* (New York: Garland Publishing, 1990), 397.

[7] Lionel Tiger, *U.S. News and World Report* (July 1996).

[8] *Journal of Social, Political, and Economic Studies* 20 (Spring 1995): 20.

[9] *Handbook on Abortion* (Hiltz Publishing, 1970), 54.

[10] National Center for Health Statistics (NCHS) (Feb.12, 2002), final health statistics; www.nchs.gov.

[11] All definitions are from *Webster's Dictionary of the English Language*, Unabridged Encyclopedic edition (J. G. Ferguson

Publishing Company, 1977).

[12] www.census.gov.

[13] *University of Chicago Medical Tribune* (September 8, 1971).

[14] United States Agency for International Development; www.usaid.gov.

[15] Susan J. Belcher, Will County, Illinois, NOW chapter (1999).

[16] Gynecological Cancer Foundation statistics (September 2003).

[17] Susan J. Belcher, NOW Tubal Ligation Resolution (July 3, 1999), Will County, Illinois NOW chapter.

[18] *Family Planning Perspectives*, 33, no. 4 (July/August 2001): 35-41, 49.

[19] Belcher, 1999.

[20] *Family Planning Perspectives*, 33, no. 4 (July/August 2001).

[21] Tubal ligation fact sheet; www.tubal.org

[22] www.tubal.org.

[23] Belcher, 1999.

[24] Neil Lauersen, M.D. and Eileen Stukane, *Listen to Your Body*, p. 354.

[25] S. D. Hillis et al, "Tubal Ligation and Long Term Risk of Hysterectomy: Findings from CREST-United States Collaborative Review of Sterilization," *Obstetric Gynecology* 89 (1997): 609-14.

[26] www.qis.net/~pvietz/history.htm.

27 *Lancet* 1,356 (August 2000): 9,229.

28 *The New Ourselves: Growing Older* (New York: Touchstone, 1994).

29 FEMISA fact sheet from the Hysterectomy Association of UK.

30 *American Journal of Epidemiology*, 138, no. 7(October 1993): 508-21.

31 NCHS (National Center for Health Statistics) news release (June 25, 2003).

32 M. J. Drake and D. Cranston, "The Chequered History of Vasectomy," *British Journal of Medicine*.

33 *American Journal of Public Health* 5 (May 1995): 644-9; National Institute of Child Health and Human Development website, www.nichd.nih.gov.

34 McMahon, *British Journal of Urology* 69, no. 2 (February 1992): 188-191; Choe J. M. Kirkemo, "Questionnaire-based Outcomes Study of Nononcological Post Vasectomy Complications," *Journal of Urology* 155, no. 4 (April 1996): 1284-1286; Stanley A. Myers, Christopher E. Mershon, and Eugene F. Fuchs, "Vasectomy Reversal for the Treatment of Post Vasectomy Pain Syndrome," *Journal of Urology* 157 (February 1997): 518-520.

35 Shahani SK Haddikudor NS, "Immunological Consequences of Vasectormy," *Archives of Andrology* 7, no. 2 (September 1981): 193-99

36 Anthony H. Horan, "Complications of Vasectomy," *American Family Physician* 48, no. 7 (November 15,1993): 1,264-1,268.

37 www.engenderhealth.org.

To contact RACHEL SCOTT:

RachelMScott99@aol.com

Printed in the United Kingdom
by Lightning Source UK Ltd.
107552UKS00001B/93